NO MORE MEDIOCRE

NO MORE
MEDIOCRE

A Call to Reimagine
Our Relationships and
Demand More

LAURA DANGER

PLUME

PLUME

An imprint of Penguin Random House LLC
1745 Broadway, New York, NY 10019
penguinrandomhouse.com

"Doing the Laundry" by David Gate originally published
on davidgatepoet.com, used by permission of the poet.

A tweet by Raina Brands reprinted by permission of the author.

LIBRARY OF CONGRESS CATALOGING-IN-PUBLICATION DATA

Names: Danger, Laura author
Title: No more mediocre: a call to reimagine our relationships and
demand more / Laura Danger.
Description: New York, NY : Plume, [2026] | Includes bibliographical references.
Identifiers: LCCN 2025017908 (print) | LCCN 2025017909 (ebook) |
ISBN 9780593474785 hardcover | ISBN 9780593474792 ebook
Subjects: LCSH: Work-life balance | Work and family | Motherhood | Self-realization
Classification: LCC HD4904.25 .D36 2026 (print) |
LCC HD4904.25 (ebook) | DDC 650.1—dc23/eng/20250612
LC record available at https://lccn.loc.gov/2025017908
LC ebook record available at https://lccn.loc.gov/2025017909

Printed in the United States of America
1st Printing

The authorized representative in the EU for product safety and compliance is
Penguin Random House Ireland, Morrison Chambers, 32 Nassau Street,
Dublin D02 YH68, Ireland, https://eu-contact.penguin.ie.

Some names and identifying details of certain people mentioned have been changed.

To Charlie, Frances, and Jack

Contents

PART 3
Community:
A Future Rooted in Collective Care   261

NO MORE MEDIOCRE

Introduction

I n OCTOBER 2019, I stood in my kitchen staring at a birthday card, which sparked a full-blown identity crisis and eventually led to my burning a lot of my life down (in the best way). The card, which read, *Happy Birthday, Mom! You're the best wife and mother in the world! We ♡ you!* was well-intentioned and sweet. But as my eyes traced the words in front of me, I struggled to catch my breath. The room suddenly felt smaller, the walls closing in around me.

It was my thirty-first birthday. That morning, my husband and kids presented me with a handmade birthday card in an envelope and some garden-picked flowers. My six-month-old sat in her high chair next to my three-year-old. They beamed with pride at what they'd made me.

As I stood in the kitchen holding the birthday card, I was running on fumes, barely holding it together. I was deep in the raw, never-rested fog of my youngest's first year while also navigating life with a threenager. On top of everything, I was only eight weeks into a new teaching position at a new school. I'd had the rug pulled out from underneath me that June when, just days into my maternity leave, my position was eliminated and I'd been laid off. After a summer of uncertainty, I started a new job in September and now, two months in, I was still scrambling to find my footing. I was pumping on my prep periods, grading papers after bedtime, and using periodic child-free trips to the grocery store as my main source of self-care. I'd worked hard to hold on to bits of myself through my transition into motherhood—staying involved with neighborhood organizations and finding creative projects I could do from home—but those things were the first to go as I struggled to maintain balance. I'd been powering through the days and weeks, but I was beyond exhausted.

Right as I was reading the birthday card, my husband, Jack, announced that it was a "whatever Mom wants to do" day! My heart sank. I was the "best mom and wife" according to them, and yet, all I wanted for my birthday was to not figure out the plan. A real gift would have been an entire day during which I didn't have to make a single decision. I didn't want to have to think about what kind of activity everyone would like, what restaurant had the chicken strips the kids might eat, or take into consideration how we'd work around nap and nursing schedules. Even on my birthday, which was supposed to be a celebration of me as a person, I was a mother and a wife first. Despite all the good intentions and love being launched my way that morning, I couldn't help but notice how suffocated I felt.

Jack was doing everything in his power to encourage me to put myself first, but what wasn't clear to either of us at the time was how many barriers were in the way of actually making that possible. He thought he was being supportive, but by tossing the reins to me, my husband was unintentionally giving me more work. Just telling me to do "whatever I wanted" disregarded all the mental and emotional labor that went into having a fun day with a family of four. The Mom Day and the card that addressed me by my roles, with no mention of me as a person, felt like clear proof of what I'd feared: that my value was measured by what I was to others, and that the work I was doing was invisible. I didn't want to force my family into doing something I wanted to do; I wanted them to notice what might be enjoyable and then make considerate plans for me.

The sting of sadness that came with my gifts was paired with shame. I felt like an ungrateful brat for being bothered by the sweet gestures of the people who loved me. I felt like I had no reason to be upset. I thought I was being a total fool for not being satisfied. I didn't have the energy or the understanding to express what was actually going on with me. So rather than ruining the mood by confronting whatever weird feelings were coming up, I sipped my coffee, choked back confused tears, and picked a place for lunch that I knew had something my kids would eat.

On the surface, that birthday looked the same as all the others— buying a few plants and getting ice cream—but something in me had changed. I'd frequently found myself in a cycle of rumination and resentment, acting like a nag or denying my feelings so I wouldn't come off like one, but as the day went on, rather than pushing away the feelings that came up for me, I let them linger. I realized I'd been walking around most days with a rain cloud over me, going through the motions without giving myself time to process anything. I was so tired and worn out, exhausted from making decisions all day every day about the kids, the house, my job, and the groceries. I wanted a break. A *real* break. Not just a solo trip to Target. But I was so tired that the thought of the effort I'd have to put in to getting that break made me want to scream. The thought of picking out what I wanted to eat for lunch felt like one decision too many. On the day of my thirty-first birthday, rather than wallowing in familiar self-pity, I allowed my feelings of resignation to transform. I couldn't accept a future full of tearful birthdays during which I felt like a ghost. That card propelled me forward.

YOU GOT THIS, MAMA

I'd been told through Instagram and Facebook posts featuring tired but happy moms that the struggle would be worth it, and if I could just try to be present, motherhood would fulfill me. I was smart and resilient and had great support, so whenever I felt like I was hitting a wall, I figured if I kept moving forward, things would eventually ease up. I thought motherhood was a muscle I needed to keep exercising, and if I continued to pick up more responsibilities, I'd just get stronger and more capable, like all those model mothers online. I'd heard every variation of "It's just a season, Mama!" but the seasons just kept hitting, always with inclement weather. Standing in the kitchen on my birthday, fighting back tears, I didn't feel strong. I felt deflated and defeated. I felt resentful and alone. I had been quietly Momfluenced and had internalized the ways motherhood requires martyrdom.

I was Jack's wife, Charlie and Frances's mom, dedicating myself willingly to those roles and then quietly resenting them for how much I'd felt pressured to sacrifice for them. I'd allowed myself to be swallowed up by those titles to the point where I didn't recognize myself that morning. I was a wife and a mother, and I loved my husband and kids, but who was *Laura?* Believing my primary contribution to the world was how I could provide for the needs of others, especially as a mother, I wasn't sure how to provide for my own anymore. In fact, I wasn't even sure what my own needs were.

How had I gotten to that point? I had always seen myself as a progressive feminist. I'd been outspoken about women's issues since I could remember. I was involved in local activism, studied social issues, and read feminist theory. I wanted the world to be fair and equitable, and I carried that core belief with me in everything I did—in my friendships, in my work in my community and as a teacher, and, I thought, in my marriage.

Why then, three years and two kids into parenthood, did I feel convinced that I needed to make myself smaller for the sake of being a certain kind of parent or partner? I was so out of practice considering my needs and desires in decision-making. Where would I go if I had a week to myself? What would I eat for dinner if it were really up to me? I didn't know. I'd pushed myself so far to the sidelines that when opportunities came up—weekends away with friends, a leadership role at work—I turned them down without giving any serious consideration to how I could make it work. I cleared my plate of what I felt extra or optional, the personal interests and passions, and tried to suppress the grief of letting go. Dedication to my roles was supposed to bring me all the connection and fulfillment I needed.

Why didn't pouring myself into those roles feel like enough for me? Where had I picked up this belief that I needed to sacrifice myself in order to make myself valuable? I was so terrified to tell the people in my life what I really needed. Why did I feel like my family would stop loving me if I chose to love myself?

I pictured myself as a powerhouse take-no-shit mom with a career and a family, just like any man could have. Unknown to me, I had bought into a toxic version of the American Dream, believing self-reliance was a virtue. I was applauded for "balancing it all" and wore my hard work, tired eyes, and hustle like badges of honor. In an effort to feel empowered in an anti-woman world, I'd unintentionally slipped into a position of hyperindependence, basically writing the same story of inequity but in a different font.

Throughout my twenties, I'd watched as friends began making major life decisions: moving in with partners, relocating for new jobs, getting married, having kids or choosing not to. I'd assumed we'd be different. We were artists, musicians, misfits— "nontraditional" in so many ways. Despite that, we transitioned through milestones, and familiar trends began to emerge. As our couple friends became parents, many of the new dads continued to grab weekly postwork drinks while their wives traded their trivia nights for virtual book clubs or "mommy and me" yoga. Sure, the women in my life were taking on leadership positions at work and the men wore nail polish, but the postwedding thank-you notes always seemed to arrive scrawled in my girlfriends' handwriting. Halloween parties were organized among wives and girlfriends, who coordinated shared dishes ahead of time and began to clean up while saying their goodbyes. Antiquated gender norms reared their ugly heads in my partnership, in my friendships, and in the lives of the people around me. In hindsight, it's obvious I was playing out patriarchal expectations and contributing to my own suffering, but while it was happening, it just seemed like the way things were. Much of it felt like a choice—the marriage, the kids, even the casseroles. The novelty of early adulthood and my sense of belonging made it easier to gloss over the more subtle inequities that were compounding in my life.

An especially glaring example of this was that when I looked at the caregivers around me, martyrdom was not only completely acceptable—it was expected. In the Facebook "mommy" groups, on TV, and in viral videos, I saw the same thing: "Motherhood is hard! Hang in there, Mama!" The motherhood forums made it clear that it was customary to be a little bit (or a lot a bit) miserable, evidenced by the dozens of daily posts about never having enough personal time or venting about husbands. In between stories outlining how to ask reluctant bosses for pump breaks were posts about "husband chore charts," under which hundreds of women would laugh together in the comments about the challenges of getting their husbands to pitch in. When one of them shared, "I left the house for a girls' night and the kids stayed up past 10!" the group's members responded with similar stories and gave suggestions for how to better prepare next time.

Carrying the world on your shoulders is a part of the mother archetype. No matter who you are or what your circumstances—whether you're a lesbian parent in a dual-income household, a middle-class straight stay-at-home mom, or a working single mother—against any and all struggles, you're supposed to be able to get shit done. This was the story that was spun in online spaces I hung out in. Mothers endure! We make it work! We do it all! That's our superpower! Don't you forget it! *You got this, Mama!*

The feeling of overwhelm and loss of identity were considered part of the gig. Senses of isolation and self-abandonment were the norm—not just side effects of motherhood but part of what defined the role. And we overworked moms were expected to bond around it. A lack of support was inevitable, so moms encouraged one another to embrace superhuman strength with pride.

In those first years of motherhood, I turned to my friends online and in person to help keep me going. As often as I could swing it, I'd get together with my mom friends for a picnic brunch, where we would bring our babies to a local park. We'd do a little catching up before shifting to commiserating. We'd air our grievances about feeling constantly tired and overwhelmed, share about our partners casually turning on the TV instead of tackling the dishes, complain about unsympathetic bosses, and then send one another off into battle once more. Each visit, I left wishing we could savor that space of connection and validation for a little longer, always feeling like we'd just scratched the surface and never fully confronted what we'd all been dealing with behind closed doors. Any complaint of motherhood came furiously Bubble-Wrapped with dozens of reasons why it was the most magical thing to ever happen to us, lest anyone be judged a bad mom. "Wouldn't trade it for the world!" Any criticism of a partner who wasn't pulling their weight was met with chuckles and downplaying. "He's a fool, but he's my fool!" "Is it really love if you don't also want to kill them sometimes?" It was comforting that we were all going through a bit of a hellish time, but the comfort also seemed to make us complacent. We were all struggling in our own ways—with finances, health, relationship issues—spread thin and let down in ways we hadn't expected. But we laughed it off. We coped. We softened our disappointment with sarcasm and wore our ability to tolerate it proudly. We were tough. We were chill. We focused more on how things could be worse than how they could be better.

I always walked away from these gatherings feeling less alone, equally grateful for the community and discouraged that this was the reality of modern motherhood. We were living lives that were okay. Good, not great: mediocre.

When I say our lives were mediocre, I mean that motherhood and, more broadly, whatever version of the American Dream we each embodied, had overpromised and underdelivered. I wasn't alone in feeling misled. Everyone I knew was grappling with their own reality checks when recounting their life's decisions. For every achievement and milestone, it seemed there were unexpected costs. We'd been upsold on the college degrees, the dream jobs, and the little nuclear families, and had also gotten burnout, debt, and an absence of autonomy. The parts of our lives we were told would be remarkable came with consequences we hadn't counted on. I felt duped, and I know I wasn't alone in that.

My thirty-first birthday was my turning point, when I gave myself permission to truly acknowledge the depths of my anger, to take a critical look at my own choices, and to be honest with myself. I was used to smothering little bursts of frustration after attempts to fix their cause fell flat.

That morning, the unsustainability of it all was undeniable. I was so angry that so many of us felt compelled to be productive and independent past our capacities, despite the costs. I hated myself for willingly accepting a role and then allowing myself to resent it. For turning my anger on myself. In those first years of parenthood, I couldn't escape the message that it was my own fault for being unsatisfied after lying in the bed I'd made for myself. I wanted to be a mother and a wife so badly, so I thought I must be weak or ungrateful if I had any criticisms of either. I spent so much time believing that becoming a mother and wife would add to my identity, but I'd allowed those roles to consume so much of who I was that I hardly recognized myself.

With the clarity that comes with righteous anger, I began to recognize many of the ways I had been encouraged to adapt to my own discomfort. Memes and viral videos romanticize and make light of the weight of modern motherhood. Hashtags like #couplescomedy and #marriagehumor are cesspools of exaggerated examples of toxic relationship dynamics, their comment sections full of laughing emojis and "omg so true! Lol!" If you aren't laughing along, you're taking yourself too seriously. For a while, I joined in. I giggled along to the relatability of mainstream jokes that poked fun at situations without realizing that those same situations were making me and my peers miserable. I barely gave it a thought that the punch lines were often women losing their personhood, adult men lacking meaningful connections, and couples who hate each other. When queer TV show characters like Cam and Mitchell from *Modern Family* fell into familiar marriage humor traps, I unconsciously filed these scenes away as evidence that inequity and resentment were just universal relationship truths rather than socially constructed conditions we'd been taught to accept.

These dynamics have been normalized repeatedly and through countless aspects of our lives, discouraging us from questioning and encouraging us to resign ourselves. No wonder so many of us have felt like we need to accept less than what we deserve. We never stood a chance.

In October 2019, as I processed my daily life with a new perspective, I hit pause on making any dramatic changes . . . and then came the pandemic.

SOMETHING'S GOTTA GIVE

Prior to the pandemic, my husband worked thirteen-hour days outside of the home and traveled a minimum of one long weekend a month. I worked a full-time job and handled most of the housework and childcare. He participated actively when he was around, jumping in on childcare duties and taking on chores, but the way the responsibilities were divvied up, more landed on me.

Our division of labor was lopsided, but it wasn't just because of his long work hours, and it didn't just start when we had kids. We'd contributed to our shared life in different ways from the beginning of our relationship—I tended to take on a larger share of the mental load and administrative work, and Jack was more likely to tackle the physical follow-through of tasks. Over the years, we found ourselves caught in a loop.

Because I was responsible for so much, I was burdened with the work of asking for help. Because I shouldered so much, my husband struggled to jump in without being given directions. We butted heads often, both of us defensive and exhausted by the pattern. We'd initially entered into our partnership with the full intention of being equals, but it wasn't the reality we were living in. I was drowning, he felt helpless, and neither of us knew what to do about it. The gridlock was miserable. On top of that, the inequality and imbalance at home were so out of line with what I stood for, I could hardly bear to face it. I felt like a fraud, a bad feminist, facilitating everyone else's life in a way that felt simultaneously embarrassing and enraging.

I've never shied away from challenging overt misogyny—it's easy to argue with a coworker who insists that "female comedians aren't funny." But it was much harder to turn that same critical eye inward. It felt riskier to be honest about what was creeping into my most intimate relationships, to hold firm boundaries, or to name the ways I was adapting to dynamics that hurt me. Confronting casual sexism in the world felt easier than recognizing how deeply ingrained norms were shaping our roles at home. When the call is coming from inside the house, the stakes feel much higher. Facing the everyday sexism woven into our personal lives requires us to acknowledge the harm of our habitual behaviors and make a choice to either continue perpetuating the status quo or to do the work of growing.

And just as I was waking up to that reality, the world changed.

When the Covid lockdowns went into effect in early 2020, my kids were nine months and three years old. I was teaching special education in a Chicago public school, and when everything shut down, I was suddenly thrown into the position of needing to parent and teach simultaneously. My husband's travel schedule stopped, but his long work hours and day-to-day responsibilities didn't. I taught online from our unfinished basement and did whatever I needed to do to keep my kids quiet. It was a blur of endless *Cocomelon*, Goldfish crackers, and mess. With hardly any time to myself, I often caught myself mentally escaping, even pondering what it would be like if I just drove off and never came back.

The pandemic tested every aspect of my and my husband's relationship, and with so much of my energy spent keeping my shit together in front of my students and kids, I couldn't find an ounce of patience to "ask nicely" when it came to housework. I either spoke with frustration or shoved that frustration down. We were in survival mode, with very little energy left over to address larger concerns. We functioned like ships passing in the night, and because tensions were often so high, when we had downtime together, it was frequently spent sitting on separate couches, scrolling social media or immersed in video games.

Those years were dark. I've dealt with mental health issues my entire life, but symptoms I thought I'd had pretty well managed consumed me. Pulled in so many directions, I felt like I was failing at everything. I was a horrible mother who snapped and yelled, could only muster up the energy for Lunchables and fast food, and had my kids in front of screens for way longer than recommended. I was passive-aggressive and short-tempered with my husband. I was a bad friend who couldn't keep in touch and a bad family member who could barely muster the emotional energy to send a text on a birthday. All the while, I logged on to my online classes each day and taught lessons, feeling helpless as society's failures played out in front of me and my students and their families lost jobs, housing, and family members.

The pandemic, the protests in response to the deaths of George Floyd and Breonna Taylor, and our government's failure to address any of it in a way that prioritized our humanity shattered much of my ignorant understanding of how our society was structured. I dug deeper, burning through books on history, abolition, feminism, disability justice, and systemic oppression. I ramped up my involvement in local organizing and activism. My worldview shifted as I watched my neighbors show up for each other, committed to caring for one another in a prolonged moment of crisis. I felt the impacts of our government's disrespect for our humanity intimately, in a way I'd been insulated against for much of my life. As I struggled to keep my kids cared for and to show up for my students and their families reliably without the childcare or social resources I needed, the total disregard for our value as people by many members of society smacked me in the face. I felt trapped. Duped. Angry. In the fall of 2021, I hit a wall. As I prepared to go back to in-person teaching for the sake of the economy, I had to ask myself if I could participate in systems I wasn't sure I believed in anymore.

Whatever had been cracked open in me because of that birthday card back in 2019 finally exploded just a few weeks into the 2021 school year. I was a shell of myself. I was constantly on edge and wavered between feelings of hopelessness and intense anxiety. From the lowest of my lows, I took a look at my life and realized I wasn't just overextending and self-sacrificing at home and at work. Bleeding myself dry was something I'd always done, a behavior present in everything I did and in every relationship I was a part of. I'd gone into teaching because I thought it was a way of affecting positive change in the world. I wanted to do good and be good. But the longer I worked that job, the more I saw the flaws. I was never going to be the teacher I wanted to be, the wife I wanted to be, the mother or the person I wanted to be. I couldn't do it. I was never going to be able to do it.

I'd gone into teaching because I wanted change. What I realized was that by overextending myself to make change possible, I was feeding the very machine that I was fighting against. When I worked past contract hours to fill in the education system's gaps, my self-sacrifice kept the exploitative system afloat. There were deep foundational beliefs I needed to confront if I was ever going to thrive. I knew I wasn't going to solve my problems by outsourcing cleaning, making better lists, or learning to work more efficiently. Martyring myself as a mother or as a teacher wasn't going to save the world. I needed individual change *and* cultural change. I was finally ready to burn it all down.

LIGHTING IT ON FIRE

Up until that point, everything I'd ever learned about how to create value in the world had been tied to how to serve others. But trying to create value that way had pushed me to a place where I seriously considered how much better off the world might be if I weren't in it. I'd poured every ounce of myself into trying to be a good wife, mother, and teacher, and yet I felt like a failure at all of those things. I could no longer act lighthearted about how much being a super-mom was crushing me. I felt so much shame for not enjoying my life, even though in every way it looked like I "had it all." I felt biologically broken, because none of the things I thought would come naturally to me, like housework or soothing a child's tantrum, *did*. It felt safer and more in my control to keep moving forward as a shell of a person or to drive off and never look back than to verbalize what I wanted.

I gave my two weeks' notice mid-September 2021 after a hellish workweek and yet another message from daycare telling me my kids would have to be home for the next five days because of a

Covid-19 exposure. I felt like I'd been fighting a battle for basic things. Fighting my school district to get the resources I needed to meet my students' needs, scrambling to find childcare to get the needs of my children met, desperately searching for time and energy to keep my household running.

I was unraveling. I wasn't eating or sleeping. I was snapping at my kids over nothing, my body shrinking as the stress hollowed me out. I had been on a downward mental health spiral for months at that point, but in the weeks leading up to quitting, it had gotten significantly worse. The path I was headed down wasn't just unsustainable—it was dangerous. I felt like I was in a losing battle with life. As I considered my options, one thought rattled around in my head: if I died, my admin's first reaction to hearing the news wouldn't be grief at losing me. They'd wonder whether I'd left lesson plans for a substitute. The issues I'd been grappling with were so much bigger than just what was happening at home. It was all connected—my overextension, my exhaustion, the systemic failures. I was depressed, furious, and desperate for a way out. So I quit my job.

Between the fall of 2021 and the spring of 2022, I reevaluated every part of my life.

Rather than walking away altogether, I walked away from the parts that were making me miserable. For so long, my career in the classroom had felt like a fundamental part of my vision for a stable life. But when I paused to look beyond it, I started to see a much larger picture. I took stock of the skills I had developed over the years—teaching, facilitating, creating learning experiences—and began to imagine other ways I could put them to use beyond the traditional classroom. Letting go of my rigid ideas of how I thought my life should look opened up new possibilities, including the opportunity to redefine motherhood on my own terms. In the process, the invisible lines I'd drawn between home, work, friendships, and community blurred.

Leaving my job wasn't just about rethinking my career choices; it was about fundamentally questioning my relationship to care and asking whether my efforts were upholding or disrupting. The inequities at home, the impossible demands on teachers, and the failures of social systems weren't separate problems—they were all part of the same broken structure. Care work is the foundation of everything, and when we rethink our relationship to it, we don't just find balance—we change the way we live, relate, and build the world around us.

Change wasn't something I could achieve alone. Through social media, online communities I've been a part of, and in-person connections, I found encouragement and solidarity. I stopped tiptoeing around my resentment and loneliness and trusted that the outcome of self-advocacy would lead to something better—something more authentic and secure. Despite how scared I was that things would fall apart, I took the leap to ask for what I truly wanted. I realized that if I didn't explicitly ask and make room for what I needed, I was guaranteeing I would never get it. By staying stuck, I was making a choice, and I decided to make new ones. I risked harm either way, but if I had the courage to self-advocate, the possible rewards were endless.

My husband and I began to tackle our relationship from all sides, seriously assessing what it actually took to run our household, implementing official meeting times to review tasks, during which we took notes and even came up with stressful-conversation safe words. We ramped up our efforts, and although our progress was messy and nonlinear, improvement in our division of labor and household communication happened.

We each took personal ownership of our parts of the imbalance.

I stopped assuming responsibility for tasks like packing for trips and cleaning out the fridge without talking about it with him first. We invested time in doing tasks together during evenings and weekends so that we could talk through processes and expectations in real time. Sorting dusty bins in the basement, coordinating hand-me-down disbursement, and filling out camp registration packets became group projects instead of things I'd invisibly tackle on my own. Rather than hanging back and looking to me for guidance on things like when to replace the kids' shoes and where to get the best deal, Jack asked me if I was cool with him taking the lead and jumped into action. Our consistent resistance to old habits helped us carve out new ones. The more we did together, the more confident my husband felt making decisions that considered everyone's needs. We slowly and deliberately tipped the scales, giving us both more peace of mind and freedom—him to make choices without feeling like he needed to check in with me, and me to release responsibilities confidently.

Talking about the little stuff encouraged us to connect over how we wanted our lives to look in the long run. We had explicit conversations about what we needed and wanted—from ourselves, each other, and life in general. We asked ourselves and each other: How do we want to spend our time? What kind of impact do we want to leave on the world? Why?

As my relationship changed, so did I. Balance at home gave me mental and emotional space back. It also gave me more time and flexibility. I knew things would be okay if I had to run out of the house at the last minute. I felt confident nothing would fall apart if I went away for a weekend. I paid attention to what made me feel excited. I rode my bike, went on walks, said yes to coffee with friends. I hiked our local forest preserve, listened to audiobooks, and embraced solitude. I started taking solo trips. For the first time in my life, I spent a sustained amount of time just observing—myself, my surroundings, and the complicated web we're all part of. As I began to look at the world through my relationship to it, I was confronted with all the ways we've been coerced away from truly and deeply caring for ourselves and each other on a grand scale—in our homes, communities, and society at large.

I had no idea any of that was ahead of me when I made the decision to leave my job. All I knew was that something drastic had to happen. Feeling defeated and anxious on my last day as a teacher, I made some cheesy TikTok supercut of myself packing up my classroom set to a sentimental tune. On top of clips of my near-empty classroom, I wrote, "Today I hung up my hat. I don't know what's next. But for now, I'm burning down my nest with the hope that I can rebuild from more fertile soil." At that moment, I felt like I had no other option but to leave, and I was clinging to the hope that I was on the edge of a new beginning. When I made that TikTok, I had my fingers crossed that I was having my phoenix-rising moment. Looking back now, that's exactly what it was.

FANNING THE FLAMES

That TikTok in which I said goodbye to my classroom was just one of the many I'd posted since I first downloaded TikTok during the initial Covid-19 lockdown a year and a half earlier, in March 2020. Initially, I logged in as a casual observer, scrolling to kill time. But as the months dragged on, with no end to the isolation in sight, I let it become my creative outlet, a space to converse and connect. I made videos where I shared my garden, talked about social issues, reflected on trending topics, and shared my personal experiences. My first videos only ever got a few hundred views each, but the more I shared critiques of cultural norms, the clearer it became that I wasn't alone in my rage. People were excited to talk about what so many of us had been dealing with behind closed doors.

Because very few people in my real life were on TikTok, I felt free to express myself openly with little consequence. I spent months talking about whatever interested me with relative anonymity and minimal viewers. The TikTok algorithm had me pegged as a millennial mom, so my For You feed regularly had clips and skits I was expected to relate to. Every day I saw reminders in video form of how I was expected to be selfless, how I was supposed to laugh off inequity and get used to the mediocre version of adulthood being sold to me. On my Instagram, where I was mostly connected with family and old friends, I saw signs of increased inequity as schools remained closed and childcare continued to be an issue. I couldn't stop seeing the ways we'd all been conditioned to give ourselves up.

Almost a full year into the pandemic, during one of my midday Instagram scroll sessions, I came across a post from an old family friend who had recently had her third baby. It was a picture of her husband sitting in the lobby of her gym, grimacing at her, their three-month-old in one hand and a cell phone in the other: "Best hubby! He let me get thirty minutes at the gym for the first time since baby! ♥" He *let* you get thirty minutes?

While the post made my hair stand up on end, I recognized that every single facet of our world tells us that we're not real mothers if we aren't in a constant state of overextension and sacrifice. I was so mad for her, because I also saw myself in her. I was sure just asking for personal time took a lot for her. Despite the volume getting turned down over time, there's still a lingering voice in the back of my head that tries to tell me that time and space for myself should be considered a special gift rather than a given. Despite the frustration her post sparked in me, her marriage and family dynamic were none of my business, so I closed out of Instagram, opened TikTok, and turned the camera on myself.

I let my frustration loose. I said, "If I see one more post of a mother like, 'Awwww, dream man—watched my baby while I took a shower,' 'Daddy watched the kids while I ran some errands. How'd I get so lucky?!' I'm going to flip. A. Table."

Within twenty-four hours, this video had been seen more than half a million times and had nearly fifty thousand likes. The comment section erupted with hundreds of comments echoing the same sentiment.

"Stop. Praising. Mediocre. Men."

"Yes! Dads are parents, too! They need to step it up and act like it."

"Or 'He HELPED with the housework.'"

"OMG THIS! They're your kids, too! It's not babysitting!"

It felt like I'd put my finger on something we'd all been dying to get out in the open. Over the course of the next few months, I kept talking about gender roles, domestic inequity, and relationship dynamics. I launched the #WeaponizedIncompetence hashtag and yelled into my phone. I commented on trending videos, pointed out misogyny in popular marriage jokes, and began to build a platform of thousands of followers. I had a space to be furious, and my anger was validated and welcomed. Alongside my followers and the millions of people interacting with my content, I was expressing our collective frustration. I started getting tagged in viral videos of "dumb dad" jokes and "nagging wife" content, asking me to tear them apart. This dissatisfaction with the status quo was a flame to be fanned, and I was happy to be given the opportunity to blow on it.

TikTok provided me with both a platform and the safety of anonymity—and the added bonus of not having to protect the comfort of the people closest to me. On TikTok, the only people who saw my content or engaged with it were the ones who wanted to hear more. Whether they felt validated and empowered by knowing they weren't alone, or challenged to unpack the realities of their relationships, my messages resonated. People were pissed. Overwhelmed caregivers being expected to continue to be full-time caregivers, full-time workers, and abandon their own needs for the "greater good" were at their wits' end.

THE MORE I talked about these topics, the more hyperaware I became of their prevalence. I witnessed imbalances and inequities everywhere I looked: in the relationships of friends and family, at work, and in my personal life. I pointed out examples of weaponized incompetence, something we'll discuss in depth in the following chapters. I saw disconnection and imbalance everywhere, even in less-traditional relationship structures, and it all made me feel indignant.

Underneath the wisecracks from women and other primary caregivers about having to make dinner and monitor online school while sick with a 104-degree fever, I saw all the ways our social standards had been set. Because I couldn't go back in time and scream at past me, I made videos about the things I wish I'd known earlier. I processed verbally and told the internet the things I wish someone had told me. I hoped my videos would grace the timelines of anyone who felt tempted to make light of disparity in their partnership or convince themselves that we should all resign ourselves to unsustainable dynamics.

Over the course of 2021, I gained nearly two hundred thousand followers on TikTok. I trained with the Fair Play Policy Institute as a certified Fair Play Method facilitator and started to work with individuals and couples to confront domestic inequity in their homes. I hosted workshops to help families build systems and practice communication, and coached people through the process of finding new ways forward. I've taken opportunities to present internationally on the impacts of social media on domestic expectations and partnered with brands to amplify the importance of boundaries and balance. In partnership with Swiffer and the Fair Play Policy Institute, I've put my educational background to use to develop a family and consumer sciences curriculum that gives explicit language for things like the mental load and teaches young people to collaborate rather than make assumptions. While I continue to facilitate discussions and partner with organizations to develop curricula, my community of over 800,000 continues to grow.

I am growing along with this movement, one voice in a powerful crowd. The narrow, imbalanced version of success we've been taught to accept depends on our silence. As long as we see mediocrity as inevitable, we'll keep settling for imbalance and disconnection. We can't afford complacency. Together, we have to keep raising our voices and pushing for change.

FERTILE SOIL

After a certain point, my platform grew large enough that my face started popping up on the timelines of friends and family. I started getting texts from the people who knew me in real life saying they saw me reposted in a mom group or that a friend had sent them one of my videos. Increasing numbers of men, even the ones from my personal life, began following me and embracing what I had to say. Where I'd expected defensiveness, I've instead found a surprising amount of self-reflection and hope. The overwhelming sentiment has been that the discomfort inherent in facing our problems doesn't need to be something to fear but rather something to embrace as a necessary aspect of change.

This book is my way of taking the power of collective rage I've found in my online community and pushing it further into the world. My videos have been sent in group text threads and shared in Instagram stories as a way of saying "Look! We're not the only ones who are pissed off! We deserve to be pissed!" My hope is that this book will be passed among friends in the same way. To be a part of the thread that connects us all is a joy I never imagined I could feel.

We've been convinced to seek comfort in consumerism and grind harder to combat the isolating conditions of the nuclear family and capitalism. We're all losing out by subscribing to that version of normal. I don't want us to simply feel comforted that we're all struggling together. I want this book to contribute to a future where we're bonded together by our radical hope and pursuit of a new normal. The purpose of this book is not just to act as a curtain pull to reveal the many ways we've been conditioned to settle for less than we deserve but also to provide actionable steps. I hope it will act as a compassionate push toward necessary boundary-setting and encouragement toward courageous curiosity and liberated futures for us all. *No More Mediocre* is a battle cry for better.

We cannot hesitate to raise the bar—beyond the limits we've been conditioned to accept and toward the standard we've always deserved. We can't let fear hold us back from seeing what's possible. If we want real change, we have to be willing to face the ways we've been conditioned to accept less, both in our personal lives and in the world at large. We must be willing to dig down to the roots of our problems, to recognize the interconnectedness of injustice, and to trace the lines back to ourselves.

The first section of this book is focused on the way things have been. It's a look at how easy it is to slip into inequity without noticing. It's an investigation into invisible labor, the weight of building a life, and the lessons so many of us internalize because of the normalization of contempt and disconnection. Sitcom-style comedy is constantly recycled and repeated in modern viral videos, and like the shows of the past, these videos teach us to brush off behaviors that would be alarming without a laugh track. We exist in a culture that overemphasizes the importance of marriage and romantic love and tells us it's okay for those relationships to hurt. Cheap jokes repeat social norms for laughs and discourage us from seeking relationships that are truly fulfilling. By exposing how we've been conditioned into mediocrity and shifting our perspective on the daily work we do, we can move forward and disrupt the ways these outdated beliefs show up in our lives.

In the second section of this book, we'll look at rejecting outdated roles and embracing conflict as an opportunity for connection, identifying tools for stronger communication. The invisibility of domestic labor explored in section one shows up in the ways we define nagging and nitpicking. This section will expose the way rigid roles impact us all, regardless of gender, sexuality, or status as parents, and propose new, more collaborative approaches to household systems. Competition and perfectionism are pitting us against one another, and section two is about how we can come together to fight back.

The third and final section of this book is about letting go of mediocrity. We may not be to blame for the messages we've picked up incidentally throughout our lives, but when we know better, we can do better. Just acknowledging imbalance or overextension isn't enough. This section is about rethinking the ways we show up for one another, swapping individualism for a more collective approach. Quality connections come from mutuality, vulnerability, and reciprocity of care. The expectations to fit within certain cultural norms are strong, and section three is the space to explore, to be curious, and to reject the idea that having standards and expectations is a bad thing. We cannot have what we need unless we give ourselves permission to consider what our needs might be and how we can all have more of what we need by moving from our atomized families into community. The mediocrity we accept in our personal lives stems from mediocrity at large. It comes from ill-fitting social norms and systems that leave our lives lacking. We get to decide for *ourselves* what we want, and in this section, we imagine what's possible.

I'm writing this book from my perspective, which is informed by my intersecting identities both in how I am perceived in the world and how I perceive it. Many of the issues explored throughout this book are rooted in capitalist, patriarchal, ableist, white supremacist social norms. These norms affect us all differently. We internalize them differently; they influence our behavior differently and impact our relational dynamics differently. I am a cisgendered white woman in a heterosexual partnership. I am a mother. I have invisible disabilities, a college education, and grew up financially secure. My experiences, my relationships, my access to information and resources have all shaped the lens through which I see the world, and though I'm committed to an ongoing pursuit of growth and understanding—and not for lack of consideration—my viewpoint is limited.

In these pages, as we confront the ways our culture plays out in our intimate partnerships, it's essential that we also look at the ways these norms reinforce the broader oppressive social systems that benefit from our burnout, individualistic thinking, and divestment from quality connections.

Learning to connect more deeply, build community, set limits, and grow together doesn't just benefit our closest relationships. These practices are acts of resistance against broader systemic social issues. I encourage anyone reading these pages to explore the works of those most impacted by these social systems, especially those who experience multiple intersections of marginalization. Read, listen to, witness, and discuss the stories of others whose identities and experiences differ from yours. Some of the voices that have had the greatest impact on me over the past several years have been Koa Beck, Mia Birdsong, Angela Y. Davis, bell hooks, Mariame Kaba, Mikki Kendall, Robin Wall Kimmerer, Audre Lorde, Leah Lakshmi Piepzna-Samarasinha, and Alice Wong. Evidence of the impact of others on me can be found woven throughout these pages. So much of what I continue to discover about community, interdependence, sustainability, and love has been influenced by the invaluable works of these and other brilliant storytellers, organizers, theorists, authors, and educators. None of my growth has happened in a vacuum, and I am forever grateful for the gifts that others have put into the world by sharing themselves, their ideas, and their perspectives.

Some portions of this book will directly confront heteronormativity and gender roles, but that is not what this book is about. This book is meant to challenge what we see as "good enough" for ourselves. My hope is that you'll feel validated and motivated by this book but not directionless. There are concrete steps we can take as individuals and as a society to live more connected and joy-filled lives.

Throughout the following chapters, alongside the critiques of what is currently normalized for us, I'll provide examples and actionable steps to help you align your life with what you truly want. I'll share resources, lessons learned, and real-life examples of what it looks like to leave mediocrity behind. Because race, religion, disability, socioeconomic class, employment status, age, and location are some of the factors that affect how we are impacted in society and how we experience the world, diversity and inclusion are a priority for me. The stories you'll find in this book come from firsthand accounts; interviews with friends, acquaintances, clients, followers, and experts; and responses from my social media following. The experiences shared in this book are real; however, I've often changed identifying details, and in some cases, I've taken similar experiences from multiple people and combined them to illustrate a shared experience in a way that protects the storytellers' identities.

The path that's been forged for us, the roles we've been told we should play, and the values we're encouraged to adopt are not our own. There are countless ways to live in community, to maintain bonds, and to meet our own and one another's needs.

More important than playing the role that was handed to us is taking the chance to write our own story. Instead of settling for a limited definition of adulthood, relationships, or success, we have a daily opportunity to invest in living a good life. We don't have to accept mediocrity as the best we can hope for—we can demand more. We each get to decide what good means to us. *We all deserve lives that are more than mediocre.* It's my hope that this book will empower you to have such a life.

PART 1

At Home:
Notice, Get Mad,
Change Expectations

CHAPTER ONE

Domestic Engineer

What We Miss When We Undervalue Care

USED TO THINK I grew up with a dad who worked and a mom who didn't. My dad woke up every weekday and went to his job. In exchange for his time and efforts, he brought home a paycheck. There was no question that his work was work. Meanwhile, in my mind, my mom was just a mom. When asked what she did for work, without skipping a beat, I'd tell someone she did nothing, carelessly rendering her days invisible. In reality, she worked tirelessly. She handled the unpaid daily demands of managing our household, including being the primary caregiver of me and my two brothers. Often unnoticed and definitely undervalued, she spent countless hours every day and the majority of her mental and emotional capacity on the work that made our lives special.

I believed my mother didn't work because that's the understanding I'd picked up from the world around me. The language I'd always heard used to describe primary parents, homemakers, and life-builders was passive. They stayed home. They were "just" moms. What do they do for a living? Nothing! I'd unconsciously absorbed the idea that the work that kept me alive and thriving was not *actually* work.

I was appreciative of how my mother cared for us, but my understanding of the mental, emotional, and physical efforts it took to keep our family together was shallow and misguided. My mother planned and coordinated while my head was bent over a Game Boy or I was at playdates she'd planned for me. She made phone calls and grocery lists, filled out forms, and switched loads of laundry in between carting us around to sports and dance classes. She knew our teachers' names, where our friends lived, and when our last physicals were. Top of mind, she was always considering what life lessons we needed to learn, how we could learn them, and what she could do to support us. Not only was she sure to check the pantry to note which of everyone's staple foods were needed before heading to the grocery store, but she also shook off her own feelings whenever her children needed comforting and made hard decisions about how to handle the minefield that is teenage rebellion.

I appreciated the fruits of my mother's labor, but I never gave a second thought to the fact that I wasn't categorizing her efforts as *real work*. I took them for granted, seeing what she was doing as simply what any mother would do. The heavy lifting of orchestrating a home life, to me, wasn't labor. I saw what she did all day, every day, as something else—some kind of natural expression of what it meant to be a woman. To be a mom.

THE SHAMPOO FAIRY

It wasn't until I was living on my own that I started noticing how many small details and tiny tasks I'd taken for granted growing up. The efforts that had gone unnoticed then hit me in the face when they became my own. There's nothing quite like getting stuck home alone with no toilet paper to realize your mom always made sure there was a stash of extra rolls in the bathroom cabinet. My mom was a "Shampoo Fairy." She'd notice when our toiletries were running low and add them to her shopping list before they ever ran out. We'd mention a diminishing stock of Q-tips or toothpaste to her in passing, and more would show up a day or two later like magic. Forms left out for field trips were completed and placed in backpacks; carpools were coordinated; and sports jerseys were stain-treated and laid out clean before big games.

But the idea of a Shampoo Fairy is absolute bullshit. Our home wasn't run by mystical spirits. There was no magic wand. *There was domestic engineering.*

There was the mental labor of planning and organizing, the emotional labor of raising well-adjusted kids, and the physical labor of the daily demands of family life, all orchestrated and executed with precision.

To me, those tasks I hardly noticed or saw as minor were essential aspects of what made me feel safe and secure as a kid. My mom's reliability and problem-solving skills helped me grow. She noticed what we needed. She paid attention. She considered each detail and looked at the long- and short-term consequences of our daily activities. She assessed our immediate and bigger-picture needs and made things happen. All of that took work. The magic of our lives ran on my mom's invisible engineering.

Though I'd wrongly assumed the labor that went into caregiving was innate, there was nothing effortless about it. My mom was meticulous and careful, came up with processes and systems, and aligned each element of our family's needs and schedules in order to keep our lives running smoothly. She navigated household management with imagination and creativity. A household is like a giant machine with switches and gears that can easily become misaligned and broken. Keeping things on track takes careful planning and coordination, quick response, and an eye for detail. Domestic engineering is a science, and the consequence of any miscalculation can be severe. It was never the case that my mother didn't work. The work she did was just going unnoticed and unvalued.

ESSENTIAL AND EXPLOITED

The fact that I didn't consider the essential labor of domestic engineering to be *real* work wasn't a fluke. The fact that I often didn't see it *at all* wasn't just that I was some ungrateful kid. I was ignorant in not valuing domestic and care work, but not willfully. I'd just picked up on the ways our society assigns value to certain types of work.

The term "domestic engineering" was born in the early twentieth century as a reaction to the way domestic work had historically been belittled and pushed to the margins. Colleges across the United States were starting to offer home economics programming and advertised domestic engineering degrees, drawing a clear distinction between the study of physics and mathematics and the study of child development and nutrition. Over the years, the term "domestic engineer" has been a part of an ongoing movement to change the narrative around domestic and care work, and it's been used by everyone from homemakers to advertisers to domestic worker labor union organizers.

Domestic engineering falls under the category of work that maintains and sustains societies, and it's all a part of a process that theorists call social reproduction. There's work that makes products and wealth, and there's work that shapes the people and conditions that keep production going. The term "social reproduction" encompasses all the work that keeps us going—all the tasks, activities, and efforts that go into reproducing society within the current generation and beyond. It's the necessary time and effort that goes into birthing, childcare, education, nutrition, and healthcare. It includes physical labor like housework, mental labor like planning meals, the emotional labor of conflict resolution, and the cultural work of passing on traditions. Social reproduction includes paid and unpaid domestic and care work and labor that happens in both private and public spaces. There's work that goes into replacing a roof, and there's work that goes into packing a lunch. There's work that goes into client management and work that goes into organizing a home. All work is work, and it all contributes to the creation of the world in which we live.

The term "social reproduction" is important because it answers the question of why it's worth our attention. Does it really matter who does the cooking and cleaning? What's the point in making a big deal out of the small stuff?

It matters because the work that reproduces societies also reproduces the inequities within them. If we want to create a most just and equitable future, we have to look at the work that goes into creating our present.

The illusion that one person's labor is more valuable than another's is an essential feature of a hierarchical society like ours. When some work matters more than other work, some people matter more than other people. Encouraging us to see some work as more prestigious, important, or valuable turns work into an oppressive tool.

There were plenty of cultural reasons I'd failed to see the value in the work that kept me alive. Domestic work is often unpaid or underpaid. In a capitalist society, money equals value. Domestic work is feminized, making it insignificant in a patriarchal society. Where there's a hierarchy to be found in our society, domestic labor plays a role in enforcing it. It has also long been racialized, making it a tool to exploit and dehumanize people of color.

A clear example of this is how, in the times of chattel slavery in America, many enslaved Black women were forced to do both domestic work inside the home and physical labor outside it. Often under threat of brutality at the hands of white mistresses, Black women kept tidy homes while their white enslavers benefited from their skilled labor of childcare, cooking, cleaning, and home maintenance. Domestic and care work was both racialized and feminized, and even women who weren't enslavers felt the impact. White women with wealth and status had lives that seemed effortless, because someone else was putting in the effort. White women who were doing the work on their own were discouraged from letting their efforts be known, in order to distance them from lower-status work. It was desirable to host a beautiful, delicious meal, but undesirable to let other people know how much hard work went into making it. It was important to have well-behaved kids whose clothes were clean, but the valuable work of discipline, education, and laundry was disregarded. The product mattered more than the process, just like everything in a capitalist society. The value of domestic work and the domestic worker disappeared. The hierarchy of whose labor was seen as valuable aligned with whose lives were assigned value.

The retellings of this time in history that focus on the violence and dominion of white men over all others and paint white women only as disempowered in their homes miss an important truth. Many white women of the time weren't interested in upending existing power structures. Their advocacy aimed to secure their own place within them. Rather than fighting for equal rights for all, they prioritized securing the legal right to enslave people, expanding their financial and social power, and reinforcing systems that upheld their own dominance over others.

This has been a trend for mainstream feminist movements—they've been more focused on increasing access to power and privilege within the existing system than transforming the system. This kind of feminism, often referred to as white feminism, does nothing to disrupt inequity on a grand scale. It's an exclusionary form of social change that re-creates the same oppressive mess in a new way—giving power to one group while holding another down. Author of *White Feminism*, Koa Beck, describes white feminism as an ideology and approach to gender equality that "focuses more on individual accumulation, capital and individuality—accruing power without any redistribution or reconsideration of it." The goal of white feminism isn't to dismantle or alter the systems that oppress women but to achieve individual success within them. By focusing on gaining power within the existing system, white feminism reinforces the same inequity it claims to fight against.

The devaluation of domestic work and domestic workers has played a major role in how certain social systems have oppressed women, and any lasting and inclusive social movement should consider that.

Despite chattel slavery being outlawed, in the centuries since, women of color have continued to be overrepresented in subordinate domestic roles, underpaid, and in positions of disempowerment compared with the people, often white women, who hire them. In imagining more personal freedom, many people buy into the idea that a sign of success would mean not having to wash one's own dishes or cook one's own meals.

If they can avoid this work entirely, it becomes a symbol that they've truly made it.

The theorist Nancy Fraser is well known for her work on how society values different types of labor. She argues that the divide between work done within the home and work done outside it, and the placement of paid labor as more valuable than unpaid, creates an imbalance of power as well as an opportunity for exploitation. Fraser has emphasized in her work that though care and domestic labor often go unpaid or underpaid, those types of work are actually at the root of what creates all social and economic value. Treating this labor as if it doesn't build bonds, maintain the health and well-being of communities, and facilitate all other work is one of the greatest and most impactful lies our society tells us. The hierarchical divide of labor and the workers who perform it is not an accident. That divide makes it into a weapon of maintaining power and control.

Domestic workers, who provide essential labor like childcare, elder care, cooking, washing, cleaning, and gardening, have historically been among the most exploited workers in the world. Through strikes, protests, and collective bargaining, grassroots organizations and domestic worker unions have fought for and won legal protections like paid leave and safety standards. And still, domestic work remains one of the least-protected sectors—often excluded from the labor laws that safeguard other workers.

Despite their critical role, domestic workers are three times more likely to live in poverty than other workers. In the United States, their median annual wage is just $20,926—less than half of what other workers earn. And in the South, where labor protections are weakest, that number drops even lower, to $18,252.

Many of these inequities were built into the system by design.

Domestic workers have long been denied the same rights as other workers, excluded from key labor protections that vary by location. In Delaware, for example, domestic workers are left out of the state's minimum wage law. Live-in domestic workers nationwide are exempt from federal overtime pay requirements. And while the Fair Labor Standards Act (FLSA) was amended in 1974 to include some domestic workers, the National Labor Relations Act (NLRA) still denies them the right to organize or collectively bargain. These are just a few of the historical exclusions that still shape domestic workers' vulnerability today.

These gaps in protection disproportionately impact women, who make up nearly 90 percent of all domestic workers—and especially Black, Hispanic, or Asian American and Pacific Islander women, who make up more than half of the workforce. Many are also immigrant women working in informal, precarious conditions without legal contracts, access to healthcare, or the right to organize.

Instead of being treated with dignity, domestic workers are often seen as disposable—denied basic labor protections and treated as if their work contributes nothing to our daily lives or the economy. But this labor is not only essential, it's holding everything together. The unpaid labor of the women and girls who do the majority of this work adds an estimated $10.8 trillion to the global economy every year.

This means domestic workers aren't just keeping households running—they're sustaining economies and generating massive amounts of wealth without retaining any of the power their work creates. They're doing some of the most valuable, life-sustaining labor there is, yet they remain among the most invisible and undervalued workers. Meanwhile those at the top with the most power, wealth, and privilege—the ones who benefit most from our social systems—continue to write the rules to a game only they can win.

While this work is woefully underpaid and often exploited in the workforce, when caregivers do this work at home without compensation, that's when society truly brushes it off as nothing.

I think there's power in putting the domestic work of family life into capitalist terms, to highlight how it's been used to disempower some for the benefit of others. Keeping the work of running a household separate from a monetary value and unattached to a fixed wage are ways we've been kept ignorant of its worth. Since money is what speaks in our society, let's put it in financial terms.

According to 2019 data from Salary.com, if stay-at-home mothers were compensated for their labor, they would be making a median salary of $178,201 annually. This prepandemic survey found that stay-at-home moms spent an average of 97 hours per week running their households. A follow-up survey by the same researchers found that the increased demands of home life throughout 2020 and 2021 had stay-at-home moms putting in an average of 106 hours a week of domestic and care work. The estimated value of that labor based on market prices and hourly demands was just under $185,000. The role of stay-at-home parent requires long hours and also demands wearing dozens of hats. They take on the roles of dietitian, educator, event planner, housekeeper, chef, chauffeur, therapist, personal assistant, and so much more. The cost of outsourcing these positions would be astronomical, meaning that domestic engineers not only contribute immense time and effort but also save their households tens or hundreds of thousands of dollars annually. Even if you could afford to outsource all the cooking, cleaning, transportation, and other tasks, the energy it takes to check references, share pertinent information, and communicate with professionals on top of the cost itself often makes it so outsourcing isn't worth it. It costs an average of $43,000 to employ a full-time nanny in the United States. That cost only covers care for standard daytime hours, and the emotional and logistical burden of finding and managing a quality caregiver is immeasurable. Weekly cleaning can cost between $300 and $800 a month, and that doesn't account for daily tidying or the time required to pick up before cleaning can even happen. Outsourcing just the cooking of weeknight dinners can cost between $45,000 and $78,000 annually for a private chef or between $15,500 and $22,000 for takeout. But even with the chopping and searing done for you, decisions around meal planning, food preferences, and dietary restrictions still need to be made. Obviously, most people aren't hiring chauffeurs, assistants, and personal shoppers to keep their lives running, but considering the market value for these skills and how much time these jobs take are two ways of visualizing what we, as a society, have failed to acknowledge.

Domestic labor is labor. Care labor is labor. The mental, emotional, and physical demands of simply *existing* require work. Very real, very important work. Adjusting our understanding and approach to this work are key factors in how we can create change in our personal lives as well as in society as a whole.

It's been in the best interests of the people who benefit from domestic labor to keep it undervalued, to the detriment of the people who perform this essential work day in and day out. When we disregard and diminish the work that maintains and sustains us in our homes and in our communities, we contribute to a society that disregards and diminishes our value as humans. Disregarding and diminishing domestic and care work also disregards and diminishes the people who require that work to survive—which is, ultimately, all of us! Discounting the value of the labor that keeps our lives running has been done purposefully, so we have to be purposeful about valuing it, acknowledging its importance, and embracing how essential it is. And in order to make progress happen on a wider scale, we must first dispel some of the more ingrained notions around domestic labor that play out in our homes.

WHEN'S MY WEEKEND?

We feel the impacts of domestic and care labor acutely in our intimate relationships, and in the same ways this labor can create inequity and protect power in society, it can do the same at home. *The unfortunate reality is that most American households deal with domestic inequity.*

And while heteronormative expectations and compulsory behavior put cis-het households at a higher risk of slipping into domestic and care inequity, compared with queer, same-sex, or polyamorous partnerships, it isn't gender, sexuality, or even job status that causes imbalance to be the norm. *Norms cause imbalance.*

The American Dream version of family life, with a man as the primary earner and a wife who handles the household, clearly defines two roles with specific responsibilities, and the complementary setup of one person working and the other handling the home is sold as a recipe for equality. This standard for partnership misses so much of what it means to be in a relationship, and the nuclear family structure with a single male earner isn't the reality of most American households.

As of 2023, the "traditional" straight, married, male-headed single-income household is no longer the typical American family structure. More than ever, people are living on their own, cohabitating with roommates or long-term partners, single-parenting, choosing not to have children, or living in multigenerational homes. Not only has the nuclear family structure become far less common over the past several decades, but the financial structure of American households has shifted as well.

Today, about half of all married American households are dual income, and the number of women who earn the same as or more than their male spouses continues to rise. Analysis from the Center for American Progress has shown an upward trend of women bearing a significant financial burden within households. As of 2019, about 65 percent of mothers were sole or co-breadwinners—with rates reaching as high as 85 percent among Black mothers. While there's been an increase in financial equity, the progress toward domestic and care equity has been much slower. The primary caregivers carrying more than their fair share are rightfully pissed.

This "second shift," a term coined and popularized by the sociologist Arlie Russell Hochschild, is the work that happens at home after paid work is done. Unfortunately, when men and women are partnered, women are doing more of it.

Research from the Pew Research Center looked at cisgender, heterosexual married couples and found a clear imbalance in household labor. In families where both partners contributed equally to finances, women averaged 4.6 hours more per week on caregiving and housework than their husbands. Even when women were the primary breadwinners, they logged about 6.9 hours on caregiving and 4.6 hours on housework per week, while their husbands spent 5 hours on caregiving and 2 hours on housework. Whether women contributed none, some, or most of the family's income, they consistently spent more time on unpaid domestic labor—between 6 and 24 hours of caregiving and housework per week depending on their financial contributions. It was only when wives were the sole earners that husbands took on a greater share of the housework and caregiving, particularly in households with children, where fathers took on about 5.6 hours more per week than their wives.

All of this data reveals that when two people earn the exact same wages and/or dedicate the exact same amount of time to paid work, domestic equity is not the guaranteed result. Simply put: equal earnings do not necessarily lead to equal domestic labor.

While there's been progress, the domestic care gap persists. The amount of time men spend on housework per week has more than doubled since 1965. Fathers today spend about two and a half times the amount of time dedicated to childcare compared to dads of the seventies. Yet, on average women still do more housework and childcare and spend less time on leisure than men, with men averaging more than five hours of leisure time than women per week.

The way married men and women split chores is only one piece of the puzzle. We need to get to what's underneath it. Looking beyond just what's happening within cis-het households can help highlight what's holding us back and paint a clearer picture of how unchecked social expectations are impacting how we spend our time and how we relate to one another.

Relational dynamics matter—women generally do more housework than their male partners. But across the board, women still do more than men, whether they're partnered with men, women, or no one at all.

Researchers have found that, compared with cis-het couples, queer and same-sex couples tend to divide the mental and cognitive labor more evenly and are less likely to report feeling like their division of household responsibilities is unfair. They are also more likely than cis-het couples to make explicit agreements and divide labor along lines of individual needs and skill sets rather than running on gendered assumptions about household roles. And while there's evidence to suggest that queer and same-sex couples are less likely to trip over unequal housework troubles, *that doesn't mean same-sex partnership is the solution to the problem.*

The issue of expectations and assumptions has the potential to rear its ugly head in any relationship structure and between any number of people. It can show up within blended families living across multiple homes, between roommates who play chicken with the dishes, in friendships where one party is always doing the planning, or in families when siblings rely on the eldest to organize the holiday events.

The disproportionate demands of time and physical labor between primary caregivers and the people they live with come with costs. Studies have linked an unequal household divide with sleeplessness, mental health problems, lower relationship satisfaction, and less intimacy. A recent study of the division of cognitive labor in households, published in the *Archives of Women's Mental Health* in 2024, found evidence that being the member of the household who is the "knower of all things" in particular had the potential to cause serious injury, not just to a relationship but to the health and wellness of the person carrying more of the mental load. Researchers found that mothers who bore the brunt of their household's mental workload experienced increased stress, depressive symptoms, and burnout, along with a decline in relationship quality.

More time running households means less time for personal or professional pursuits. Being in charge of tasks with time constraints, like taking kids to extracurriculars or serving dinner before everyone gets grumpy, can mean having to select jobs that fit family schedules. It can mean turning down social or creative opportunities. In these and so many other ways, inequity can increase one person's access to autonomy and personal wellness while limiting the other's.

Professional responsibilities, wage contributions, and unequal time demands are all important pieces of the puzzle when it comes to confronting inequity in our homes, but they don't make up the whole picture. How long a task takes doesn't define its value or account for how much energy or effort it might demand. How much that task would cost to outsource is a weak measure of its importance.

EXCUSES, EXCUSES, EXCUSES

Inequity in our relationships can hold us back and significantly affect our quality of life. And yet, efforts to address it globally and in our close relationships are often met with resistance. When the issue comes up, it's often excused away.

Here are a few of the comments I get the most:

Excuse: "But I go out and work; they stay home and handle the rest. I break my back so they can stay home!"

Reality: Financial contributions are important, and whoever is doing that work often faces a lot of unique pressures: long hours, stressful work conditions, and the weight of providing. The oppressive conditions of wage earning in our society, especially with the rising cost of housing, food, and other necessities, can feel disempowering. They *are* disempowering. But coming home and guarding your time, or expecting someone else to overcompensate by carrying the mental and emotional demands of the household, is just carrying over the exploitation we face in our work lives and inserting it into our closest relationships. Using the frustrating conditions at work—of, say, tyrannical management or the demands of endless productivity—as an excuse to expect more of a partner than of yourself is passing on that disempowerment. You're expecting a partner to keep a household afloat, because burnout-inducing economic conditions make *them* the Band-Aid to a broken system. Letting the exploitation bleed into home life does nothing to improve the conditions that create it.

The work of managing home and family life still happens in the evenings and on weekends. Not only does household management require being on call twenty-four hours a day, but demands are relentless. When are the sick days? Vacation days? How about retirement?

Excuse: "I do the outside stuff, and they do the inside stuff! In fact, I do more than my fair share! I help out around the house, too!"

Reality: A traditional gendered divide of housework where one person takes on the cleaning, meal prepping, calendar management, and laundry, and the other handles the yard work, car maintenance, and home repairs isn't inherently equal. Each task takes a different amount of time, demands different amounts of mental and emotional labor, is more or less challenging, repetitive, or uncomfortable, and so on. Yes, it's true that compared with past generations, men are spending more time on unpaid domestic labor, but when you consider how rare it was for men of previous generations to share even in diaper duty, the silliness of this argument becomes clear. And let's be real. Many of the "manly" household tasks that get brought up in these arguments are one-time projects, often done without children in tow, and are sometimes even enjoyable. When comparing housework and childcare demands, do you think you'd rather be in charge of mowing the lawn, during which you can get some sun and listen to a podcast, and have a clearly defined endpoint? Would you rather be tasked with cleaning the gutters and getting the oil changed a few times a year, or the ever-present chores of sorting, washing, drying, folding, and putting away the endless onslaught of laundry? A tree branch that needs trimming will not throw a tantrum. When you get an oil change, you get to check something off a list. The daily demands of the household never end. The second you finish a load of laundry, there's more. Dishes keep coming. Trying to feed a household on a budget, get enough protein and fiber into everyone, and not scream when you spend time and money on a meal that everyone complains about is a very specific kind of hell.

The tough part about all of this is that no one hands you a job description for a domestic engineer before you take on the role. None of us is given a list of all the mental, physical, and emotional responsibilities we will be expected to perform. Then when we're faced with the reality of all this unexpected work and a bit bamboozled, we feel like we have no one to blame but ourselves.

PISSED ABOUT DISHES

The truth is, anyone doing any job would feel cheated about being tasked with duties they didn't realize they were signing up for. Seen in that light, it's not foolish to feel upset about laundry that literally never ends. It is completely understandable to feel overwhelmed by keeping all the lists and scheduling all the appointments. It's not that you can't keep up with the vacuuming and the dishes; it's that those tasks are just the tip of the iceberg, with much, much more beneath the surface.

Even after living on my own for a while and gaining a better understanding of how vast the demands of a household really were, a lot of that work—just like my mother's—remained invisible and unaccounted for. Early on, our flow felt simple. I put my headphones in and washed the dishes or folded laundry while watching a movie. My husband helped when I asked, and it didn't feel like a significant issue to be the person asking. If he ever forgot something or did it in a way that didn't meet my expectation, it was no sweat to give a reminder, share my opinion, or do it myself. He never outright asked me to take responsibility for the home, and I never outright accepted it. It happened without clear acknowledgment, and it didn't feel like that big a deal at first. The inequity and all its consequences piled up over time.

I knew something was holding me down, but I hadn't let go of the Shampoo Fairy mindset that reduced daily essential labor to magic. Because I couldn't see all the work that I was actually doing, I couldn't validate my own experience. Because I'd seen my experience satirized on TV and on social media so frequently, I brushed my own concerns aside. Even though I knew I was consistently stretched too thin, I'd been desensitized to taking my own concerns seriously. And because I didn't want to see myself as being petty or harsh, I often downplayed my own exhaustion.

But after the birth of my second kid, the crushing weight of the additional responsibilities forced me to shift my focus. My time and energy resources were even more limited than they'd been in the past, and I could no longer keep myself and the household afloat by asking for help or doling out directions. I was more strapped for time than ever and physically couldn't keep up. Instead of trying to convince myself I was overreacting about the housework, I faced it head-on. Instead of trying to convince myself I was being silly and sensitive, I paid attention to the domestic and care work I'd been dismissing. I started mentally inventorying what I did throughout the day and kept tabs on the time and effort that went into each step. I committed to noticing every last detail, from the phone calls I took on lunch breaks to the toddler socks I turned inside out before tossing them in the laundry.

When my maternity leave ended and I transitioned into the role of a full-time working mother of two, my new awareness was both a breakthrough and a burden. On one hand, I was getting better at describing ways my husband could help, but on the other, knowing how much help I actually needed stoked the flames of my increasingly valid frustrations. Getting my hands on Eve Rodsky's book *Fair Play: A Game-Changing Solution for When You Have Too Much to Do (and More Life to Live)* a few weeks before that fateful birthday card pushed me right up to the edge. Eve does the work of breaking down a typical household into one hundred tasks and describes each one in detail. As I listened to the audiobook through my car's stereo one evening on my commute from work to daycare pickup, thinking about all the things I needed to take care of during my second shift at home, I broke down.

I'd been going through the motions, simply doing what I expected of myself without acknowledging what those expectations really were. I realized I'd never consciously accepted much of the work I found myself doing daily. I just did it. I hated that I felt like I had to be the one to ask for help. Just having to ask implied it was my responsibility in the first place. I'd never asked, or agreed, to be put in charge!

The more closely I paid attention to where my time, energy, and efforts were going, the more obvious it became that the division of labor and discrepancies in expectations in my home were issues worthy of making a big deal out of. I wasn't overreacting. I was overwhelmed, because what I was doing was overwhelming. It all felt like too much because it was.

It's reasonable to feel upset or unimportant if you don't feel like you can rely on a partner to notice and take the initiative to get things done in a way that keeps things moving at home. Feeling frustrated about "help" in the form of half-finished jobs doesn't make you ungrateful; it's an understandable response to never feeling like you have real relief. On top of that, when someone says they "can't see the mess," it can feel like they can't see all the things you do. It can feel like they don't see *you*.

Like the gears of a clock, the inner workings of a household fit together delicately, and each aspect takes time, energy, and care. We're often taught to see issues of the home as inconsequential, even though a delayed meal can set off a domino effect of disasters. Truly seeing domestic labor and valuing it appropriately are essentials to building healthy, collaborative households. To be on the same team, you need to know what you're tackling—making the invisible labor visible, not only by paying attention to the physical tasks our daily lives demand but also by acknowledging the mental and emotional labor, too.

WHAT'S MONEY WITHOUT EMOTIONAL LABOR?

Emotional labor is the work that underpins our lives. It's the thought and care that goes into everything, from what meals to make to what discipline style to use to deciding the best time to have a hard conversation. Emotional labor is what creates and nurtures communities and connections, and it's present in every interaction we have. In 1983, Arlie Russell Hochschild, the same sociologist who defined "the second shift," also coined the term "emotional labor." It was originally used to refer to the emotional work required of a job such as a flight attendant or therapist, but the term has adapted and expanded to describe similar work in any setting.

A flight attendant who needs to manage their own emotions while being condescended to by a drunk passenger must read the feelings of others, predict their behavior, and respond in a way that creates a certain emotional environment. The same work is present in planning holiday meals, delegating tasks on Sunday cleaning days, and facilitating relationships between in-laws and their grandkids. Navigating everyone's needs, wants, personalities, behaviors, and expectations takes empathy, consideration, and care.

The author and journalist Rose Hackman delves deep into the topic of emotional labor in her 2023 book, *Emotional Labor: The Invisible Work Shaping Our Lives and How to Claim Our Power*. On a call with me, Rose shared her definition of the term. Emotional labor, as she defines it, is "the editing work of emotions you will do on yourself, or a person will do on themselves in order to have an effect on the emotions of the people around them. It's a smile that you will give to the people around you, regardless of whether you're feeling good inside, in order to make other people feel good inside."

Emotional labor, whether it's paid or unpaid, with customers or between loved ones, is skilled work that demands effort and energy. Emotional labor is ever-present, tangled up in every interaction we have, from how we deal with receiving dressing on our salad when we asked for it on the side to coming out to our parents. While the term itself is most often used to describe the internal processing and decision-making that influences how we interact with others, emotional labor is inextricably connected to all other work we do in service of our relationships with others.

When a friend loses a loved one, emotional labor is present in the lowering of shoulders and softened tone when offering a hug. It's linked to the mental labor of picking out a black dress and ordering flowers in preparation for funeral attendance. It's connected to the domestic work of cooking a casserole and preparing for childcare so you can be there. It takes emotional, mental, domestic, and care work for us to make one another feel secure, loved, and supported. These efforts are the glue that bonds us. This labor creates and nurtures communities. It's the work that goes into making us feel how we feel. This real and necessary work contributes to how we love, connect, and grow.

Emotional labor, like other domestic and care labor, has also been used as a tool of exploitation. There's all kinds of messaging about how women are "emotional creatures" or "just better at" feelings. This isn't a biological truth. Sex or gender does not determine someone's ability to be empathic. It doesn't determine whether someone can consider others' feelings, respond with care, or achieve a meaningful emotional outcome. Empathy, or the ability to assess other people's feelings and put yourself in their shoes, is something we need to practice. Identifying our own and other people's feelings and considering the needs of multiple people in decision-making are skills that need developing.

Throughout society, this feminized and often racialized work is disproportionately demanded of the oppressed to protect the power of the oppressor.

Rose explained that, in her research on emotional labor, she heard plenty of arguments that women are naturally better suited to read the emotions of others compared to their male counterparts,

but she found that so-called women's intuition isn't a female phenomenon. Women often learn to pay attention to the feelings of the
people around them because it's a survival skill. When I get cat-
called, I have a split second to assess the situation before deciding
to flip him off, to pretend I don't hear him, or to smile. Rose describes this emotional labor as coerced, where the person performing it has to make a series of often self-betraying choices in order to
avoid punishment.

This kind of emotional labor isn't just women's work. Rose
shared that, in her years of research, she's come to understand that
emotional labor and intuition have far less to do with gender and
much more to do with power. You see this anytime one group is
being centered in our society and another is expected to cater to
their feelings.

For example, Rose described a hypothetical scenario where a
Black man and a white man work together. If a disagreement happened, the Black man would have far less freedom to express frustration or communicate with directness than his white colleague.
Our culture of white supremacy protects and privileges white people and holds racialized groups to different standards. Studies have
shown that Black men are more likely than white men to be perceived as dangerous. Even if he used the exact same tone and body
language as his white colleague, the Black man's behavior is more
likely to be seen as threatening than the white man's.

Because of racist social beliefs, stereotyping, and discrimination, there's a power dynamic between the two men that encourages the Black man to protect the feelings of his colleague above
his own. Among other possible consequences, expressing his emotions could lead to him getting passed up for future promotions or
even fired.

Even though there's no woman, and thus no "woman's intuition," in that situation, one person is expected to predict and react to protect the feelings of the other. Rose explained that a "woman's intuition," or the ability to predict and react to someone else's emotional state, is better described as a "subordinate's intuition."

More examples of this:

- A disabled employee may wait to ask for an accommodation until they know their boss is in a good mood, then play up their positive attitude to raise their chances of getting their needs met.
- A friend may suppress their disappointment in not being picked as maid of honor, because they worry that being honest might set off the bride and get them cut from the bridal party altogether.
- An adult child might ignore hurtful comments from an emotionally immature parent so that their own children can maintain a connection with their grandparents.

Anytime one person is expected to create and maintain a certain emotional environment without equal effort from the other party involved, emotional labor becomes a tool for subordination. Within relationships, one person's lack of emotional management and regulation creates a situation in which the other person is forced to make up the difference, keeping them in their place. This becomes a tool for harm.

As Rose explained, "Not only do we live in a patriarchal society but a deeply hierarchical society." When you're coerced or forced into a position of having to put your emotions to work for the emotions of other people in such a hierarchical, rigid society, she explained, "it ends up being the literal expression of a secondary-role position." One person's unwillingness to do their fair share of emotional work forces the person they're in a relationship with to do it for them.

Yet emotional labor is the glue that binds us together. It keeps us safe, helps us grow, and makes us feel cared for and loved. Done in service of care and connection, it's how we build intimacy. When emotional labor is given freely and reciprocated, our relationships thrive. So how do we reclaim emotional labor from the ways it's used to exploit us and put it to better use? It starts with rethinking what it means to relate with each other.

TO HAVE OR TO BE A PART OF?

A reciprocal approach to relationships is different from a transactional one. In a reciprocal relationship, giving time and effort and care is done with the understanding that it's in service of the relationship, and trusting that the care will be returned but not keeping score. A transactional approach frames interactions as trades, tries to quantify and define who is giving what, and sees efforts given as entitlement to receive.

A reciprocal approach respects the fact that when we're in relationships, we have responsibilities and obligations rather than rights or entitlements. Care should be given freely, not coerced. Trying to approach our responsibilities to each other in our relationships by identifying even trades misses the point of what it means to be in relationship with other people.

When it comes to the value of the work that goes into our daily lives and its impact on us, a dollar amount or even counting the hours the tasks take fails as an effective unit of measure. A transactional capitalist lens with its tidy tit-for-tat framework doesn't do this work justice. It also places two people who are supposed to be in relationships with each other as opposing forces. Finding balance within our homes and our closest relationships isn't about simply counting chores, tallying numbers, or cutting checks; it's about putting in effort for the sake of building lives together.

Perhaps most important, intimacy is something you have to create. Cash alone doesn't make you feel seen or heard. You can use it to pay someone for their attention and care, but money itself is not *love*. A stack of bills can't remember your birthday, figure out how to handle family illness, or decide whether you'd rather book a vacation at the beach or in the mountains based on how they hope you'll feel when you're there. A human, using care and intention, has to do that. Emotional labor is essential to the development and sustainment of love. Money can help you afford to outsource tasks, but even recognizing the value in hiring help is an act of care in and of itself. Someone has to decide that putting money from the budget toward a cleaning service is a worthwhile investment because of the relief and comfort it would bring. Someone has to do the mental, emotional, and physical domestic and care labor to make a life.

Our culture tells us that to have more is to be worth more. Our culture wants us to *have* a partnership, not necessarily experience nurturing a relationship. Our culture wants us to *have* a house, not necessarily experience maintaining a happy home! We overvalue the cash that affords us the chance to buy the bigger house or send our kids to a private school and undervalue the labor of remembering your partner's favorite meal or comforting your kid through their first heartbreak.

At any given moment in the world, there are masses of people digging in drawers for a partner to a sock, ordering birthday cakes, scraping cheese off pans, sneaking stuffies into washing machines, researching nut-free school lunches, and doing all the simple yet oh-so-special daily tasks that make up a life. That scam, that money is the key to giving yourself a good life, is what makes us miss out on the value of the little acts of domestic and care labor that actually facilitate the moments of goodness. For as long as we miss what really matters, we'll miss out on truly experiencing it in our pursuit of something better.

SIGN UP FOR IT

Too often, we end up unconsciously playing out harmful dynamics despite our best intentions. We lean on models of partnership from our families of origin and subscribe to social expectations, because it's what we know. To rewrite the scripts we've been handed, we have to adopt a practice of paying attention. We have to ask ourselves questions about our needs, our feelings, and our behaviors. Rather than acting on what we've been convinced to find valuable by a society that doesn't give a shit about us, we have to decide for ourselves what matters.

This change has to start with a new worldview. One that focuses on the ways we are connected to one another and values the work that strengthens communities. Giving the labor that creates our lives the respect and value it deserves is one of the most important and immediate shifts we can make when building something better.

When we have choice over how we spend our time, what are we choosing to prioritize? Are we skipping meals with family so we can put in extra hours at work? Are we competing with each other for prestige or validation? Too often we treat household tasks like a game of hot potato—passing them off, avoiding responsibility, deferring them, or pretending they don't exist. We act as if the work that contributes the most to our well-being is an inconvenience—something to pawn off, to minimize and push to the bottom of the priority list. And when the avoidance becomes a standoff, it poisons our relationships. The empty toilet paper roll sits on the holder, the laundry pile grows on the stairs, the recycling overflows on the back porch—each of us waiting to see who will cave and do it first.

Ignoring the tasks doesn't just leave them undone. It corrodes the quality of our lives and relationships. When we disregard the work that keeps our homes and relationships functioning, we devalue the people doing it. It breeds resentment, fosters imbalance, and turns shared responsibilities into power struggles.

But care is in the details. It's in vacuuming up the crumbs so they don't stick to your loved one's feet, in matching their socks so their morning runs smoothly. It's in remembering they wanted to increase their iron intake and looking up a few recipes, in deep cleaning the kitchen bins before the smell becomes a problem, in labeling storage bins so the holiday decorations are easy to find each season. It's the little things that make life easier, that show we're paying attention. This is where we live. Not just in the big moments, but in the everyday acts of care that turn a house into a home. Small, thoughtful gestures—often unnoticed—are what make a home feel like a place of care rather than a battleground of score keeping.

Cleaning the house is worth closing your laptop for. Grocery shopping so that you and the people you care about have what they need is just as important as the paycheck that buys the groceries. If we find ourselves avoiding or abandoning domestic and care work, it's important to ask ourselves why. To what end? Do we work to live or live to work? How can we draw boundaries and move things around to align our lives with what really matters?

We have to learn to **notice**. Notice the care, notice the consideration, notice the decision-making. We have to notice the work we do for ourselves and one another and what that work provides for us. If we want lives that are fulfilling, we have to notice what makes us feel fulfilled. If we want to feel secure and connected, we have to notice what makes us feel secure and connected.

Think about a time you felt really cared for. Try to visualize it. What contributed to that feeling? What were you experiencing? Who was involved? What actions and behaviors affected how you felt? What emotional and mental labor contributed to it? Let yourself linger on the details. Take yourself through any sensory experiences that may have been a part of how you felt: tastes, smells, something you touched or heard. Think about the work that went into each aspect of what contributed to how you felt.

Care can look like a friend taking the time out of their day to pick you up from the airport. It can look like a package sent to your house on your birthday. It can also look like someone brewing coffee before you come over and remembering to keep creamer in the fridge for you, even though they take their coffee black. Care can look like helping you move a couch up two flights of stairs, and it can also look like being supportive when someone needs to take space or talking it out when your feelings are hurt. The little moments of noticing, the tiny tasks that might seem so insignificant, simply aren't.

THE POET AND AUTHOR OF *A REBELLION OF CARE*, DAVID GATE, whose writing and visual art "centers around care for the individual (heart, mind, body & soul) and the nurture of community (culture, the earth & environment, the dignity of others and spiritual communities)," aptly redefines the work that goes unnoticed and undervalued in his poem "Doing the Laundry."

DOING THE LAUNDRY

Doing the laundry
and the dishes
and meal preparation
are not tasks of the mundane
because being clothed
and clean
and fed
declares the dignity
of human life
and nurtures us
into new days
into new eras
they are not mundane, no
they are the rituals of care

How would these tasks change if we stopped seeing them as mundane and instead saw them as *rituals of care?* Maybe the repetitive work of dishes, laundry, meals, and cleaning can feel tiresome and never-ending. But it's also a part of the bigger picture of what facilitates living. *It's part of what life is made of.* When we do these tasks for ourselves, we grow. When we do them for each other, we grow together. Paying attention to each other, showing up for each other, and allowing ourselves to be shown up for in big and small ways *is what life is all about.*

Capitalism has little to gain when we invest our time in each other, when we get together as a family and have a cleaning dance party instead of putting in extra work away from each other in order to pay to outsource that cleaning. As long as we see acquisition as more valuable than how we impact one another, capitalism wins.

Mediocrity wins. Having a family doesn't mean you're a part of it. Having a house doesn't mean you have a home.

The erasure of domestic labor has been purposeful—so our pushback on it has to be, too. To value this care, to take it seriously, to honor the weight and impact it has on us is an act of personal *and* social liberation. Valuing this work for what it is—that's at the core of building equitable partnerships *and* an equitable world. *These rituals of care will nurture us toward the future we imagine.*

5 THINGS YOU CAN DO RIGHT NOW

1. Take Note

Start a list of the little things that make you feel good. Keep a notebook with you or a running list in a document on your phone. When you notice joy, ease, or pleasure, take note. Is it hot coffee in the morning in your favorite mug? Turning on your postwork playlist before starting dinner? A favorite food, a way a certain person approaches you, rubbing your feet together under your covers like a cricket before falling asleep? Jot it down. Then, with as much precision as possible, describe how you're feeling. Safe, secure, cared for, easy, empowered, or comforted? Use this activity to incorporate the practice of noticing into your daily life. Learn to recognize what matters to you. When you can connect the dots between your needs and what contributes to them being met, you can invest your time and energy accordingly. Done with a friend or partner, this can be a powerful way to learn how to show up for each other.

2. Roles and Responsibilities

We each have different understandings of what it means to be in a relationship or to fulfill a certain role. Rather than running on assumptions or unspoken expectations, define roles and responsibilities clearly and explicitly. Studies have shown that equality, or equal splits of chores or financial responsibilities, isn't what creates relational satisfaction. A better predictor of satisfaction is when expectations, *whatever they are*, align with reality. That, and the ability to have open conversations, which often result in efforts being made to meet everyone's needs. For everyone to feel good about a household system, being able to talk about it and establish a sense of understanding and agreement matters—oftentimes even more than whether tasks are split evenly. Like in all other situations, *consent* matters.

YOU MAY HAVE signed up for an "equal partnership," but your and your partner's definitions of that may have been different from the jump. Your definitions also may have *changed*. Consent should be ongoing. You're allowed to change your mind or renegotiate!

SET A ONE-YEAR goal for your household. What will the division of labor look like? What would you like each party's roles and responsibilities to be one year from now? Be as clear and explicit as possible. Who would do what? How would time be spent and which decisions would be made together and which separately? Is there anything each person would like to spend more or less time on? Once you have a vision in mind, decide on two or three actionable steps you'll take to get there.

3. Connect Consistently

Daily or weekly, in-person or virtually—it doesn't matter! Carve out a consistent time to connect with your partner about the division of domestic responsibilities and talk about your short-term and long-term family goals. Put it on a shared calendar and reschedule if you miss it. This is an opportunity for alignment, awareness, and appreciation of what goes into creating your lives. Create a shared document where you can drop notes between meetings, so neither of you carries around the anxiety of figuring out how or when to bring something up. Write it down and get it out of your head! Consistent meetings are also a good time to check in with each other about personal capacities. How much emotional capacity do you have? How much time do you have? The clearer you can be about how much capacity you each have to deal with certain tasks, the more aligned you can be on what to prioritize. Connecting regularly is less about what exactly you tackle in that time and more about a commitment to creating a life together. Consider the pain points in your relationship—where communication breakdowns or labor imbalances are taking a toll. Are they leaving you exhausted? Is the imbalance creating loneliness, stress, or limiting your opportunities? Those are the areas where consistent effort will bring the biggest payoff. *Set the time aside and then show the heck up!*

4. Household Manual

Imagine you had to hand off the running of your household to a stranger. Create a digital master document or get creative with it—get yourself a scrapbook and bedazzle it! What would you need to communicate to someone to make sure everyone in your household's needs were taken care of? How would you describe your family's top priorities? What details would they need to know, not just to pull off the bare minimum, but for a *fully* functioning home? In the household manual, include details like doctors' names and phone numbers, preferred takeout places, which family members get holiday gifts, when you usually start on your taxes, how often you service appliances, and so on.

A few ways of starting this process:

Task by Task: Pick a household task and write it on the top of a piece of paper. Draw four columns with headings: "daily," "weekly," "monthly," and "yearly." Brainstorm the mini-tasks within a bigger task and fill in each column. Write down every aspect of that task and every detail you can think of, including the mental, emotional, and physical labor involved. For example, dishes are washed, dried or put on a rack, then put away daily. Whoever does them needs to notice what's dirty and what needs to be cleaned before each meal. Weekly, you may bleach the sink or disinfect brushes, search the house for loose cups, and take water bottles apart. Monthly, you might scrub the drying rack and restock dish soap. Yearly, you may replace any broken or misplaced kids' utensils or water bottles. Be detailed and don't forget to include the visible *and* invisible aspects of a task.

Room by Room: Pick a room in your home and list all the tasks that keep it functioning. For example, list everything that happens in the kitchen: groceries and meals, cleaning, appliance services, trash, stocking home supplies, backpacks and homework, and so on. Use each task as its own heading and outline how each one is done.

No need to rush through this project. The *process* of talking through household tasks and how your family does them is what's important.

For printables and additional resources, visit my website: www.lauradanger.com.

5. Equity in Autonomy

Where there's an imbalance in household responsibilities, there's almost always an imbalance in access to autonomous time—time in which you have choice in how it's spent. If you need a place to start in making your household more equitable, start there.

Does one person have the freedom to "run out real quick" but the other has to ask permission to do things like shower? Does one person have the ability to come home late without much warning while the other would have to plan well in advance to do the same? Is one person structuring their personal and professional pursuits around the needs of the household, while the other fits in household tasks around their own goals? What happens when the household gets sick? Who gets time to heal, and how well does the household function when they're down for the count?

Aim for equity in quantity *and* quality of autonomous time.

Consider how much time each person gets when they're completely off the hook for meeting other people's immediate needs. Not just time when the baby is napping, when you're still tethered to the house and on call if anything happens, but time when you're free to focus on yourself.

Ask yourself what *quality autonomous time would feel like.* Would it be time spent connecting with friends? Uninterrupted time to make art? A night out where you don't have to rush home to help with bedtime? Taking a twelve-week pottery class or joining a soccer league? A daily walk?

What would need to happen to give all parties equal access to quality autonomous time?

What information needs to be communicated? What adjustments could be made to time or budget? Are there resources in your community or people in your network who can help make rest happen?

Are there ways to create more time by freeing up schedules, sharing responsibilities differently, or letting go of nonessential tasks? And when the time is available, how can it be more restorative, fulfilling, or meaningful?

You may be facing challenges like shift-work schedules, deployment, and complex care responsibilities. You may lack access to childcare, time, money, or support. You may not feel safe or interested in leaving your child in the care of others. But even the small changes can add up. Consider both the resources you do have access to and the barriers in your way.

Instead of asking "if" rest is possible, approach it with a mindset of "how."

CHAPTER TWO

Sitcom Syndrome

The Hidden Harms of Laughing It Off

ONE NIGHT WHILE out for a friend's birthday dinner, I was seated across from a couple, Maggie and Brian, whom I'd never met before. Maggie and Brian were in their mid-thirties, had been married for ten years, and had a toddler and a new baby. As we all introduced ourselves, Brian told me about the tech startup he worked for that kept him busy with long days and frequent evening and weekend wining and dining. Maggie shared that she'd recently accepted a full-time in-person position after working part-time from home and managing childcare for the past few years.

When it was my turn to share and I explained that I work in the realm of domestic labor, Maggie excitedly leaned in and remarked, "I bet you're never short on work!" She said she'd been panicked about how she was going to manage everything once she made the job transition, but before she could finish what she was saying, Brian cut her off. He explained that she had nothing to worry about because having the kids in daycare would make everything way easier. She gave a playfully unsure face and looked like she was going to continue, but Brian spoke over her again, reminding her that he'd agreed to cook on the nights he was home and was always happy to pitch in whenever he had the time. "You'll be fine! I'm here to help!" he assured her.

As we kept talking, and the topic shifted to what we all liked to do for fun outside of parenting and work, I felt a noticeable tension from across the table. Brain explained that except for work-related entertainment and travel, Saturdays golfing with his brother on his nontravel weekends, and his Thursday-night soccer meetups, he really didn't get to do much. As Maggie listened to Brian explain how he spent his time, her jaw clenched and her body stiffened, but she kept her smile. When it was her time to share, she said, mockingly, "Well, I mean, except for my fancy macaroni dinners and traveling to Target with the kids . . ." I gave her a polite smile as she trailed off. "No, but really," she went on, "I'm dying to find some personal time." Brian turned to her and laughed. "For what? So you can take your book somewhere and read?" He looked at me and explained that all she ever wants to talk about is her books. To her, he said, "How many more hours could you really spend reading? You don't get enough time for that when the kids are asleep?"

Her smile bent into a wince, and she furrowed her brow as she shot a wounded look at Brian. He laughed again. "What?! It's not like you're a social butterfly. Name one friend you'd go out with!" She stared at him with an exaggerated look of shock as he went on. "You haven't had a hobby in years! Don't lie! Are you telling me you wouldn't just do the same thing you do at home?" She kept staring back at him wordlessly, clearly searching for how to respond. I kept my eyes glued to her, ready to follow her lead.

She shook her head and rolled her eyes as if to say, "Men, am I right?" As her husband continued to tease, Maggie gave a defeated sigh and laughed, then swatted at him. She gave me a resigned smile, turned the joke on herself, and said to me, "He's not wrong," before changing the subject to appetizers.

I'd been in her shoes before, not just with partners but also with bosses and friends, having to weigh whether to stand my ground or accept what felt like defeat in a conversation that was never meant to be a competition. I recognized the tactic as a way to diffuse and distract, so when she tossed me a comment about the spinach dip, I took the conversation pivot and ran with it.

TAKEN HOSTAGE

I gleaned from the situation that Brian and Maggie had different ideas about what it looked like to share household responsibilities. Clearly, they also had different definitions of personal time. On top of the opportunities for traveling the world and eating incredible food, Brian had consistent access to chunks of time away from his family responsibilities during his off-work hours. Meanwhile, Maggie was struggling to fit her career and personal interests into the cracks, working around the demands of facilitating family life. Brian's commentary suggested that he had very little understanding of just how much went into keeping a family functioning and the ways their family dynamic was uniquely impacting all parties. His behavior suggested he had very little empathy for Maggie.

Brian's busy schedule and the overwhelming demands of domestic engineering undoubtedly contributed to Maggie's losing touch with some of her friends and hobbies. Many primary parents and homemakers pick up hobbies that can be done flexibly, from home or with children in tow, like crafting, baking, or, in the case of Maggie, reading. She very well might have loved to spend long stretches of time with friends on her weekends, but someone had to watch the kids while Brian was traveling or out golfing. Hearing him comment on her lack of interests and friendships had to have felt like getting the wind knocked out of her. Even as an outsider, *I* felt his words like a punch to the gut.

So why did she laugh in the wake of his hurtful commentary? Brian had made her into a situational hostage.* She was unwillingly put into an uncomfortable position and given a series of bad options for how to react. She'd felt hurt by her partner's commentary, but because of the social setting and the expectation to maintain peace, the *least* bad option was to laugh it off.

She could either laugh along or be honest about the harm he'd done. She could point out the problems, but she risked escalating the issue and causing a scene in front of others at the dinner table. She risked him feeling embarrassed.

Our patriarchal culture expects women to protect men from shame. It expects anyone in a lesser place of power to protect whoever has more of it. We learn that men can be dangerous when they're upset, saying things they might not mean, withdrawing emotionally, or raising their voices. Maggie chose to accept hurt feelings over the risk of blowback, deciding that emotional self-betrayal felt safer than being honest about her feelings. She chose to laugh along to break the tension, but it didn't disappear. She just absorbed it.

---

* This term was introduced to me by a workshop attendee. It's brilliant!

TGIF

Growing up, I spent my Friday nights watching TGIF on ABC. It was a block of popular family-friendly sitcoms that aired every week from 1989 to 2000 and featured shows like *Boy Meets World, Hangin' with Mr. Cooper, Full House,* and *Family Matters.* Every Friday I'd air-pop popcorn and settle down in front of the TV with my brothers, where we'd sit for hours watching our favorite characters and laughing at their antics.

Those shows left an impression on me. They transported me into the fictional living rooms of people who felt familiar, whom I liked. Those shows shaped my beliefs about what was acceptable, typical, and worth taking seriously. With their planned pauses and studio-audience laughter, they made a massive impact on how I felt about common experiences in my most formative years. For me and the tens of millions of other impressionable viewers, sitcoms contributed to some of our most foundational beliefs about what to expect out of life. For those who watched with their beliefs already established, the shows served as reinforcements.

TGIF was entertainment that I could watch with my brothers, meant to be comforting, satirical, and silly. The writers and producers of these shows intentionally played it safe in order to cast a wide net and wrote stories that most people would find enjoyable. We were meant to see the families on TV as the kind who could live next door.

Therein lies the problem. *Comedy is sneaky.* With lovable characters, relatability, and canned laughter, various forms of media play a major role in what we see as normal, acceptable, and laughable. They stay within the bounds of what the dominant culture sees as moral, and so they also strengthen the bounds of what we see as normal.

These days, sitcoms may not have the cultural influence they had in the TGIF era, but other forms of comedy affect our current beliefs and norms. When stand-up specials and viral memes confront common experiences like hating our jobs or feeling let down in our partnerships, they can either frame familiar dynamics as unserious or highlight the absurdity of what we accept. If comedy isn't done carefully, it runs the risk of taking painful matters and normalizing them rather than encouraging us to challenge them— on *and* off the screen.

All media has the opportunity to uphold or challenge the status quo. Because of that, the entertainment we consume as kids, and then as adults, is a key player in accepting mediocrity in society and in our everyday lives.

I LAUGH SO I DON'T CRY

Sitcom syndrome is the internal laugh track that overrides red flags when we see harmful dynamics. It's the self-gaslighting that happens when something feels really off, but you've been taught your whole life that it's not a big deal. The fights you keep having about housework? Sitcom syndrome is the voice in the back of your head that tells you to stop being so serious and to learn to lighten up. The cycle of criticism and defensiveness you and your partner keep finding yourselves in? Sitcom syndrome tells you to get over it! That's just how marriage is! It frames frustration as funny. It takes righteous rage and labels it ridiculous. Sitcom syndrome takes widespread social issues and, rather than encouraging change, ostracizes anyone unwilling to laugh along.

Sitcom humor is akin to pointing and laughing when someone trips. But in the case of situational comedy, the people who are most harmed by social issues are the ones tripping and getting laughed at. It's the mom who is so underwater with housework that she can't keep a job. It's the dad who gets berated by his boss but can't quit. TikTok videos, Instagram reels, and YouTube shorts, just like sitcoms, often take the modern misery of being exploited at work or feeling lonely and disconnected from your family at home and tell us to "Cheer up, buddy, you're not alone! We're all a little bit miserable. Laugh!"

Sitcom syndrome causes us to not see the seriousness of our issues. The stereotype of women being overemotional and anxious teaches us to roll our eyes and brush off their concerns. If we pause to consider why that stereotype exists—rather than assuming women are just being unreasonable—we might recognize a deeper cause behind the overwhelming stress many experience. If chronic stress weren't framed as comedy, we'd see it for what it is: a real problem.

We see our troubles on-screen and are comforted to know that we're not alone. But there's a fine line between comforting an audience and normalizing the struggles we face. When inequity, toxicity, and harm are depicted as lighthearted jokes, we become desensitized to them instead of inspired to disrupt them. Rather than critiquing harmful cultural norms, the rough edges get rounded off. We end up getting comfortable with them. We don't think to challenge domestic inequity because we are told to laugh at it.

We are taught to laugh at things that hurt us to spare other people's feelings. Without tools for real communication, we learn to choose laughter over change in our own lives.

#BRINGINGWORKHOME

Those of us who grew up religiously camped out in front of the TV on Friday nights are now adults. And though prime-time sitcoms are much less of a thing these days, we still find ourselves seeking the kind of entertainment that gives us relatability, comfort, and laughs. Many of us are finding that through our phones. At any hour of the day, we find commiseration through memes, skits, and parodies on YouTube, TikTok, and Instagram. And the situational comedy is still everywhere, just now on small screens we hold in our hands, accessible anytime, anywhere.

In a weird demonstration of "same shit, different day," the kids who sat down in front of their TVs on Fridays are now the adults who spend hours scrolling on their phones, seeing the same cheap, punching-down comedy fill their feeds. The fictional TV families have been replaced by family vloggers and couples accounts, but they all make the same jokes we've heard a million times before.

TV sitcoms and their modern equivalents give us entertainment that acts like a Band-Aid. It's surface-level comfort against the harsh realities of modern-day demands. Situational comedy is supposed to be lighthearted. It isn't meant to make you think too hard. And that's exactly why it's so dangerous. If we see painful cultural norms as things we shouldn't give too much energy, they'll never change. When we don't give it a second thought when we see a dad being so incompetent that his wife has to give up her dreams or that his kids don't trust him to take care of them, it quietly enforces the idea that the only thing we can do in the face of it is to laugh. We come to expect the behavior.

What makes modern online couples comedy even more insidious than TV sitcoms is that the family vloggers who go viral acting out tired marriage tropes are real people. When clips of influencer couples go viral, the only context we're given as onlookers is whatever fits in the sixty-second clip and whatever is typed in the caption. We don't know for sure if what's being shown is satire, slightly exaggerated, or the truth. And because of how uncritically social media is often consumed, not many people take the time to consider what they're being shown—they just file away whatever they see as another example of what's normal.

Couples comedy relies on archetypes and exaggerated stereotypes, the same way sitcoms always have. They take situations and needlessly turn them into gendered generalizations—like how men are babies when they're sick and women power through—making unfair trends out to be the result of biological differences rather than unequal social expectations.

Every month or so, there's a new viral video of a dad who promised to get up with the kids so mom could sleep in and disaster ensued. Videos in which men are made out to be buffoons fly under the radar as harmless in part because of how familiar the trope is. On the surface, it seems like these jokes land their punches on men. But marriage humor that makes men out to be jesters isn't simply showing the punch line as them being fools. When these dynamics play out in real life, the punches land on the kids who can't rely on their dads and the wives who have such unreliable partners that they have to make sacrifices and overcompensate.

Some of the most common couples tropes reinforce fathers as domestic duds, but one of the most popular themes in mainstream relationship comedy is the burnt-out breadwinner. These jokes boil down to the idea that men, or more broadly whoever is working a "harder" or "better" job, shouldn't be expected to be reliable at home because they've paid their dues and are entitled to be taken care of. We laugh at the guy who deals with the misery of waged work all day and let him off the hook for lollygagging at home—hiding in the bathroom for an hour when it's time to clear the dishes or being too tuckered out to toss his socks into the laundry basket. The ever-present undercurrent of the jokes about domestic inequity is that we all know how demanding bosses and clients can be and how stressful many workplaces are. An alarming 80 percent of American workers say their workplace conditions have negatively impacted their mental health. Meanwhile, wages have failed to keep up with rates of productivity, and the rich get richer. Analysis from the Economic Policy Institute found that compared to CEOs of the 1960s, who made about twenty times that of their workers, as of 2022, CEOs of similar-size companies were making around three hundred times that of the average worker.

Avoiding the tasks that help us meet our basic needs or pushing them off onto each other because we're so exhausted by work isn't a gender issue—it's a capitalism issue. It's an issue of a society that makes it hard for us to have enough time or energy to do basic things like eat, sleep, keep our homes clean, and spend quality time together. We don't have enough support at work, and we don't have enough support at home, but mainstream comedy has long encouraged us to point fingers solely at each other and to accept these conditions as inevitable. When we laugh at the played-up comedy version of the person who comes home after work and dodges responsibilities, we miss an opportunity to place blame where it belongs—on the social conditions that have us feeling like we're in such a perpetual pinch.

Opting out of work at home because you're burnt out is a common comedy trope, but the crisis of exploitative work conditions *isn't funny*. To see the true impact of this kind of comedy, we must consider who's actually harmed in the realities being satirized. Many waged earners get belittled at work all day, then come home so drained that they accept letting their partner overcompensate for them. With their lack of participation, they send the contradictory message that the work of the home is simultaneously less challenging, important, and valuable than their waged work, while also being *too much* for them to participate in.

It's a serious problem to be so drained by conditions at work that you have nothing left to give when it comes to caring for yourself or others, but that doesn't mean we should accept offloading that misery onto our partners. Using the frustrating conditions at work and the demands of endless productivity as an excuse to expect more of a partner than of yourself is passing on that disempowerment, not doing anything to improve the oppressive conditions that create it.

What if we zoomed out? What if we took this dynamic at face value and investigated how we could make the situation rare rather than relatable?

Who benefits when we take our dissatisfaction with the status quo home with us and play out normalized power dynamics between ourselves? Who benefits when we see the isolating and unjust social conditions as normal? When we laugh at familiar misfortune, the systems that create it avoid being held accountable. They're left unchallenged.

IN ON THE JOKE

There's a particular brand of social media content that deserves an especially close look: the questionably candid kind.

In one video posted on a couple's account with more than one hundred thousand followers on TikTok, a husband films his wife as she glares at him. She stares at him, aware she's being filmed, surrounded by mounds of laundry, piled on top of the machine and spread across the floor. The video appears to cut in midway through a conversation they were already having.

The caption playfully reads, "Have a great trip . . . we'll miss you <3 #deerseason #huntingwidow #husbandandwifecomedy."

The first thing we hear when the clip starts is him laughing at her from behind the camera, asking her to repeat whatever she'd just said so he could get it on video.

He chuckles, "What was that? What did you say?"

She starts shuffling around the room, picking up clothes and sorting them into piles, moving quickly, and in a matter-of-fact tone responds to him. "You're leaving for hunting today, so what does that mean for me? You'll be gone for ten days. That means for the next ten days, I have to take care of everything: chores, house, school, kids, work, cross-country, you name it." She ends with a defeated sigh and a sarcastic, "So I hope you have a *super* good trip."

The camera cuts. This video and so many others along the same lines riddle online spaces. They capture what seem like candid or "unfiltered" moments and present them as if they're funny, but they tell a serious story. The overwhelmed, self-proclaimed "hunting widow" is a woman who appears to be managing a career and a household, who is well past her limit, clearly expressing frustration and resentment, and instead of engaging with her in a meaningful way, her husband gets his phone out to capture her complaints as content. She's explaining how overwhelming and unequal their dynamic is, and he doesn't express empathy or understanding. Then he laughs in her face. The video captures a significant issue and presents it as unserious.

We don't know the people who posted the video. We don't know their lives or what led to the moment they posted. With only the context we're given, we're left to wonder if what we're being shown was staged, exaggerated, or a candid clip. There's a lot of context missing, and the intention behind posting the video isn't clear. The caption says it's comedy, but what parts are we supposed to be laughing at?

If this video showed up on your feed, you might not give it a second thought. Conflict is hard. Their dynamic may feel familiar. It's just a short clip in a sea of online vlogger content and viral videos, an insignificant social media moment in the grand scheme of things.

What's worth looking at is how we're impacted by what we casually consume every day. We know household inequity is normal, so when we see "real" content of how other people handle it, it affects how we see our own lives.

Clips of dysfunction and imbalance are everywhere online, and, especially when they reflect our own painful realities, they have the same effect that TGIF did. When we mindlessly scroll, we subconsciously absorb these scenarios as okay. Social media scrolls are generally meant to be a time to turn off your brain. We're not critically examining what's being shown in clips that cross our feed. But a closer look can be valuable, *so that's exactly what we're going to do here.*

The hunting widow is expressing her feelings clearly and directly while also being recorded, likely knowing the video will be made public. She toes the line of sharing her annoyance while keeping her rage reined in enough to not make it seem too serious. Her self-editing is a herculean display of emotional labor in action. When the camera first starts recording, she's more heated, but her tone changes as the video goes on. She's very clearly feeling frantic and frustrated but remains measured. What we see is an honest look at a woman who really is struggling while her husband looks on and laughs.

The video was seen more than a million times and received

thousands of comments. Many came from fed-up wives cheering on the woman in the video for speaking her mind. Some claimed to be hunting widows just like her. There were echoes from folks commiserating, plenty of comments telling her to lay off her "hard-working husband," and even more encouraging them to call a divorce lawyer. If the couple posted the video because they thought it would be relatable, *they were definitely correct.* The issue of whether it was *funny* was where most people disagreed.

The fact that the comment section had such a split opinion of what they were looking at is a clear indication that we should collectively be giving the topic a bit more thought. Why do we laugh off such a common experience, even when it causes anger and resentment? Why do we dismiss how common it is to feel misunderstood and hurt?

We don't have context for the lived experience of the couple who posted the video. We're all shaped by the conditions we grow up in, and instead of singling out individuals as the root of the problem, we can focus on the bigger picture: the cultural norms that make these dynamics feel normal. Rather than attacking one person for a bad joke, our energy is better spent calling out the jokes themselves and challenging the culture that makes them acceptable in the first place.

LIGHTEN UP

Evidence of why we need to take a closer look at relationship norms ends up in my inbox on a daily basis. On top of being tagged in cringeworthy couples comedy, I see far too many clips of desperate and defeated primary caregivers who make pleas for support. What hurts to see is that the folks who turn to their phones to make videos in hopes of finding camaraderie are often seeking outside validation because something has convinced them their feelings aren't reasonable. It could be family or friends who brush off their concerns, or socially conditioned self-doubt, but what's for sure is that the "jokes" that fill our For You pages contribute to a culture that downplays pain. Every day in my inbox, next to the clips of real people who are vulnerable and hurt, I also get skits satirizing the behavior that hurt them.

In one especially heartbreaking video, posted in June 2022, a young parent leans in close to the camera and quietly vents. The words "I'm not mad at my husband, just tired" are captioned at the top of the screen. She sighs and says, "So this afternoon, after a long day of being a stay-at-home mom / working mom, my husband comes home and— Oh, is this a doozy! The first thing he does is ignore the children, lay straight down on the bed, and go to sleep. And I know he's tired, but so am I. Just because you clock out of work doesn't mean you clock out of parenthood." She goes on to explain that despite begging for help, her husband refused. She explained that she'd been battling a cold, had a colicky baby, and desperately wished her husband would work with her. "But no, he's in there sleeping right now, and I'm up trying to get the toddler to bed, cleaning up the dinner mess, doing the laundry, cleaning up the rest of the house, and desperately trying to sort out our financial stress. Everything is on me. Everything is on my shoulders. And he wonders why I have such a short temper." She continues. "My patience is starting to wear thin." Anyone in her shoes would be running out of patience. She claimed she wasn't mad, but she had every right to be.

This exhausted parent and the hunting widow downplayed their experiences—one with a clarifying text above her head and the other through comedy hashtags in her caption. Both burnt-out caregivers were clearly angry and hurt, but something held them back from turning that pain into something useful.

The lack of context that comes with viral content and the performative nature of social media blur the line between fantasy and fiction in the content we consume. If we're not careful, casual consumption of couples comedy and motherhood content will continue to reinforce the same inequities that caused the tropes in the first place. Women will continue to be made out to be "hysterical," and nobody will blink twice at a dad who doesn't know how to change a diaper. Anything outside that will be an exception, not the rule.

Even though the woman in the hunting-widow video was the one suffering from the situation, the video's existence on their shared account suggests she agreed to post it. As it gained traction and went viral, they even pinned it as a featured post on their profile. She may have helped write the caption or even laughed at the comments. Why? Probably because it felt like the safest option. When your pain has been consistently made the butt of a joke, refusing to laugh at the harm that's being done to you can cause new and different problems. What would it mean to have these scenarios not be facts of life? Of inevitable mediocrity?

I'M A LOT OF FUN AT PARTIES

Some of the most popular jokes are also the most harmful. But because so many people engage with them, when anyone dares to push back on whether they're worth laughing at, they're told they "must be a lot of fun at parties." Despite what naysayers would claim, failing to find humor in putting down, punishing, humiliating, exploiting, or dismissing another person or their needs doesn't make a person humorless. Part of the culture-changing work of disrupting social norms is changing what kind of media we engage with. There are entertainers and influencers out there making relatable content that doesn't ask audience members to find humor in things that hurt.

The comedian Clare Brown, author of *New Nigeria County* and @clarabellecwb on TikTok and Instagram, is one example of a creator who is using comedy to make change. In an interview, she told me that one of the biggest problems she sees with the situational comedy popularized on online couples accounts is the way women are nearly always made to be the punch line. That kind of comedy furthers power dynamics rather than disrupting them. While mainstream situational comedy takes real experiences and presents them at face value for laughs, Clare's skits take common situations and use shifted context and strategically placed exaggeration to elevate the underdogs.

In one of her most popular videos, captioned, "If we spoke to young boys the way we speak to young women," she rocks a baby doll and speaks to someone off-screen, rattling off condescending commentary like, "Watch your brother until your daddy gets back"; "This is what your body is meant to do. Carry babies. That's why boys have such strong upper bodies"; "Look at you, little papa!"; "Sweetie, put on a sweater. If you show everything off now, you'll have nothing to give your future wife"; and "Look at you cleaning up—you'll make a great little husband one day." In another video from a series titled "If white people experienced racial microaggressions," she plays the character of an HR professional who stumbles over how to pronounce the name Megan, claiming it's a mouthful, before reprimanding her white employee for her "unprofessional" flat hair. Clare highlights how ridiculous it is that we accept oppressive dynamics by flipping them. By placing the oppressor in the shoes of the oppressed, she ridicules the power dynamic, not the people being harmed by it.

Clare told me that when she's creating her jokes, she always starts by figuring out her motive. She decides where she wants the joke to land. "At the center of good satire is someone who is voiceless, nameless, and faceless without power," Clare said. "Bad satire gets away from that and ends up giving the person that has the power too much voice." Clare explained that comedy and tragedy are two sides of the same coin, and what some of the most viral couples comedy content does is make the victim the butt of the joke rather than empower them.

On the sitcom *Black-ish*, which aired on ABC from 2014 to 2022, writers regularly used common tropes and toxic beliefs in their storytelling. But like Clare's jokes, the punch lines are placed intentionally—punching up at power. Rather than asking viewers to laugh at the existence of painful experiences, the writers elevated the voices of those hurt by sexism, racism, and classism and let victims be the ones to come out on top. Like the episode in which Bow, the mom of the show, chooses to return to work after having a baby. The audience watches as Bow grapples with her decision. The script plays with patriarchal gender norms by having her husband, Dre, nudge her away from her career, but they end the episode with him sharing that he only encouraged her to stay home because he wanted her to know she had *options*. Their conversation touches on identity, gender, race, and class as they open up about their family histories, values, and beliefs. The episode concludes with Bow empowered to make her own choice.

Shows like *Black-ish* are proof that popular, relatable entertainment can be realistic without perpetuating the worst parts of what's considered normal.

AS FOR THE bumbling dad archetype, the comedy duo that makes up the Dumb Dad Podcast uses humor to push back against toxic norms. According to the podcast's description, the hosts, Kevin Laferriere and Evan Kyle Berger, "believe the only way to erase the stigma that Dumb Dads get painted with is to parent harder, not dumber." On top of their regular podcast episodes, the two create short skits about relatable parenting problems, like how hard it can be to wrangle a toddler into a car seat and the nightmare that is parenting through daylight saving time. They also tackle unequal expectations head-on. In one video, Kevin acts out common casually sexist experiences that dads face. It opens with a mom on the playground saying, "Oh, look at this! Dad's babysitting today!" Then his child's school calls about allergy information, and even when he tells them he has that info, they insist he put his wife on the phone. When he arrives to pick up his kids from daycare, the teacher tells him to take his time and asks if he needs help finding his kid. The Dumb Dad duo doesn't create content that makes them seem exceptional for doing the same kind of parenting you'd expect from a mom. They don't rely on the stereotype that dads are different and less capable than moms to carry their comedy. They get laughs in more creative ways, while normalizing dads just being parents.

There are countless examples online of loving relationships—romantic, platonic, and otherwise—and they help normalize joy simply by living it out loud. One of the ways that sitcom syndrome works is by convincing us that there's no use in hoping for better. We can fight falling for that hopelessness by consuming content with varied representations of the countless ways to find love and happiness. We can engage with content that challenges the norms we wish weren't so normal.

MAYBE I *AM* A MISERABLE SHREW

Even more important than changing *what* we choose to engage with, we have to change *how* we engage. When we see a skit or a storyline depicting a relatable frustration, we can question whether we should laugh at its inevitability or if there's something we could do to eliminate it. When we see displays of normalized inequity or oppressive norms, we can change the channel, click "not interested," pick a different movie, call out the harm in the joke, or write an honest review. We can be angry at a culture that frames dissatisfaction and double standards as funny. With intentional engagement, we can challenge beliefs and change norms.

When we notice our experiences being reflected back at us in comedy and romance, it's up to us to decide for ourselves if what's being presented is actually laughable or not. Like Clare Brown said, we have to ask ourselves whose voice is given power when we laugh and whose is being silenced. We have to ask who's actually being made a fool and, based on the answer, decide what we want to do about it.

Simply presenting a situation as a joke doesn't make it funny. If something is causing friction or pain in your life, you won't find joy through forced chuckles. Sitcom syndrome makes us believe happiness will come from laughing along and learning to lighten up in the face of dysfunction. In reality, *true happiness comes from allowing ourselves to feel what we feel. True happiness comes from allowing ourselves to see anger as information.* If you feel hurt, ask yourself why!

ANGER IN ACTION

Many of us have been taught to fear anger in ourselves and one another. It's presented as if it's a dangerous emotion, innately violent or punishing. We're taught to see avoidance of anger as the safest approach, protecting comfort and dodging disruption, even when it means adapting to painful and oppressive conditions. We're taught to fear anger more than what makes us angry.

Dismissing or downplaying the feeling doesn't solve whatever problem caused it in the first place. Underneath anger is unmet needs. If you breathe deeply through pain, you might endure it better in the moment, but without tending to the source of the issue, the hurt will remain.

The feminist author and activist Audre Lorde wrote about this in her 1981 speech "The Uses of Anger." Throughout her career, she was often invited to speak at conferences, where she gave speeches, presented on panels, and read her essays, often as the only Black woman among mostly white peers. She was sought out to speak to large rooms of mostly white academics who wanted to learn about sexism and racism from her. They wanted her—a queer, disabled Black woman—to teach them about the social inequities that harmed her and made her rightfully angry, but they didn't want to witness her anger or acknowledge their participation in contributing to it. When treated with ignorance at these events, she was asked to be tolerant, patient, and cautious of her tone.

Audre Lorde recognized that anger was a necessary and powerful tool of change, and rather than shying away from it, she stood firmly in it when she presented "The Uses of Anger" as the keynote speaker at the National Women's Studies Association conference in 1981. She stood in front of a crowd of progressive, mostly white women who were eager for social change and pointed out that their unwillingness to be witnesses to anger and their fear of feeling anger themselves was protecting oppression. Their avoidance of anger and discomfort wasn't a passive harm. Choosing passivity out of fear of anger—theirs or others—made room for harm to continue. In the face of injustice, the fear of anger is more dangerous than anger itself. Anger at oppression is righteous and powerful, and if we avoid it by deflecting, downplaying, or letting it sit idle as *guilt*, it's wasted.

Lorde underscores that anger is the appropriate response to racism and sexism. It's appropriate to be upset about injustice and inequality. It is appropriate to feel anger at structural oppression, hateful attitudes, and harmful cultural norms. Feelings like anger, disappointment, or dismissal are *completely reasonable*. Anger is a feeling, and feelings are reactions, not morally good or bad. Lorde said, "Anger is loaded with information and energy." Feelings are connected to our needs, and when we feel angry, the questioning we do can help us better get those needs met—individually and collectively. Why do I feel angry? What contributed to that anger?

In "The Uses of Anger," Lorde wrote, "Every woman has a well-stocked arsenal of anger potentially useful against those oppressions, personal and institutional, which brought that anger into being." Anger is ripe with potential for changemaking. If we shoo it away, we may temporarily take the tension out of the room, but at what cost? What kind of change could we make as a society if we honored anger and used it as a force for progress?

Lorde said, "And when I speak of change, I do not mean a simple switch of positions or a temporary lessening of tensions, nor the ability to smile or feel good. I am speaking of a basic and radical alteration in all those assumptions underlining our lives."

Inequity in our homes, exploitation at work, burnout, and

isolation are all oppressive conditions, and when we dismiss the anger those things bring up in us, we maintain their normalcy. Letting sexist, ableist, homophobic, or racist jokes fly out of fear of rocking the boat, being called a "Debbie Downer," or being kicked out of the "old boys' club" is letting the threat of discomfort outweigh the threat of hateful attitudes. Calling out a joke, belief, or behavior takes anger and turns it into a powerful tool. The clenched jaw and hot feeling that comes from anger is *power*, and where we have power, we need to put it to good use dismantling its source.

Anger is not the enemy; it is a powerful tool.

5 THINGS YOU CAN DO RIGHT NOW

1.　Poke Fun at Power

When it comes to comedy, practice paying attention to whose voice is being elevated and whose is being silenced. If the underdog is still suffering by the time the story's told, it's not comedy—it's cruelty. When we laugh at oppression in a way that empowers the oppressor, we normalize it. If we don't want oppressive conditions to be seen as acceptable, we have to identify when we're laughing them into normalcy. Engage with comedy with an eye for who's winning. Save your laughter for comedy that disrupts, not disempowers.

When picking out which shows, movies, comedy specials, or influencers to engage with, consider the impact their comedy has on culture. Unfollow, thumbs down, or give an honest review. When you're face-to-face with someone trying to crack wise at someone else's expense, take the opportunity to make change.

Don't underestimate the power of letting someone's bigoted joke fall flat. If it isn't funny . . . *don't laugh.* Try acting confused and saying, "Oh, I must not have gotten it. Can you explain?" Asking for explanations, directly addressing how a comment or behavior is harmful, and denying an affirmative smile are all ways of disrupting norms. Letting someone feel the discomfort of an awkward silence or social misstep may be the kind of necessary consequence that stops the same behavior from happening in the future.

Calling someone an idiot for defending a partner who makes them feel invisible does very little to show someone that they deserve better. Our culture keeps us ignorant and afraid, and that's important context when approaching anyone who has accepted the status quo. We can be empathetic while criticizing someone's behavior or beliefs, and supportive in pointing out the ways they're harming themselves and others. We can be direct, with the understanding that ignorance is *not always willful*. Reject the urge to criticize someone who goes along with a joke at their expense. Criticize the systems, *cultures, and beliefs* that allow for the joke or challenge the person who chose the harmful joke. Criticize complacency and willful participation.

2. Conflict as Connection

Shift your thinking on conflict. Rather than avoiding it, commit to practicing how to have healthy conflicts. When you're tempted to dismiss a harmful behavior or a painful dynamic, remember that the pain doesn't just go *away* if you find a way to cope or adapt to it. Confronting issues and setting boundaries can feel risky, but there are *also* risks to coping! *You are not obligated to protect the people who hurt you from the knowledge that their behaviors are hurting you.* Being direct about what you do and do not want creates an opportunity for deeper connections.

Though we may have been conditioned to believe that conflict is inherently dangerous, it doesn't have to be. *Conflict can be an opportunity for connection.* Avoiding conflict doesn't avoid hurt; it wastes it! Shielding someone from feedback that might make them feel guilty also shields them from a chance to love you better. It's the same when someone comes to *you* to share the ways your behavior may have hurt them.

Addressing harmful behavior and beliefs is not the same as attacking someone's character or acting violently toward them, even if the result is upset feelings. Sharing your anger or your hurt with someone is an invitation to grow together. Opening up about how you feel, even in anger, is a vulnerable act and a way of communicating to them that you believe things can improve. *When you know better, you can do better!*

QUICK TIPS FOR HEALTHY CONFLICT

Stay focused. Consider the outcome you're hoping for.

This sounds like: *"I'm feeling disconnected and want to get on the same page about this . . ."*
"I want to be honest about how I'm feeling, so we can communicate better in the future . . ."

Take responsibility for your part. Own what you can.

This sounds like: *"I should have said something sooner . . ."*
"I have been passive-aggressive about this . . ."

Slow down. When you're feeling overwhelmed, pause! Avoid walking away from a conversation completely by agreeing to a five-minute break.

> This sounds like: *"I'm feeling overwhelmed and don't think I'm communicating clearly right now. Can we take a breather and come back in five?"* *"I'm worried I'm going to say something I don't mean. Do you want to take a quick break and keep talking now or revisit this after dinner?"*

De-escalate. Make attempts to de-escalate and accept when they do it.

> This sounds like: *"I'm not trying to attack you!"* *"I'm on your team!"* *"I'm sorry, that was out of line."*

Reflect. Don't just brush off issues. When the dust settles, think about what happened, journal about it, or talk about it together.

> This sounds like: *"What worked well and kept us feeling connected through that conflict?"*

Repair and Recover. What happens after a conflict is just as important as what happens during. Reconnect in whatever way works for you: hug, hold hands, go on a walk together, laugh over your favorite comfort show, or dance in the kitchen to your favorite song. Apologize for your part and acknowledge that you're on the same team.

Not all conflicts will end with you feeling closer. We each have a responsibility to work on our own communication, but ultimately, we can't force someone else to do that work and we can't do that work for them. Recovery after a conflict might be done apart from the person with whom you've had the conflict. You may step back. Recovery may look like journaling or talking with a therapist. It may look like taking time for yourself or turning to friends.

3. Get a Context Clue

Everything is made up. What we consider *normal* has been socially constructed. Settling for a "normal life" of squabbling behind closed doors and pointing fingers at each other keeps us from fighting the systems that create tension. Investing your time and energy in learning about yourself *and* about the context you exist in is an act of love. Make a commitment to diversify the media you engage with, including the fiction and nonfiction books you read, podcasts you listen to, and influencers you follow. Especially, listen to the experiences of people who are most marginalized and oppressed within the dominant culture. The same culture that creates inequity and protects power in the world shows up in how we relate in our most personal relationships. Everything from mass incarceration to reproductive rights policies impact how we live our daily lives and have relationships.

To better understand ourselves and our interpersonal relationships, we need a better understanding of society and culture. Racism, classism, sexism, and ableism all affect us.

Recognizing why norms exist and who's benefiting from the way things are helps inform our choices so we can create a version of normal where we *all benefit*.

Reading recommendations are in the back of the book.

4. Get Messy

Self-reliance and the ability to tolerate discomfort are considered signs of strength, and as a result, many people hold a lot of the issues they face in their personal lives close to the vest. Nothing changes when we push ourselves past our limits to keep things together. Let people into your mess. Become the friend people feel safe sharing their mess with. One phrase that can go a long way in doing that is, when someone is opening up to you, "Do you want me to listen, or do you want help problem-solving?" Or "What kind of support are you looking for?" Practice offering up what you're looking for when you come to someone else for support. The trust we build by showing up for one another well makes our relationships more resilient and sustainable.

5. Collective Anger

The worst aspects of the status quo persist in part because our culture is incredibly isolating. *Collective anger is powerful.* Seek out groups online or in person that focus on issues or topics that matter to you. Independent bookstores and local libraries often host in-person book clubs and groups with specific themes that may matter to you. Online book clubs like the Noname Book Club and the Soft Heart Book Club offer virtual events and discussion spaces where you can connect with other people who can validate your anger and act as comrades in creating change. Start a discussion group of your own where each participant offers a piece of media for everyone to watch, read, or listen to and comes together to discuss. Connect, discuss, and end your sessions with the question "What next?"

CHAPTER THREE

Hey, Mama

How the Gendering of Care Holds Us Back

I DON'T THINK I'VE gone a single day of the last decade without seeing or hearing "Mama" at least once. I was called "Mama" long before I became one: a "little mama" with baby dolls, a drawn-out "Mamaaa" from car windows. In motherhood, I hear it constantly, not just the dozens of times a day from my kids, but everywhere. It's printed on T-shirts, embroidered on hats, bedazzled on mugs, splashed in bios, and used alongside anything related to home life. It's usually meant affectionately, but its overuse and broad application have consequences. "Mama" may reflect a real relationship, but it has also been stretched into a role built on self-sacrifice, bundling care work into a single identity. Language has power, and "Mama," with its light tone and far-reaching definition, hides the impact of its mean left hook.

"Hey, Mama" is dispensed like a badge of honor. It's a term that makes motherhood look like an exclusive club that anyone would be lucky to join. It's thrown out with a wink that reduces the unsustainable expectations of motherhood to "just what it's like to be a mama!"

Sure, we're meant to thrive despite a lack of social support, but if we just "Hang in there, Mama!" it'll be fine! Mamas are overburdened, but it's okay, because, we're told, "Mamas have what it takes!" The term is tossed around casually, stripping women of their individuality and turning "mama" into a bloated identity loaded with unrealistic standards. It assumes that nurturing and selflessness are natural duties for women and frames any struggle with motherhood as a personal failure, reducing real challenges to just part of the role.

"Mama" is often found in places it has no business being. Productivity apps target "busy mamas," pediatricians provide "child nutrition for new mamas" pamphlets in waiting rooms, and Amazon algorithms serve up deals for shirts and mugs that read "Mama needs wine." The problem with the "Mama" rhetoric is that it reinforces housework, domestic work, household management, and relationship-tending as women's work. The message is loud and clear that mamas are the ones who should care about back-to-school shopping, healthy recipes for kids, and steam cleaners—no one else.

The comedian Eilise Patton poked fun at the phenomenon of "Mama" in a quick video with the caption, "every comment on every mommy bloggers [sic] IG." With her signature Midwestern motherly twang, she embodied the shallow encouraging phrases from comment sections: "You're a rock star, Mama! Your superpower? Bein' a mama! LOL. My hubby is the same way. *You got this, Mama!* Can I join you on that vacation, Mama? Strong mama! Great kiddos—even more, *great mama!* You inspire me, Mama! I'm coming to your house for dinner, Mama! Ha-ha!"

Immediately after she posted it, her video bounced around group text threads and was reposted by countless Instagram accounts. The commentary and infantilizing pronunciation of "Mah-Mah" resonated because it was ripped from real life. When mothers share the pressure and challenges of motherhood online, the response is that they're cheered on but not given a hand. Any talk of feeling run-down, not having time for oneself, or feeling buried under housework is celebrated as a superpower rather than questioned. Craft projects, home-cooked meals, and family vacation photos get positive attention, and the rest gets reduced to the burden meant for mamas to carry. It's maddening.

The cheering on and celebration of mama-hood too often stops at validating any of the challenges and experiences with "I see you, Mama!" in a way that says, "This is your lot in life!" rather than "I see you, Mama! That anger you're feeling? Let's explore that." The Mama rhetoric teaches women to cope rather than fight for change.

Yes, motherhood changes your life drastically, and it does become a large factor in the decisions you make and the way you spend your time. But women are not biologically better at wiping butts. Women are not naturally more capable of caregiving and empathy. Gender has nothing to do with someone's ability to develop those skills or thrive in a caregiving role. Planning parties where everyone's food preferences are considered, taking kids to their doctor appointments, and checking on them when they're sick— these are things anyone can do, not just mamas.

All caregivers should be invited to take parenting classes, shop for new school uniforms, and book date nights. The classroom parent emailing, "Hey, mamas, we're organizing a class bake sale," sends the message that fundraising is for women. The post from a sleep expert that reads, "Hey, Mama, I know you've been up all night with the baby," sets the expectation that men have no reason to be waking with a restless child or doing sleep-training research. The frequency at which "Hey, Mama" is slapped on top of general caregiving tasks and information reduces women to their caregiving role and excludes anyone else who doesn't identify with the label. When we claim that being considerate, anticipating the needs of others, and acting empathetically is "motherly," we feminize that behavior and discourage the development of those skills in boys and men. The problem isn't necessarily with "Mama"; it's the expectations and rigid roles it reinforces. "Mama" is just one drop in the bucket of the subtle ways that women are restricted and reduced.

DIAL-UP

I'm a child of the internet. I've been perpetually online since I could first access dial-up. I spent hours alone in my room writing in my LiveJournal, chatting on AIM with my friends, and uploading drawings to DeviantArt. I expertly curated my AOL away messages to include the lyrics of songs I knew my crushes loved. Though I now spend most of my online time on Instagram and TikTok, over the years I've had accounts on Friendster, Myspace, and Tumblr. The internet has provided me with a creative outlet, a space to learn, and a way to connect. Like so many other people my age, it has played an integral role in how I've built my identity.

While I've gotten older and better at discerning what to let influence me, I am definitely still influenced by what I see online. I screenshot cute haircuts and click links that creators share in their IG Stories. Over the years, what I've seen on the internet hasn't just nudged me toward vintage-inspired stoneware and string lights; it's had an impact on some of my most major life choices.

I learned what was worth celebrating by witnessing which life events got the most engagement on Facebook. Hearts and comments poured in for marriage and pregnancy announcements and trickled in for graduations and career changes. As I entered my twenties, and friends and acquaintances started posting their engagement and maternity photos, I felt the itch to be celebrated in those ways. The vintage-clothing influencers I followed started posting wedding content and then eventually started documenting their perfectly round baby bumps. When I began thinking about having kids of my own, I started Pinterest boards and bookmarked nursery inspiration based on what I saw on my feeds.

In a way, social media influenced me toward becoming a mother, and then it influenced me on how to be one. Just as sitcoms programmed my childhood views of family and marriage dynamics, and then passed the baton to social media to further shape what could be seen as "normal" or funny, AIM and Tumblr gave way to Instagram and TikTok, meeting me in my twenties with a more powerful agenda: joining the "Mama" community.

MOMMY FB

While Facebook used to be a lively place, it's morphed into a forum for used furniture and a way to keep in touch with extended family and random people you met once and added as a friend fifteen years ago. These days, I generally only log in so I can lurk in the local neighborhood, gardening, and parenting groups.

I first dipped my toe into the online motherhood realm through fertility forums back in 2015. These groups were places for aspiring parents to share tips and tricks for getting pregnant. Up until I found the Trying to Conceive (TTC) forums, I was just an ordinary person. Once the admins approved my application, I became something new. Before that point, I'd found online connections through shared interests like art, gardening, and my love of strange real estate listings. When I clicked "Join" on those first "mommy groups," I gained an official new label: "mom." Everything I used to enjoy while scrolling was immediately overtaken by content about how to be a better mom.

The mommy groups are a raw and wild place. Facebook groups were just becoming commonplace when I first got pregnant in 2015, and at the time, our local "Mama Tribe" group (yes, incredibly problematic) only had a few thousand members. (Today it sits at nearly forty thousand members and has changed its name to Mama-Hive.) To join I had to click "Yes" on a series of rules. "Be Kind. Be tolerant. Respect everyone's differing opinions. This is a space for motherhood, not politics!"

Those mommy groups were incredibly influential in how I understood myself, my journey into motherhood, and what I expected of myself and others. I turned to them for advice, camaraderie, and entertainment. Those mommy groups were incredible resources, but they came with many flaws. First, they were "man-free" spaces. "We want this to be a safe space where we can talk about issues unique to mothers. We also need some space to vent about our husbands. ::wink::" Every post started with "Hey, mamas" or "Hi, ladies!" I didn't love the exclusionary language, but I brushed it off. It was a space full of people who understood what I was going through. At the time, the group felt like an empowering resource, full of shared wisdom and support. I was far more focused on the value it gave me than the flaws I might have seen.

On any given day, the mommy-group feed would be filled with posts giving honest reviews of daycares and pediatrician offices, recommendations for kid-friendly museums and restaurants, as well as requests for advice on how to handle bedtime battles. At least once a week someone would post something controversial like "Should we circumcise?" or "Should I let my kid cry it out?" and the comment section would explode. When we had our first baby, the mommy Facebook group became the place I turned to with any parenting issue. I liked that I could pop into the group and use the search bar to find someone else asking the same questions I had. I loved reading the passionate takes of people I didn't know, and I ended up forming a lot of my opinions about parenthood by figuring out how I felt lurking in those comment sections.

In my first few years as a mother, I got a lot out of the Mama-Hive. But since it was an explicitly man-free zone, if my husband had a parenting-related question or curiosity, he had to relay it to me. If I stumbled upon an important piece of information while scrolling through the group's feed, I had to screenshot and share it with him. Quickly, we fell into roles where I was the teacher and he was the student. The group of moms that made up the MamaHive created an incredible community and a priceless resource and then withheld it from everyone who didn't identify as a mother. The relaying I had to do because of the mommy Facebook group felt like a fair trade for the wisdom and community it gave me, but it set up unequal expectations in our household that proved sticky and hard to undo. Within our household, I slipped into the position of the assumed expert because I had more access to the information, picking it up incidentally. This placed me in a position of consistently explaining and teaching.

Without realizing the impact it was having on me, I began taking on a disproportionate amount of the mental load of parenting. I took on little tasks like researching child nutrition and signing up for park district accounts. I took on the mental tasks of sorting through recommendations and measuring them against our values, and the emotional load of considering everyone's needs. I found time to communicate about important decisions and facilitate conversations. Because my husband didn't have access to the group, his Facebook feed wasn't filled with reminders that the dance class registration would open at 9 a.m. on Monday. He didn't get the recommendations for potty training books or American Academy of Pediatrics updates on sleep safety. When a mom posted a picture of her kid incorrectly seated in their car seat, he didn't witness the pile-on in the comment section or feel the pressure to research the correct way to buckle them in. I spent weeks searching for a budget-friendly car-seat-safe winter jacket for our kids based on what I saw in those groups. None of it felt odd, and yet so much of it was invisible, and hard to counteract once it was established.

It set the stage for how information came into our household, contributing to an imbalance that snowballed. Because of how often I engaged in those parenting groups, the algorithms pushed them my way. My social media feed was overflowing with posts of parenting tips from friends and strangers, while my husband wasn't even allowed to join. It became easier for me to research, set reminders, and schedule appointments, because I was the one with the information. I did my best to keep my husband in the loop and a part of major decisions, but doing that was also work. It was tiring to solicit input, especially when he didn't have the background knowledge to give as informed an opinion. As a new mom, the silver lining of the disproportionate parenting load was that by being the resident expert in our home, I also felt like I was doing the things that *good moms* do. I was proud to do more.

At the time, I was ignorant of the impacts of exclusionary mommy groups—on myself and others who felt ostracized and left out. I naively thought that because my husband and I were progressive and well-intentioned about being equal parents, we'd be aware of inequity creeping into our lives. I was unable to see how this one aspect of modern motherhood was shifting the scales of the mental load in our home. This resource, meant to make the lives of tired moms easier, was actually bringing me and the other mamas in the group further from real relief. Instead of sharing the mental load with our partners and empowering each other to step into equal roles as parents, my fellow moms and I just became more efficient so that we could carry more.

One of the greatest mistakes we make, and what leads many of these spaces to become "mommy" spaces rather than simply parenting or childcare spaces, is equating those skills to motherhood. Everyone, regardless of gender, should be encouraged to participate in more than just the hands-on portion of parenting. Having spaces to connect with people who have similar experiences or identities as you is important—and that's what the mommy groups attempt to be. But we have to be mindful of what parts of parenthood we believe to be *mama-specific*. By categorizing school forms, uniform sales, and baby food as *motherhood*, we discourage other caregivers from taking responsibility for those things. There's a time and a place for closing a door to create a safe space. *Keeping parenting and caregiving resources locked in a room where only mothers are welcome doesn't make the world safer for mothers.*

EMERGENCY CONTACT

In 2022, the gender-bias expert Dr. Raina Brands tweeted in a four-point thread:

Our son has been in daycare since the beginning of the year. If he is sick and needs to come home early, they call me. If they want to give him paracetamol [acetaminophen], they call me. If he has injured himself they call me. So what?

I have repeatedly asked them to call my partner first. I have asked them to put a note on my file about that. I have asked the manager. Today they called and I asked them to always call my partner first and 2 hours later THEY CALLED ME AGAIN. What makes this more absurd is the fact that my partner has always been the main point of contact! He filled out all of the forms, he did all of the settling-in sessions, and he drops our son off every morning. But they are incapable of viewing him as a primary caregiver. When I say gender inequality is a self-reinforcing system, this is what I'm talking about.

As a parent and a former elementary school teacher, I've been on both sides of phone calls home, and it's not very fun being on either end. I was terrified the first time I had to call a student's parents. I rehearsed what I was going to say as I looked for my student's name in the main office's emergency contact binder. It was up to me to figure out which number to dial, and as I looked at my class list, I immediately noticed that of the twenty-seven students I had, all had numbers available for mom but only about half had one filled in for dad. I quickly considered which parent I thought would be more likely to pick up and less likely to yell at me. Though I had the option to call either parent, I decided to call my student's mom.

On numerous occasions throughout that first year of teaching, I added to the overburdening of my students' mothers by making the mistake of letting my assumptions lead my choices. My decision to call mothers first was influenced by a culture that expects them to be endlessly available for their kids and for fathers not to be. My choice to call mothers first as a default was not only a result of unequal gendered expectations, but it also actively reinforced them.

Initially, I let my own biases influence how I handled calls home, but it didn't take long for me to realize there were better ways to handle things. By my second year of teaching, I started sending home a detailed survey asking my students' families explicitly how they wanted home contact handled and giving them the opportunity to tell me what they needed rather than assume.

Since becoming a parent myself, I've repeatedly been the recipient of the same treatment I first doled out. For most of my time as a mother, I've been the less flexible working parent, but I have still had to beg teachers to include my husband on emails and to call him first. Dr. Raina Brands and I aren't alone in this. Research published in 2023 found that mothers are nearly one and a half times more likely to be contacted than fathers. Even in cases where it's been made clear that the dads are more available than the moms, mothers were contacted 26 percent of the time. Assumptions like these can have major consequences.

A follower of mine shared this story with me:

> When my kids were in school, even when their father was the primary contact, schools would contact me first, or sometimes only contact me. I worked in mental health and would be in counseling sessions and unable to be interrupted. The school would call my mobile, leave a message, and wait for me to call back. They didn't call my workplace, who could have interrupted me in an emergency; they didn't call my partner, who was in an office job and always contactable; nor did they call my mother, who was retired and lived close to the school. Once, the school called me when my daughter was very unwell, and it was two hours before I realized there was a message on my phone from them. Then it took me twenty-five minutes to get there. She needed to go to the emergency department. She had a bleeding ovarian cyst and was left crying for hours because they only called me.

Anytime my own child's school shows up on my caller ID, my stomach drops. Those calls are rarely ever good news. If it's a school nurse calling about a sick kid, whoever fields the call has to stop what they're doing and immediately figure out the quickest way to pick them up, mentally scan the medicine cabinet, and make a mental game plan of how to juggle the inevitable domino effects of the rest of a household getting sick from the same bug in the following days. Not only does receiving a call from the school usually require mental energy for logistical planning, but it can also spark panic and anxiety in scrambling for childcare, keeping up with deadlines, or facing wage loss. By assuming women should be the primary contact for kids, we place demands on women that require immediate attention. On top of everything, a sick kid is usually a sad kid, and figuring out how to manage the disruption also requires sweetness and the emotional presence to comfort a kid who needs a little extra care. This kind of thing is a normal part of parenting, *not just motherhood.*

I don't want to place blame on individual childcare providers here. *I've done it myself!* This is just one of the well-intentioned but insidious ways we perpetuate inequity. Our cultural beliefs about who's better fit for care are stubborn, and women are still being forced into managing more even when teachers and coaches are begged to reach out to dads. Gender has nothing to do with how well someone manages calls home, but gendered beliefs and implicit biases have us looking to Mama every time something in this realm needs handling.

Parenting, caregiving, cooking, cleaning, and even planning and organizing have all been attributed to skills women are innately better at. This is a lie.

This socially constructed "truth" has had far-reaching negative social impacts, and the health and science journalist Chelsea

Conaboy has made it her mission to correct the narrative. In a 2022 *New York Times* article, Chelsea defines the "myth of the maternal instinct" as the belief that "the selflessness and tenderness babies require is uniquely ingrained in the biology of women, ready to go at the flip of a switch." So much of the pressures we face as women boil down to this widespread idea that we're "made for motherhood." Parenting is a behavior and a skill, not something you turn on the second you get a baby in your hands. Parenting isn't just giving birth or nursing; it's clipping toenails, negotiating bedtimes, signing field-trip forms, and helping teenagers handle peer pressure. It takes research, coordination, consideration of values, and billions of careful choices to parent. So much of what gets categorized as motherhood-specific is actually just domestic engineering— emotional labor, mental labor, and physical labor that *anyone* can learn to do.

In her book *Mother Brain: How Neuroscience Is Rewriting the Story of Parenthood*, Conaboy explains that "researchers today have clarified that 'maternal behavior' is, in fact, a basic human characteristic, not uniquely maternal at all." I connected with Chelsea on Zoom and picked her brain about the lies we're told about motherhood and the consequences of them. She found that parenting *does* change the brain, but regardless of gender or biological relation to a child, those changes come from engaging with children and developing the skills of caregiving. Chelsea explained: "Experience is what shapes the parental brain. You don't have to have a pregnancy or even be biologically related to your child in order for your parental brain to adapt." Mothers' brains change and grow in profound and lasting ways when they become parents, but *all kinds of caregivers* have the potential to go through changes when they accept responsibility for the care of a child. "It's about your commitment, in a deep way, to your child. And that's not a soft idea. The parental brain is changed by hormones and experience, and if you are a parent in any capacity, you go through that. If you are a parent, whether you're biologically related or not and whether you're a mother or not, you have the opportunity to experience those changes."

We become caregivers by caregiving. The people in our care are nurtured by us when we learn the skills necessary to nurture them. It isn't just relatedness or physical proximity or even an instantaneous magical moment that turns us into parents or caregivers. *Caregiving is active.* Actively engaging in the learning process has so many benefits—it gives the caregiver a stronger bond with their family members, a sense of accomplishment and belonging, and skills that extend outward toward a more fulfilling social life and thriving within their community. *Everyone deserves the opportunity to participate in that work.*

But the roots of cultural conditioning pushing girls toward this work and boys away from it run deep. Data from the Bureau of Labor Statistics found that in teens ages fifteen to seventeen, girls already spend more time on errands and housework than boys their age. Girls spend more time volunteering and doing unpaid care work and less time on leisure activities even as high schoolers. Little girls are being socialized to be community-minded, to tend to bonds, to volunteer, and to find purpose in domestic and care tasks, while little boys are socialized away from those activities. Because of the emphasis on the gender binary, same-gender peers get together and practice certain skills together. When girls are more likely to be encouraged to learn the inner workings of the home than their male peers, the outcome isn't just a gap in physical skills but gaps in mental and emotional ones, too. Girls learn how to make decisions that consider interconnected tasks and develop the

skills of surveying collective needs. Girls are provided more opportunities to practice anticipation and empathy, and boys are directed
toward more competitive skill development.

As an elementary school teacher, I once asked my sixth-grade
class who they turn to when they have something hard happening
in their lives. The girls in my group could each name at least one
friend to confide in. The boys blushed, embarrassed by the suggestion of being vulnerable with their bros. Many boys are taught to
prioritize the skills that will make them good breadwinners, and
when it comes to housework, they learn to take direction passively
within the home rather than see themselves as having an equally
important voice and presence in everyday home life. We teach them
that to feel, to communicate, to practice empathy, and to invest in
the skills of caregiving are all things girls do. The impact of those
unequal expectations shows up in adulthood. Girls are not naturally more thoughtful or prone to domestic engineering; they're
taught to find value in it, are held to higher standards, and are encouraged to find pride in leading at home. Boys are not less capable
of caregiving; they just don't have the same practice and encouragement.

THE MAN BOX

The reason we automatically look to women to provide domestic
labor and shoulder the mental load has just as much to do with
what we think of men as it does with our tendency to say, "You got
this, Mama." Patriarchal ideas of manhood claim that men show
up for their families through their paychecks and their ability to
protect against physical threats. They're supposed to bring home
the bacon and grab the bat when you hear an unusual sound, right?

Because we believe men are suited to those duties and women are born to nurture, we expect mothers to shoulder more of the child-care burden. But these expectations, rigid and binary, aren't just inaccurate or unfair to moms—they cost us all in both big and small ways. In the same way that womanhood has been falsely defined by the ability to care for and do housework, men face a rigid and restrictive definition of manhood.

The Man Box was a term introduced by the writer and activist Paul Kivel in the eighties and built upon by the author and educator Tony Porter in the nineties. Both men were committed to identifying the confining expectations of patriarchal masculinity in an effort to encourage a healthier definition. Building on that work, violence prevention and gender equity groups like A Call to Men and Equimundo have used the term to raise awareness of the harms caused by patriarchal definitions of manhood and to change the culture that makes it dangerous for men to step outside of the box.

In 2017, Equimundo: Center for Masculinities and Social Justice published key findings from a study based on surveys and interviews with thousands of young men from the United States, the UK, and Mexico, and defined the Man Box using seven pillars: self-sufficiency, acting tough, physical attractiveness, rigid masculine gender roles, heterosexuality, hypersexuality, and aggression and control. The same study that helped define these pillars also found that men whose behavior landed them well inside the box, compared with outside of it, were less likely to have close friends, reported a higher incidence of depression symptoms, were more likely to abuse alcohol and drive recklessly, and were dramatically more likely to bully and sexually harass others.

The Man Box has many victims. It harms the men who must abandon parts of themselves to fit within it; it hurts the people inside it who feel like they need to compete and harm one another to prove they belong; it hurts the people who exist outside it and become victims to the violence and disconnection it causes. The Man Box also has many enforcers. Researchers at Equimundo found that despite the serious physical and mental risks that came with fitting inside the Man Box, choosing to opt out wasn't a simple or easy solution. In their findings, they wrote, "Young men reap certain benefits from staying inside the Man Box: it provides them with a sense of belonging, of living up to what is expected of them. . . . The Man Box demands that they pretend to be someone they are not, and study results show how lonely the resulting life can be."

The Man Box discourages men from truly being present in their relationships and teaches them to seek value through their productivity and power through dominance. As a result, they're taught to love in unloving ways. But there is room for men in family life, not just if or when they bring home paychecks, *but as whole people*. It's far more acceptable for little girls to aspire to one day do things that were once believed to be reserved for men, but the same grace hasn't been afforded to little boys who see greatness in spaces and in skills considered to be "for women." When men are held back from things deemed feminine, they're also held back from the joys of participating in them. A man is not less of a man for desiring connection. It's up to all of us, individually and collectively, to break down the Man Box and to make room for a more expansive definition of personhood.

DAD'S CHEAT SHEET

While writing this book, I connected with Nick North, a content creator, trans-youth advocate, and full-time working husband and father. He, his wife, and their five kids live on an island off the mainland coast of British Columbia.

On his Instagram, he brings followers along with him on his day-to-day. He feeds his chickens, shows off the stunning views, gives updates about his professional projects, and provides a steady stream of selfies from the front seat of his car, where he often finds himself on dad chauffeur duty. In between posts about recipes he's tried and how hard it's been to draw boundaries around work, he peppers in casual captures from his bustling home—kids with their hoods pulled exhaustedly over their faces, living room messes, eating dinner standing at the kitchen counter. He shares about his relationship: how he and his wife navigate waves of burnout with solo getaways and the decision-making they do around parenting, such as bedtime enforcement and having multiple kids on different extracurricular schedules.

When we spoke, Nick explained that society's assumptions about fatherhood have impacted how he shows up in his roles, both in public and in private. In his daily life as a dad, he's noticed that he's been overlooked and left out of things like carpool scheduling and group chats for school-event organizing. He's felt the need to consciously step forward and be clear about wanting to be included. While the mothers of his kids' classmates are assumed to want to be involved, he's gotten the sense that for him and other dads, the expectation is that they'd rather *not be*. He notices the ways he's treated differently than his wife, such as being celebrated for the simplest things like showing up on time.

Nick's content, while not an explicit callout to caregiving double standards like the *Dumb Dad Podcast*, similarly pushes back at dominant narratives about fatherhood. His content isn't flashy or filtered. It's curated, *like everything is online*, but the moments he chooses to highlight tell a story of a father who's really *in it*. He's not a bystander or someone who shows up to pay bills or follow orders. He's a fully integrated member of the family. He's a decision-maker. And by sharing his life as an engaged parent and partner online, he's helping to change the culture that sees that behavior as the exception and not the norm. By embodying a kind of fatherhood that includes caregiving, personal growth, and communication, he helps to expand the limited definition of fatherhood we've inherited.

Nick's influencer status isn't limited to the online space. We *all* have influence in our day-to-day lives. Being unabashedly present and taking responsibility for caregiving is changemaking on a peer-to-peer level, but his behavior also impacts how his kids and his kids' peers view a father's role. When he's present at school functions and swim practices and when he cooks dinner when friends come over, he's actively influencing how those kids understand caregiving and partnership.

Research backs this up. A study published in June 2022 found that "the most powerful predictor of children's gender-role attitudes . . . was the amount of time fathers spent on housework during children's adolescence, both absolute and relative to the amount of time mothers spent on housework." In other words, when fathers take on more unpaid labor at home, it directly shapes their children's beliefs about gender roles. Our kids are sponges, so if we want equity in care work to be the norm, we have to model it in our own homes. We have to show our kids how unexceptional it can be.

In Nick's household, he and his wife sometimes come up with plans together and sometimes take turns taking the lead. They solicit opinions from each other, do their own research, and trust each other to communicate when they need or want something. Nick isn't just a dad who's stepping up. He and his wife are equally invested, and they each have an equal say in what happens in their lives.

It isn't always the lax expectations of fathers that influence them away from taking on a fair share of the caregiving. Sometimes it's an issue of the primary caregiver holding on too tightly to control. One parent taking control of the child-rearing decisions may be out of desire, necessity, or something in between. Being in charge can feel safe. It can feel like something to be proud of. It can feel like the only option.

In my personal experience, anxiety is what has driven me to seek control. Caregiving can feel like a high-risk activity. I don't want to let my kids down. I want to give them the best life possible, and sometimes that turns into a desperate attempt to maintain control wherever I feel I can. I research and think through every possible scenario. I struggle to find the line between healthy caution and harmful hypervigilance. It's not a bad thing to be careful, but when I've taken it too far, I've acted defensively, taken on more than I can handle, and sidelined my husband. I've told him with words and with actions that he's unwelcome, which isn't fair to him or our kids. We each have a responsibility to make careful decisions about our children. For my part, that includes practicing discernment around when my anxiety is being helpful in keeping me and my family safe and when it's becoming a hindrance.

Everyone has their own reasons for why they do things. Holding on to control might be a result of anxiety, or it could be something else, like pride, desire, safety, or fear. Sometimes the person in charge wants the control; sometimes they feel like they have no other option. Asking what's underneath the steering-wheel death grip can help us make sure we're not unintentionally boxing the other person out or putting more on them without meaning to. Once you have a better idea of what's behind the behavior, you can start to consider what changes you might want to make (if any). There needs to be room to talk through anxiety, ask questions, give grace, and take baby steps. For trust to grow, there needs to be room for it.

A crucial part of making progress in this realm involves not just welcoming men into caregiving roles and responsibilities in order to take the burden off women but also trusting them and having faith in their natural capabilities.

One of the most popular potty training books on the market is *Oh Crap! Potty Training* by Jamie Glowacki. It's usually one of the first recommendations on potty training advice threads in mommy Facebook groups. The book includes more than two hundred pages explaining a six-step foolproof process for getting your kid to use the toilet, but of those pages, only two are meant to be seen by dads. In the back of the book, taking up the front and back of one printed page is a section titled "Dad's Cheat Sheet."

The list has some solid pointers, but peppered in are reminders of how we expect fathers to act and reinforcements that this behavior is normal. One bullet point reads, "Don't act helpless. You know your kid just as well as your partner, but in a different way." It's a call to action and an encouragement to step up, but the fact that it's even included suggests that many fathers might opt for acting incapable. In another bullet point, Glowacki wrote, "Be casual and cool. You probably already have that role anyway. You can be casual and nonchalant and good cop and still watch out for pee." The insinuation is that mothers are more likely than fathers to be enforcers of routines and strategically planned life lessons. This sentiment is echoed when Glowacki wrote, "Your partner is going to go cuckoo. I promise she'll return to normal very soon. Get her drunk. It's okay." And "Do your best to help, even if you don't want to. This has to get done. Might as well be now." The list repeatedly reinforces the idea that it would be a total surprise for any man to care enough to read a book on the topic of potty training, while expecting a woman to. It makes it seem like a typical dad would be reluctant and put out by the suggestion that they should be part of the process, even in the execution of it.

The intent behind "Dad's Cheat Sheet" is probably pretty good— the author is trying to explicitly encourage men to take part. But coaxing them into a position that's still nowhere near equal has the effect of being disempowering, not empowering.

I don't want to single out *Oh Crap! Potty Training*. It's just one of countless books, blogs, videos, and classes sending a clear message, though not always that explicitly, that Mommy Knows Best and Daddy Definitely Doesn't Know Shit. The assumption is almost always that parenting books, cookbooks, and home DIY books are written *for women* unless they have "FOR DUDES" printed in bold letters on the cover. The messaging about men and caregiving is that they're just not good at it—biologically inferior at housework and child-rearing. The subtle and overt reinforcement of this sets the precedent that men are *not welcome* unless given an explicit invitation. They're told they don't need to read the books, attend the classes, research topics, or get involved, because it's a lost cause.

Spreading the lie that men are inferior caregivers has countless negative side effects. For one, it's affected parental-leave policy, blocking men from accessing time and resources to become involved caregivers. One 2021 worldwide study found that the global average for available days for parental leave for fathers was an average of 21 days, compared to 191 for women. Another analysis of paid-leave policy found that same-sex couples have less access than heterosexual couples, and families with two fathers fared the worst. Of the thirty-three countries whose paid parental-leave policies researchers looked at, only 12 percent of them offered the same time off to gay male couples that they did to different-sex couples. Babies require the same amount of care, regardless of the sex or gender of their parents, but beliefs about *who* should be caring and *how* have held men back. Even when they have access to the time, men face criticism at work for using sick days or parental leave for their families. In 2021, when then US Secretary of Transportation Pete Buttigieg took a two-month paternity leave after adopting twins with his partner, he faced public ridicule. Among the commentators and social media voices questioning his motivation, one described his decision to take a two-month leave as "sickeningly pathetic" and Fox News host Tucker Carlson mocked him, saying, "Paternity leave, they call it, trying to figure out how to breastfeed. No word on how that went."

It isn't just public figures getting heckled. Many men catch flak from colleagues for setting boundaries around their off-the-clock hours. They risk being socially ostracized for being parents to their own kids or active and supportive partners to their spouses. They face stigma and have their motives questioned when they show interest in taking on a caregiving role. They get pressured out of bonding and connecting with their loved ones. Men don't need cheat sheets; they need to be welcomed into the world of caregiving as equally important members of the team.

Even when men are fully committed to being engaged caregivers and see it as their job, internalized messaging around gender roles and value can be damaging. I spoke with Tim and Jessica Durand, who document their experiences with equitable parenting on social media, to hear how they navigate these challenges in their home.

Prior to the pandemic, Tim and Jessica were a dual-income household that had a pretty solid equitable distribution of housework and childcare responsibilities. They saw their home as something they wanted to build together, and in many ways, they contributed equally. But with Covid-19 came a layoff for Tim and a loss of childcare for their two kids, and they went from parallel roles to a whole new dynamic in which Tim was the stay-at-home parent and Jessica was the breadwinner. The setup worked well for everybody, and they knew that, but they each dealt with their own hang-ups. "For me, I think I went through a period where I felt like I wasn't a good-enough mom," Jessica told me. "Because you hear the stories of all the moms and, like, the restless nights. That wasn't my experience." Tim struggled with feeling as though he wasn't doing enough. He told me, "When I first became a stay-at-home dad, I felt very insecure about it. That I didn't have a job, that I wasn't bringing in money." As a working parent, he was already doing the midnight wake-ups and a fair portion of the housework. When he stopped bringing home a paycheck, he felt like he needed to over-compensate, often leading to overwhelm.

They've each felt unique pressure to overperform in certain areas, and an ongoing practice of empathy and communication has gotten them through. They talk daily, about what each other needs, about the childcare and the household, and also about their personal interests and non-family-related things. They told me that one of the challenges in navigating their setup socially is a lack of community and representation. It can be isolating to be the only dad at the "mommy meetup" and to have such limited options for spaces to talk openly about experiences unique to being a non-mom primary caregiver. Since Tim became a stay-at-home parent, they've added a third child to the mix and Tim has reveled in the opportunity to be such an active participant in his family's growth. He told me that some of the best parts are "being able to spend time with my kids, not missing those moments, being there to try and help them work on whatever skills we're trying to work on." One of the greatest joys, he explained, was just being available to them as a constant, reliable caregiver. Tim and Jessica aren't immune to the influence of social pressures, but they're committed to not accepting them at face value.

We have to change the story about where men belong and how they need to behave. We have to allow for a broader definition of manhood and fatherhood—one that includes vulnerability, care, and connection. Providing can look like a paycheck, but it can also look like providing *care*. It can look like giving time and effort and putting in the work to plan and accommodate. Providing can mean providing opportunities, providing relief, or providing encouragement.

GO YOUR OWN WAY

One way to escape the confines of gendered caregiving is by creating a different family structure altogether: one with a foundation of intention and choice rather than prescription.

Markus Harwood-Jones is a Canadian author and father who is raising his toddler with his husband, Andrew, and their single-by-choice co-parent, Hannah. The three met in their early twenties, about a decade before becoming parents together. Hannah and Markus connected first, and Andrew entered the picture about a year later when Markus and Andrew started dating and Hannah and Andrew became roommates. A few years into their friendship, Hannah, who was planning on becoming a single parent by choice, began exploring her options. She asked Andrew if he might be interested in being a sperm donor and if so, what kind of relationship he might want to have with her and the child. After Andrew expressed interest, they invited Markus into the conversation and, as a group, decided that conceiving and co-parenting together would be a great option for everyone.

In preparation, Markus, Andrew, and Hannah moved in together and began the process of researching, learning, and practicing the skills they'd need to care for one another and their future child. They held monthly household meetings, attended family learning workshops, and studied up on the legal side of things. They communicated with one another and planned ahead as much as possible, and in 2022, they became parents.

Markus, Andrew, and Hannah have found a lot of benefits to having a family structure that doesn't fit snugly into the standard heteronormative nuclear family mold, and a lot of those benefits stem from having made conscious and clear choices. As their relationships have transformed and grown over the years, they've made decisions about what kinds of roles they want to play in one another's lives, talked through possible scenarios, and left as little to assumption as possible.

Culture is powerful, though. Markus, Andrew, and Hannah have to disrupt assumptions consistently. When their child started solids, Hannah took the lead on researching nutrition guidelines, which led Andrew and Markus to step back. Everyone saw Hannah as more knowledgeable, so they took directions from her. Meals were a huge part of their lives, though, and the imbalance in knowledge quickly led to Andrew and Markus feeling a lack of confidence around feeding their kid. Instances like this could easily snowball if not for regular check-ins and a commitment to mutuality.

Markus and his co-parents never expected responsibilities to be divided among them evenly. When the baby was born, Hannah spent more time on direct childcare tasks than Markus and Andrew, but they adjusted responsibilities to find a new equilibrium.

They weren't keeping tallies of how many minutes each one of them was holding the baby or exactly how many diapers each parent changed. They went into the process knowing there would be certain areas where they'd each excel or need more support, but they were committed to acting as a team.

Now that Markus's child is out of their baby phase, the household dynamic has entered a new stage. Their household has seen career shifts and schedule changes, and they've acted like a dynamic trio, navigating it all amid toddler tantrums and playdates. In the coming years, they'll be looking at childcare and schooling options and are already considering how they can streamline teacher communication and make sure every parent's information is on the classroom paperwork. You can't predict the unpredictable, but even before becoming parents, Markus and his family talked through big issues like breakups and budgets and smaller details like holiday dinners and weekend plans. Their family life has been an ongoing negotiation—something Markus knows doesn't necessarily make parenthood or partnership easy, but does make it a choice. Intentionality can make a big difference in whether any initial imbalances from the earliest days of new parenthood turn into long-term inequity.

In cis-het couples, birthing parents often end up spending more time on childcare than non-birthing parents in the earliest years of the baby's life, and there's evidence that the trend exists in queer and same-sex partnerships, too. Similarly, studies have shown that birthing parents can take a serious financial hit compared with non-birthing parents after having babies. It's a well-documented issue in America when it comes to cis-het partnerships, but one study out of Norway suggests that regardless of the sex of their partner, birthing parents face bigger drops in income than their partners. Heterosexual women saw a 20 percent decrease in wages, lesbian birth mothers saw a 13 percent drop, and non-birthing lesbian mothers saw about a 5 percent decrease in earnings.

There are so many reasons for gaps in childcare responsibilities, like biological differences, who has access to paid leave or healthcare, income differences, and other individual circumstances. In America, where childcare for two kids costs more than the average rent in all fifty states, and we have no federal paid parental-leave policy, families of all kinds often make the decision for one caregiver to reduce their paid work hours and pick up more of the childcare responsibilities when kids are young. And while early caregiving inequality within partnerships is a trend that exists across the sexuality spectrum, it's important to note some big differences between heterosexual and queer parents. That study of heterosexual and lesbian couples from Norway found that mothers in same-sex partnerships closed their earning gaps with their partners within two years and usually saw their earnings fully bounce back within four years. Meanwhile, it took heterosexual women five years or longer to recover from the post-baby income drop. Even in Norway, one of the most gender-equal countries in the world, unequal gendered expectations around caregiving seem to be sustaining earning gaps.

One study of lesbian parents found that despite the uneven divide in childcare, when it came to housework, responsibilities remained balanced. Also, the differences in time spent on childcare evened out over time, with the gap closing after the first year or so. The same can't be said about the average heterosexual partnership. American time-use surveys show that gaps persist, with fathers spending less time on caregiving than mothers from birth until the day the chicks fly the coop.

Proactivity, like the planning Markus and his family have done, is one way of defending against ongoing inequity. Another is responding to issues as they come up. There may be solid reasons for a birthing parent to do more hands-on caregiving in the beginning, but clear communication and joint involvement in decision-making ensure parenting is a group project.

So much of the built-in inequity that comes with heteronormativity has been avoided in Markus's household because they didn't aim for what was *normative*; they aimed for what *worked for them*. They have agreed they don't want to accept roles based on who society says *should* be doing something. By doing things their own way, they all have more of what they need.

Not all of us can introduce another co-parent into our household, but taking a note from Markus's family and actively choosing what roles we want to take on and what expectations we want to set can be a game changer. Well before they ever brought a child into their household, Markus, Andrew, and Hannah discussed why they wanted to become parents and what involvement they wanted in certain aspects of parenting. Because their setup doesn't fit the traditional mold, they've been given the opportunity to design their dynamic for themselves. We can all do this. When we have open and honest conversations about what we need and want, we set ourselves up for success. Regardless of how our roles take shape, it's better to opt in than to fall into defaults. We all fare better when the choices we make, especially the ones that affect our closest loved ones, are well-informed and honest. We don't need a three-parent household to have the benefits of intentionality.

CARE IS FOR EVERYONE

There was no magic switch inside of me that went off when I gave birth that made me better at any aspect of parenting compared with my husband. Any knowledge I came to the table with was learned. Every skill I had came from practice. But when I spent twenty minutes unsuccessfully trying to bounce the baby to sleep and he had her snoozing in under sixty seconds, I felt like something was wrong with me. I'd internalized that I was supposed to be better at this stuff.

I hadn't accounted for him being the oldest child in a big family, with plenty of childcare under his belt, or that I was the youngest and that the first diaper I'd ever changed was my own child's. Unpacking our deeply rooted beliefs about gender and roles, including how that's supposed to show up in parenting, has been ongoing work, but also some of the most rewarding for our family, and especially for our kids.

When one of my kids has a fever, my husband knows where to find their meds, how to calculate the dosage, and has his method for distracting them from the yucky flavor. Our kids know it's just as efficient to go to him or me to get a question answered. Our children watch their father read school emails, add food to our grocery lists, and make decisions around the house that meet everyone's needs without checking in with me first. My kids know they're safe and cared for, because they have a father who apologizes to them. He plays with them and makes them laugh, but also gets down on the floor with them when they're frustrated so that they can breathe deeply and co-regulate. My kids have a dad who isn't just "better than other dads"—he's a caregiver in his own right, good not because he's better than past versions of fatherhood but because he is present for them in ways that meet their needs.

WHEN ANYONE ACTS in a caring way, whether it's folding laundry, sending a text to a grieving friend, or modeling calm breathing for a tantruming toddler, they aren't just doing "mama" things. *Dads who watch their own children are not "babysitters"!* They're caregiving. They're showing up. Care is not exclusive to mothers. To care and be cared for is a human experience we should all be so lucky to be a part of. When we gender it or expect it from one person and not the other based solely on their perceived gender, *everyone suffers.* We have to change what's seen as ordinary so that caregiving is recognized as a shared responsibility, not something exceptional when done by fathers or non-birthing parents. Showing up for each other isn't extra—it's essential. It's how we survive.

Care isn't just about raising children, it's about how we build a more equitable world. We were never meant to be self-reliant. Depending on others and having others depend on us is natural. While I've focused heavily on childcare in this chapter, it's worth emphasizing this essential point: **caregiving is not an act reserved for adults to be provided for children.** Care exists in many forms. We all need care and we all have the ability to give it. As our lives change, so do our needs, capacities, and the roles we play in each other's lives. Everyone, regardless of gender, should be encouraged to participate in caregiving in more areas of life than just at home. We're all interconnected and should all be encouraged to consider the ways we can provide care for others and allow others to provide care for us. We can care for each other as friends, colleagues, neighbors, and chosen family. We can invest in the nurturing of others regardless of our blood relation or preconceived notions of responsibility. If we limit our imagination to simply splitting chores more equitably within households, we miss out on what we could have if, as a *society*, we centered care.

On my call with Chelsea Conaboy, she told me, "Human mothers have always been really important, and they've never been enough." That isn't a failure of mothers. Mothers were never sup-posed to be enough. Conaboy said, "Human babies have always relied on other adults to care for them. That's like a fundamental fact about our species, because we have babies in closer succession than any other primates on the planet. And because of that, we needed help." Gendered myths about biology and caregiving con-vince us we're deficient when we can't meet all of our needs on our own. But needing other people is natural. *Interdependence is natu-ral.* Caring for one another and being cared for is a natural part of what it means to exist. Our needs and the needs of others are all interconnected.

If we want healthier communities and connections, it's impera-tive not to just untangle caregiving from gender roles but to recog-nize the skilled work of caregiving for how essential it is to our success as a society. We need to value it and expand our investment in it, interpersonally and systemically. When I asked about her big-gest takeaways, Conaboy told me her work has shown just how es-sential all kinds of caregivers are. "Anywhere in the world where babies are raised, there are people who are specialized baby tenders, and those include moms, but they also include dads, grandparents, siblings, aunts, and uncles and whoever it is. Kids often have day-care teachers, babysitters, and early childhood educators. They might have a network of neighbors. If we saw them not as some kind of backstop to broken families, or to so-called bad moms, but actually as specialized caregivers who have developed the cognitive skills to connect with babies and to meet their needs, how would we pay them differently? How would we create different social policies to support them? How would we value them differently as a culture?"

These are big but important questions for us to ask. When we can accept that mothers were never meant to be solely responsible for nurturing society and were especially never meant to manage it in little nuclear family silos, we can see how essential it is to restructure society with care at the center.

Changing the narrative about who is best cut out for caregiving will take consciously considering internalized biases and challenging assumptions. Care is woven throughout our daily lives, and undoing the gendering of it will take work. But the payoff of escaping the Man Box and the unfair expectations involved in every "Hey, Mama!" message will mean we are *all* better cared for as the multifaceted human beings we truly are.

5 THINGS YOU CAN DO RIGHT NOW

1. Defining You

Playing out gendered expectations that don't align with who we really are can hold us back from so much. It can hinder our self-expression, hurt our relationships, and keep us from opportunities. Taking some time to reflect on gender, personal identity, and the ways society's expectations may be affecting us can help us identify where to make changes. Considering your internalized biases and beliefs can help you adjust your behaviors to better align with who you are and how you want to be.

Some questions to ask yourself:

- What does gender mean to me? Do I associate any specific traits with any specific gender?
- Growing up, did I feel pressure to behave in gendered ways? Has this changed over time?
- How do I see gender expectations affecting me in my daily life? How do gender expectations affect how I feel about myself?
- What are some traits I would use to describe myself? What makes me unique?
- What are some things I excel at? What do I enjoy doing? What do I dislike doing?

- Are there any ways I've felt held back by social expectations, in my relationships or other areas of my life?
- Are there any ways in which I could express myself more authentically? Are there any changes I'd like to make?

Gendered assumptions and social expectations can be sneaky in our day-to-day, so be mindful of times you may be unintentionally acting on beliefs that reinforce inequity and exclusion. If you catch yourself thinking it would "just be easier" to handle something on your own or you're "just better at it," question yourself on that! Is there a different, more intentional approach you could take that accounts for you and your loved ones' unique needs, strengths, and circumstances?

Instead of acting on assumptions: "My kid wants to have a play date. Socializing stresses me out, but I'll handle the planning because I've always been the one who handles this."

Try acting with intention: "My partner is more of a social butterfly than I am and deserves an opportunity to connect with parent peers. This is a good opportunity to handle this together, so they can take the responsibility in the future and I can take something off their plate that they'd rather not handle."

Instead of acting on assumptions: "I don't have much experience navigating home maintenance, so I'll let them handle it on their own."

Try acting with intention: "My partner has had to call out of work to deal with home-maintenance issues in the past, because I haven't had the skills to help. Even if I don't take the task on as my own, it's a good idea for me to be aware of the decisions that are made around the house and to know the basics. I'll make time to learn what it takes to handle a responsibility I've never thought much about."

Just because you have more or less experience doesn't make you the best fit to be responsible for a task. Gender doesn't need to influence how we decide who should handle insurance claims or pack for vacations. These are tasks we can tackle together, or divide based on unique elements like skill, interest, and available time and energy.

2. Gender Neutrality

We all deserve to express ourselves authentically, which means rejecting rigidity and embracing an expansive look at gender and roles. With kids, that doesn't mean encouraging boys to act like girls and girls to act like boys. Instead, give *kids* opportunities to be *kids*. Let kids pick the toys, TV shows, clothes, and interests they want to pursue with as little parental sway as possible. Focus on exposing them to a variety of interests and opportunities, while being mindful not to let your own internalized gender biases create a situation where you overcorrect. The point is to promote self-expression, not enforce different gendered rules.

Kids of all genders should be exposed to baby dolls, tea sets, dress-up, blocks, trucks, and sports. We have to create opportunities for normalizing kids of all genders enjoying things that have been considered feminine the same way we've normalized girls doing things that have previously been deemed "for boys."

When picking out a gift for a nephew, rather than typing "boy age six birthday" in the search bar, text their parents and ask what they've been into lately. If your kid wants to host a mermaid-themed birthday party, resist the urge to offer girl- or boy-specific goody bags. Some boys like mermaids more than sharks. Some girls like sharks more than mermaids. Give out one of each kind to everyone, try offering kids the opportunity to pick for themselves, or skip the bags altogether.

Subtle shifts in language can make a big difference in how much emphasis we put on gendered "rules." Whenever possible, swap binary and gendered terms for more neutral ones. Saying *fireman* or *firewoman* is a needless divide that suggests gender plays as big a role in how the job is done as fire does. *Firefighter* is a neutral and more effective way to describe the job. Police officer, legislator, flight attendant, and server are just a few examples of similarly gender-neutral terms. When getting specific, trade stereotypical terms for precise and creative ones. Describing someone as "stylish," "bold," or "creative" gives a much clearer picture than just saying they're "girly." "Resilient," "brave," or "tenacious" do a lot better job describing someone than saying they're a "tough guy." Gender is just one facet of who we are, and using more neutral language isn't about invalidating or erasing someone's identity. It's about creating a culture that allows for self-expression and individuality.

3. Mixed Company

Having diverse friendships reduces prejudice and segregation. When kids hang out only with friends in their gender group, they behave in more stereotypical ways, they have fewer positive opinions of people outside their group, and whatever resources or opportunities they have within that group are isolated. The more they separate themselves, the more they notice differences rather than similarities and see people in the other group more for their gender traits than their individuality. Talk to the people who interact with kids and discourage things like sorting team sports by gender or lining kids up by gender at school. Host mixed-gender playdates and birthday parties.

In adulthood, attend mixed-gender group events that center around an interest—music trivia at a local bar or urban birding. Encourage mixed-gender postwork drinks and networking events. Don't let gender be the determining factor in who you get to know. You may have more in common with a colleague of a different gender who loves horror movies than a same-gender colleague who is more of a fitness fanatic. For potluck dinners, make sure to include everyone on the menu-planning email thread, not just the women. When hosting mixed-gender friends, don't shy away from suggesting a movie you might think to reserve for "girls' night." Men can enjoy sip and paint, cupcake-decorating classes, and nights out dancing just as much as women can enjoy kickball tournaments and beer pong. Spending more time in mixed company and expanding what we categorize as activities "everyone would like" helps us to know one another as whole people with unique traits and interests and softens the rigid expectations that create inequity.

4. Be Influential

Modeling matters. We're all influencers. At work, within organizations, in families, in our schools, and in neighborhoods. Imagine a future where we aren't limited by narrow definitions of gender and are free from the oppression our social norms uphold. Interrogate how you were taught you should behave and decide for yourself if that works for you or not. Act with hope for a more liberated future and model that. When you have the courage to challenge norms, you make it safer for other people to do so. You set the next generation up to feel freer.

Even little rebellions against norms make a big difference. This looks like looping men into the group chat about teacher gifts instead of just assuming the moms will handle it. Or men volunteering to take notes in meetings and organizing team parties. Men can coordinate playdates, sign up to be room parents, and volunteer for the PTA. They can research weeknight recipes or potty training methods. Women can run out for beer and flip burgers while dads chase rowdy kids around barbecues. Women can take annual weekend trips or pursue a hobby while their partner stays home.

Disrupting inequity and changing culture can be as small as dropping the "Mama" in front of things meant for parents or as monumental as expanding parental leave or making childcare more accessible. We can't expect men to pick up baby books and jot notes in the margins if that kind of work is seen as emasculating. Be a part of changing what's normal.

Positive peer pressure can be powerful! In our patriarchal society, men often look to other men for influence, and because of that, in-group encouragement can be especially powerful. When a man gets involved in caregiving and other men cheer him on, they're performing powerful society-changing acts. We can all help break down the boxes men are shoved into, but men have a unique opportunity with one another to change the context in which they exist. If being "tough" is supposedly a trait of manliness, then I'd propose the manliest thing a guy can do is boldly transgress in the face of a violent system. To step fully into your role as a caregiver is both brave and rewarding. When men encourage one another to behave in caring ways, especially when they're in a place of power or influence, they are doing powerful liberatory work.

One way to lead is by pushing for leave policies that support all caregivers and by taking leave when it's offered. Prioritize care, proudly. Paternity leave seems optional when we believe that all a baby needs is its mother, so in addition to local organizing efforts to change policy, we also need to change the narrative. When men take time off to care for loved ones, use parental leave, or set boundaries around work hours, they don't just make it safer for other men to do the same; they make it safer for everyone.

Whenever any of us takes time off to tend to the care needs of ourselves or others, whether it's care for children or adults, we help rewrite the narrative around care work—both in who can or should be doing it and what priority it deserves in our lives. Capitalism often treats care work as if it's only valuable if it's in service of profit, with bosses encouraging "working lunches" or instituting strict terms for preapproved time off. Employees who they perceive to be responsible for the care of others or requiring care themselves face stigma and discrimination. If we have the time available to us, taking it is important not just for our own wellness and the wellness of the people we provide care for, but also for intentionally prioritizing care as a powerful example. We need every effort, whether it feels big or small, because the little movements we make in our personal spheres change what happens in the bigger ones.

5. Blowing Up the Nuclear Standard

Contribute to the world with the aim that everyone has the care they need—not that care structures should look any particular way. Our social expectations should allow for authentic self-expression and should support whatever family structure works best for each of us. There is no singular ideal family structure or role that works for every situation. The goal should be that everyone has the care they need, not that their family looks or acts a certain prescribed way.

- Surveys estimate at least five million children in America are being raised by an LGBTQIA parent, and studies have shown that kids raised by two same-sex parents fare just as well as kids raised with two different-sex parents.

- The portion of American households that fit the traditional nuclear family mold with children and two parents has decreased for decades, down from 40 percent in 1970 to less than 18 percent in 2022. People are living with chosen family, or in single-parent, blended, or multigenerational households. Couples are living together without having kids; people are choosing to live alone or splitting costs with roommates. There's been an increase in multigenerational households in the last several decades, which will likely only increase as millennial parents, who have had kids later than previous generations, see themselves becoming caregivers for children and for elders at the same time.

- Everyone is going to need care at one point or another, and we can each contribute to shaping the world into one where we all participate in making sure everyone gets what they need. Child-free friends can act as integrated members of families they aren't romantically or biologically connected to. Friends can act as chosen family, supporting one another and helping meet caregiving needs. Neighbors can act as extended family. We don't have to be related by blood or law to take on caregiver roles.

- In practice, pushing the needle and contributing to a caring society can happen in endless ways. Here are a few:
  - Get involved in local political movements that focus on care infrastructure and advocate for issues of healthcare, disability justice, family and sick leave, affordable healthcare, housing, and other social services.

- Consider ways you can expand your caregiving role within platonic and non-related relationships—by driving someone to a doctor's appointment or being their emergency contact.
- Start a childcare swap with a neighbor. Build connections by introducing yourself, swapping numbers, offering to help with school pickup, or lending a hand during a busy week. Over time, you can create a safety net of caring adults for regular childcare, occasional date-night swaps, family dinners, or simply being the trusted adult a child can turn to in an emergency.

Care isn't bound to a role or a relationship. We can show up for each other in many ways: across generations, with neighbors, friends, chosen family, and even the people we see in passing. When we care beyond our own households, we reinforce a vital truth: Care is for everyone.

PART 2

In Your Relationships:
Break the Cycle, Decide What
Matters, Expand Your Outlook

CHAPTER FOUR

The Nag Paradox

Trading the Trap of Imbalance for Collaboration

RACHEL AND MAY

For most of the years that Rachel and May were together, they found themselves in a dynamic where Rachel took the lead and May followed. Rachel loved looking up recipes and would collect them on a Pinterest board for them to try together. She'd figure out which stores carried the ingredients she needed, run around town tracking them down, and make sure everything was prepped so that they could cook together when May came over after work. As their relationship progressed, and they eventually moved in together, May and Rachel's dynamic became more exaggerated. At first, Rachel had felt pride in taking responsibility for so much and enjoyed the flexibility to choose the little details, like stocking the house with the eco-friendly dish soap she liked. It boosted her confidence when May looked to her for answers.

Things started to change after the two got engaged, and the wedding planning, which Rachel assumed would be a joint endeavor, fell mostly to her. When Rachel asked for input, May said she trusted her, but May's trust in Rachel started to feel like passing the buck and avoiding responsibility. Without May's active participation in the planning and organizing, Rachel felt the weight of throwing a memorable event that met their and their guests' needs. She felt pressure to predict and make compromises in the hope she was doing the right thing. With so much on her plate, she found herself pulling the trigger on things, squeezing calls in on her lunch breaks, and placing deposits, because it would be more work to ask for help than to just do it herself.

About a year into marriage, as they explored their options for expanding their family, the same imbalance kept showing up. Each step of the way, Rachel researched and presented information; then May would either give her opinion or shrug and accept whatever Rachel thought was best. Rachel grew resentful, and May started to withdraw.

After a few years of navigating a challenging fertility journey, Rachel gave birth to their baby. Despite both of them having full-time jobs and becoming first-time parents, May continued to rely on Rachel to steer the ship.

Whenever the conversation came up, they talked in circles. May brought up how demanding her job was and explained how she was willing to help out any way she could. She was increasingly frustrated being on the receiving end of Rachel's disappointment and struggled to understand why it wasn't enough that she did whatever Rachel needed anytime she asked. On the flip side, Rachel was fed up with having to repeat and explain herself. With the excitement of pregnancy gone and sleeplessness setting in, Rachel's patience was running thin.

If Rachel asked for help on a task as seemingly simple as picking out new nursery curtains, she would have to explain the need for well-fitted blackout curtains, something she'd learned from deep diving infant sleep blogs and reading parenting books. She'd have to tell May to measure carefully, to check if the curtain rod was flush to the window, give her ideas of which stores might carry the right sizes, give her a timeline so the curtains would be purchased and installed by the time they planned on transferring the baby into her own room, and so much more. May had countless opportunities to misstep, and when she gave opinions, they were uninformed. From her perspective, she didn't want to step on Rachel's toes, who she knew had put so much care into her decision-making, so she settled into her seat as the helpful passenger and tried to fight off feeling belittled. But as Rachel continued to manage May, the little relational abrasions grew. The nursery curtains became daily reminders of the growing tension between them. The groceries in the fridge, the unsorted mail, the bins of outgrown baby clothes were all inescapable acknowledgments of inequity.

The more work Rachel put into researching, learning, and carefully making decisions about their family life, the more the distance between the two grew. May took on more hours at work and started training for a marathon. Rachel felt abandoned, but anytime she brought up her feelings, it triggered a fight that cascaded through their lives for days.

She found herself stuck, hesitant to relinquish control but resentful of being expected to know best. When May would offer to get groceries or take the baby to her appointments, Rachel would turn her down, because having to make grocery lists or outline all the questions she'd need to ask the doctor was still work. If she didn't give directions, May would bring home the wrong brand of peanut butter or forget to mention a rash. Rachel would have to decide if bringing it up was worthwhile or if she should just take note to do it herself next time. It was maddening.

Rachel didn't want to be the only one figuring out how to navigate the daycare system. When their child started having mysterious allergic reactions, she wanted to be involved in the healthcare decisions, but she didn't want to be the only one booking appointments and doing research on her lunch breaks. May, with less hands-on experience and knowledge, hesitated to care for their child for more than a few hours on her own and looked to Rachel to give guidance in decisions as small as what to grab for a snack. Rachel gladly made it her business to learn everything she could and make careful decisions, but doing so without participation from her partner left her feeling underwater and alone.

May helped out and followed through on her commitments when directions were laid out for her, but she grew increasingly defensive when Rachel gave reminders or corrections. Rachel started to see herself as overbearing and nitpicky. May felt inadequate and bossed around. They both felt misunderstood and unseen, frustrated with the positions they'd found themselves in but unsure of how to change. They kept bumping their heads against this pattern, and eventually it led to their wanting to spend less and less time together, a total lack of emotional intimacy, and the end of their marriage.

LEAVE ME ALONE

Rachel and May became caught up in the Nag Paradox, which is the relationship dynamic in which one partner directs and the other is directed. The Nag Paradox happens when partners aren't sharing responsibilities equitably. It's the result of unclear priorities and an imbalance of the mental and emotional loads. In the Nag Paradox, one person is in a position of decision-making, delegating, and making requests, and the other party is on the receiving end. One partner is the "nag," and the other is "nagged."

In a scene from the 2006 rom-com *The Break-Up*, starring Vince Vaughn as Gary and Jennifer Aniston as Brooke, the two act out one of the most familiar fights couples experience. In the scene, immediately after they say goodbye to dinner guests they'd been hosting, Gary settles into the couch to play video games while Brooke announces her intent to clean the kitchen. She asks for help, explaining that having the dishes done will mean she can relax. He repeatedly brushes her off. Eventually, after some heated back-and-forth, Gary throws his controller and gets up, clearly angry, and agrees to help.

That wasn't the response Brooke was looking for, though. She didn't want him to do the dishes after being begged and pleaded with. She tells Gary, "I want you to *want* to do the dishes." They continue to argue, Brooke explaining the ways his reluctant, begrudged participation in their relationship has been a trend, not a rarity. Gary calls her crazy and says nothing he does is ever enough. Brooke gives examples of times she's felt unimportant to him, and for each one, Gary deflects and makes excuses. He tells her he feels underappreciated and nagged. He yells that all she ever does is nag him. "Nothing I ever do is good enough! I just want to be left the hell alone!" When she throws her hands up and tells him she's done, taking him up on his request, he's shocked.

In *The Break-Up*, Brooke was clearly feeling resentful for having to ask for her partner to show up for the daily demands of their life, such as doing the dishes, cleaning the apartment, and cooking. But she was also tired of asking to be noticed. She felt like Gary wasn't paying attention to her needs or making an effort to meet them without being given explicit direction. She felt rejected after being met with resistance and protest every step of the way.

On the flip side, Gary felt like Brooke was making demands of him to do things he didn't actually want to do. He wanted to play video games, go to football games, and relax rather than rush to do the dishes. Hosting parties or going to the ballet weren't things he cared about, so he didn't understand why he should be forced into doing them.

They had different ideas of what it meant to be in a relationship. They had different ideas about what they wanted out of life. And rather than compromise, collaborate, or make explicit agreements, they fell into a trap where she made demands and he begrudgingly went along with them. They were both unhappy. They were both left with their needs unmet.

In the Nag Paradox, the nag is often tasked with the mental labor of setting standards and making plans. The result is that the nag also has to hold other people to those standards. This creates an incredibly un-fun feeling of either bossing or being bossed around, depending on which role you're in. The Nag Paradox creates a complex mess of power imbalance and unequal demands. Decision-making and directing come with the power to shape outcomes, but having to dedicate time and effort to those things and overcompensate has costs elsewhere in life. Being told what to do comes with the luxury of there being lower demands on your time and energy, but it also means you have less input into how things are done. While there are benefits and drawbacks to being in either role, the whole setup harms everyone and is a recipe for relationship disaster. Real-life Rachel and May and fictional Gary and Brooke are clear examples of that.

A PROBLEMATIC PATTERN

My husband and I know the Nag Paradox dynamic all too well. The discouragement of trying hard to strike a balance and not getting it right is definitely one we've felt in our home. For years, my husband and I both felt like no matter how much effort we put into our household and no matter how hard we tried to shift the scales, it just wasn't happening.

I bought stylish family planners and made accounts for us on home-organization websites that claimed they'd simplify our lives, but the fact that I was still the one doing the research and deep diving blogs for tips added to the problem. When we tried new things, I was still in a position of explaining the protocols. It didn't seem to matter what we tried—no app, sticky-note system, list on the fridge, or pretty planner solved the problem. Eventually, the miscommunications and unintentional inadequacies became land mines.

EACH TIME WE introduced a new trick for smoothing out our division of labor, it felt like we'd found something novel. But it didn't matter if we were using a shared note on our phones or using ink on designer paper; we kept coming back to the same methods that had caused our inequity in the first place—me telling him what to do. We were still stuck in the Nag Paradox.

We played the parts, and the resentment kept creeping. We both worked full-time, but I was capable of walking in the door and immediately noticing what needed to be done. I kept track of what was in the fridge, knew when the sump pump needed to be cleaned, and knew where everyone's important documents were kept.

In some ways, I loved being in charge. I felt competent, confident,

and powerful. I ran a well-oiled machine and saw it as a major accomplishment. But I resented having to ask for help. I resented not
having the same freedom and flexibility as my husband. I turned
down work opportunities, opted out of evenings with friends, and
stopped seeing things like travel or involvement with local organizing projects as possibilities. Meanwhile, he was building a small
business from the ground up. He was off at networking events,
flying across the world, meeting celebrities, and presenting at conferences. The only dreams I felt were within my grasp at the time
were ones where I could take our kids along with me. I was proud
of the work I was doing and was glad to put my support behind my
husband, but I was facilitating their lives. I felt like I was inconve-
niencing my husband or holding him back anytime I made a request or complained. I was glad he got to do so much, but I was
jealous.

He could come and go, because he could rely on me to keep
things running. He trusted me to make decisions and knew I had
things handled. If I needed help, he encouraged me to ask. If I felt
overwhelmed, all I had to do was give him some ideas of how he
could support me, and he'd do his best. But help wasn't what I was
looking for. My resentment came partially from his having more
flexibility and time, but mostly from the loneliness and exhaustion
I felt.

I tried relinquishing control and completely handing over tasks
to him to handle, but he wouldn't complete them on my timeline or
meet my standards. Then I had to figure out what to do from there.
Should I correct him? If so, when and how? When I'm annoyed, or
wait for a happy moment and risk ruining it? Should I find a play-
ful way to mention it, schedule a serious meeting, or accept an insufficient job? I cycled through frustration that he couldn't just

come home and notice everything that needed to be done without being told, sadness at him not knowing the details of our daily routines, and guilt at my lack of patience. I was mad a lot of the time, and in the days and hours when we were together as a family, in the back of my mind I was constantly thinking of how and when I was going to bring up the issues that were bothering me. Inevitably, something tiny would break open the dam, we'd argue, and I'd end up ashamed of myself for boiling over because of something as insignificant as crumbs on the counter. The internal struggle of wanting things done a certain way but wanting to let go of responsibilities sent me spiraling. I felt trapped between coming off as critical or betraying myself. Neither option felt good.

The imbalance we were dealing with was multifaceted. I was managing the majority of the mental load at home and knew how every cog of the machine fit together. I saw the household as my responsibility, so I moved through my days tackling tasks efficiently, picking up cups on my way to the kitchen so that I wouldn't have to double back later, and placing spare toilet paper rolls on the stairwell so I could restock the bathroom when I went up to put laundry away. I knew schedules, where to find school-supply lists, the log-in info to the insurance website, and when we needed to book dental checkups. I thought ten steps ahead and always had the big picture in mind. I knew how things needed to be done, because I knew how it all fit together.

Because I was managing the mental load for our family, I was in a place of always having to give detailed directions in order for the rest of the seemingly unrelated gears of our household machine to keep running. Because I was managing things on my own, I was also setting expectations on my own. Because so many tasks relied on other tasks being done in specific ways, when something wasn't done how I needed it to be done, I got pissed. Despite our best efforts, attempts to balance housework often created more issues than they solved.

The longer this pattern went on, the worse I felt about myself as a person. I was prickly and harsh. I was weak for even having to request help in the first place. I couldn't even imagine why someone would want to be married to someone who told them what to do and made them feel like they weren't doing enough. Everything was calm when I kept my mouth shut, but the frustration kept boiling. Either way, I felt like I couldn't win.

LIFE WITHOUT PAROLE

I was desperate not to morph into the stereotype of the bitchy wife. I'd been a cool girl. I didn't want to be someone who was hard to come home to. I wanted to be easy breezy. The TV moms who handed out chore lists and interrupted their family to solicit help were always unlikable butts of jokes, and I wanted nothing to do with that.

Despite my best efforts, I saw my husband and me playing out the tropes. I was the old maid wielding a rolling pin, shrieking at my husband after he came home from work. I thought of that tired joke, "Why is it customary for women to cook for their husbands? Because the law says you have to feed the prisoners!" and realized *I was the warden*. I'd always thought my husband was with me because he wanted to be, but the longer we stayed in the cycle of criticism and defensiveness, the more I questioned whether that was true. When he met me, I was fun and exciting. Had I done a bait and switch? Had I trapped him?

I'd heard the story a million times, that women hate to see men happy and revel in sucking the joy out of their lives. Our culture is chock-full of casual contempt for women, and I'd internalized a lot of it. I felt like a bitch, because I was taught that women who ask for equality around the house *were bitching*. I needed to learn to be more effective and patient in my communication. But try as I might, that wasn't working for me. What I usually did was spin out over little details until I burst. Then, just like Rachel had with May, I'd feel ashamed for being a nightmarish wife.

The Nag Paradox is like quicksand. It's a cycle where the more you struggle with it, the more it pulls you in. It's a relationship-killing spiral of "Just tell me what to do!" then "Don't tell me what to do!" Even when both parties are trying their best, asking for help or offering to pitch in, the effort required to give directions just keeps reinforcing the imbalance. It acts like a feedback loop of criticism and defensiveness that just keeps getting louder and louder. The Nag Paradox is definitely damaging to relationships, but beyond that, the mental and emotional weight of a household could be making "nags" sick.

Asking for help takes energy and effort. It also takes vulnerability. Doing it with sensitivity to the listener while also guarding against disappointment is like walking an emotional-labor tightrope. Each step is a careful calculation of whose feelings to protect and how, how much mental and emotional reserves are available, and the most effective and efficient way to ask for what you need in a way that will get results. It's a delicate dance trying to find the line between communicating helpful guidance and giving inflexible marching orders. Carrying more of the mental and emotional load is a game of perpetual risk analysis: taking the emotional temperature of the environment, considering the options, predicting future events, and making calculated decisions. It's either do things yourself, don't do them at all, or do the work of communicating gently and effectively while fighting back feelings of frustration for even having to ask in the first place. It's not as simple as just asking for help. It's also asking: Would the feedback be helpful or harmful? What would happen if I just didn't do it? Is the way they might do it acceptable? Will talking about it start a fight or prevent one later? Will it be more or less stressful to do it myself? Is this the time to let them learn the hard way how to do something or would the consequences be too big? All of this perpetual risk-analysis while internally screaming, "Why on earth do I have to be the one to ask for help in the first place? I didn't sign up for this!"

Emotional labor is no joke. When you're underwater already, trying to make requests without coming off as condescending is not easy. Toss in any internalized beliefs about gender and personal value—*good wives don't bother their husbands*—and the trap becomes clearer.

The Nag Paradox is a breeding ground for resentment. Not just for the "nag," but for the person on the receiving end of the "nagging." Nobody wants to feel bossed around and nobody wants to feel bossy, but the inequity of the paradox makes it nearly impossible to talk about anything without it coming off as condescending or critical.

Even if the damage is unequal, this kind of dynamic can wear on both partners. Because one person is usually in charge of coming up with plans and systems, they're forced into a position of explaining how things should be done. They either have to let things go, speak up, or do things themselves. Again, all crummy options. Even sneaking around behind someone fixing mistakes to protect their feelings or smiling while giving corrections can feel patronizing or insulting to a person who just tried their best. On the flip side, when you feel criticized, it's natural to feel defensive. Being told you got something wrong or didn't do a good enough job can feel like *you* are wrong or not enough. Defensiveness, though it can be incredibly damaging, is a protective behavior. If someone is told their tardiness means they're selfish, they might lash out and call the other person pushy or demanding. Someone who feels like they're being accused of purposefully harming another might focus on why the other person is wrong for feeling hurt. Defensiveness is a way of taking perceived attacks and turning them around to place blame elsewhere.

When defensiveness is the response to feedback, it doesn't allow for problem-solving or self-reflection. Defensiveness closes the door on discussions about the mental load or shared standards. It shuts down collaboration. Like being stuck in quicksand, you're going to keep sinking. Not getting swallowed up will require a shift in approach.

BREAKING FREE

I spoke with Dr. Han Ren, a licensed clinical psychologist, about this dynamic. She told me it's a serious issue that flies under the radar, because it's so normalized. We've been socialized to see imbalance as a natural way of being together, so the eventual contempt is seen as natural, too. Han said, "When contempt is there, that's when it gets really dangerous." Because, she explained, "You end up with disgust for each other. You can't even remember to be on the same team, because you don't even *want* to be on the same team as that person." At that point, couples will often kick into high gear and try to do whatever they can to fix things, but that usually looks like splitting tasks and not, as Han said, "Let me own things from beginning to end. Let me join you as a copilot. Let's divvy up the mental load." By only scratching the surface, the person who's trying to step up and do more continues to be told they aren't doing enough, and the person who's been carrying the majority continues to feel disappointed. Both partners end up walking on eggshells around each other, and at that point, Han said, "It's less about the tasks and more about the underlying emotional needs that are just not being met."

Han suggests that to break the Nag Paradox cycle, a commitment to a huge overhaul needs to be made. More than just tweaks and tune-ups, the overhaul needs to address inequity in the division of labor and also any inequity in emotional functioning. These go hand in hand, and *both* have to be addressed to heal. The day-to-day things like taking out the trash and doing the dishes are often fuel for the Nag Paradox, and every time there's a conflict around them, the same emotional patterns come up. But the cycle of resentment isn't really about those things. "It's about how each person meets or doesn't meet the other person's emotional needs," Han said. "And then being able to take responsibility for your own emotional reactions within that."

In action, a disruption to the Nag Paradox may mean taking space, getting professional help, or taking a completely new approach to the division of labor. That could involve each person taking a weekend day to themselves once a month, seeing an individual or couples therapist, or temporarily outsourcing some of the high-conflict domestic tasks. The point is to relieve some of the pressure the Nag Paradox creates, free up some emotional and mental space, and break patterns.

To break patterns of directing and being directed, try temporarily taking a completely businesslike approach to housework. Imagine yourselves as coworkers with a job to do. *Neither of you is the boss!* Your home needs to function, so make that the weekly goal. Throw perfection out the window for a while and practice the process of talking through logistics as peers, giving each other opportunities to take full ownership of tasks and not waiting for directions or handing them out. Approach the division of labor with a mindset of "I am going to take responsibility for handling this task from start to finish. I am responsible for getting the information and resources I need to do this successfully." As you'd do on a work project, explicitly agree to certain roles and responsibilities and don't expect the other person to jump in without communicating about it. Brainstorm together about what would help the household run smoothly without triggering each other's pain points. Ask, "How would you like me to approach you if I notice a logistical issue? Are there any words I can use to let you know I'm trying to be helpful and not critical or defensive? Would you like to do quick check-ins every few days?"

As you work on the logistics, give yourselves space to process and relieve the pressure of trying to fix everything all at once. How long did it take you to wear a groove into your dynamic? It's going to take time to get out of it. Give yourselves permission to take things week by week or agree that you'll try your best for three months before checking in to see if things have changed. If possible, take weekend afternoons apart—travel to see friends or find other ways to take space. It's hard to process and self-reflect when you're in the thick of it. Distance can provide the necessary relief from a sense of urgency to fix everything all at once.

The Nag Paradox is a dynamic that won't fix itself. More lists, more delegating, more telling or being told what to do will only make things worse. The great news is, things don't have to be this way.

―――――

CLIMBING OUT

Will is a father of three who has been married to his wife for fifteen years. When they were dating, it was clear that they both valued parity and intended on an equitable distribution of labor, but they quickly found themselves stuck in the Nag Paradox. Due in part to the cost of childcare and the lack of access to job opportunities, when they became parents, they became a single-income household, with Will earning wages and his wife taking responsibility for the childcare.

Will's wife grew up with models of household dynamics that included family chores, clearly assigned tasks, and a sense of communal responsibility for the family and household well-being. Will, on the other hand, came from a family of origin where his mother was almost exclusively responsible for the kids and the house, while his father brought home a paycheck. He entered into their partnership wanting to be an equal partner, but he'd never had a clear model for what that looked like, lacked a lot of skills, and had internalized beliefs about roles, responsibilities, and work that needed to be confronted. The misalignment between what they'd wanted (equal footing) and what they got (imbalance) caused friction and resentment.

Things have changed over time, though. Will had to be honest with himself—he wasn't living up to his ideal of integrity or truly committing to learning the skills he needed to follow through on what he signed up for. He had to take a hard look at what lessons he was unintentionally acting on when he took a secondary role at home. When he waited for directions or didn't complete a task in a way that met the family's needs, it sent a message—one that made it seem like he didn't love his wife. The realization hit hard. He would feel ashamed, try overcompensating, and often end up taking on more than he could handle. But instead of fixing the problem, he found himself stuck in the same disappointing cycle over and over again.

Though she was a motivating factor in looking for solutions, Will's wife wasn't the one responsible for his growth. He had to do the work for himself. He started to recognize and disrupt patterns in his behavior as part of a broader assessment of his life and his relationships. He developed the skills to name what was going on. He credits his intentional development of emotional skills as a major factor in the positive change in his life. Things started to shift in his household dynamic, and the conflicts he and his wife faced started to soften after he began seeing a therapist for help processing events from his childhood. His therapist helped him gain the skills to recognize and communicate about his feelings as they were happening. He had realizations about the roots of his behavior, like conflict avoidance and defensiveness, and took personal accountability for learning more direct, boundary-forward ways of communicating. The issues he was having in his relationship with his wife weren't isolated. When he accepted that, he was able to move forward.

He didn't expect his wife to let go of frustration or hesitance as he learned, but she provided him with grace and trust that he was doing his best. When he ran into an issue like a skill deficit or a misalignment of expectations, he took responsibility for bringing it up, and in response, his wife made space for the learning process by setting her own boundaries and communicating her own needs. The issue was never that they didn't care about each other or that they didn't want each other to feel happy and supported; it was that they were trying to accomplish those things in ways that weren't getting them there.

The work they've done has brought them closer together. They've gained a deeper understanding of their family priorities, which has empowered Will to make decisions that meet the family's needs without having to check in with his wife. He's gotten more efficient and skilled at household tasks that he didn't even realize existed just a few years ago. Not only does he notice that the baseboards need to be cleaned, but he and his wife have learned to look beyond themselves. Social norms shielded Will from being judged for dusty ledges. They taught him to let his partner manage and held him back from learning the value of taking initiative in the domestic realm. The progress he and his wife have made in breaking their cycles has included a more balanced distribution of household labor, but the changes have been so impactful and lasting because they aimed for understanding rather than quick fixes.

Instead of relying on internalized beliefs, they redefined what it truly means to be partners. As they've grown together, they've built a foundation of trust—reinforced by action and evidence. They're modeling the kind of commitment to growth, equity, and parity that they always wanted for themselves. They're raising their kids in a home rooted in shared knowledge and values, just like they'd imagined. Slowly and steadily, they're leaving behind what held them back and building something new together.

If the Nag Paradox is like quicksand, we can take a note from nature about how to resist getting pulled under. If you find yourself caught in quicksand, the best strategy is to lie down flat on your back and relieve the pressure from your feet so that you can slow down the sinking process. The goal is to address any stress points and create the stability needed to roll your way to safety. If you're up to your knees, you can reach for sticks or other makeshift tools to help make the surface steadier. Regardless of how deep you are, the way out is cautious, intentional movements in a new direction.

To get unstuck, slow down and take a deep breath, assess the situation, and come up with a plan. Gather tools if necessary. Seek solid footing and relieve problem areas that could cancel out progress elsewhere. Keep your eyes on solid ground, take breaks, remain calm, and keep going.

IT'S NOT YOU VERSUS ME—IT'S US

When I got pregnant with my oldest, I read every book and blog I could find in an effort to feel prepared. I saw pregnancy and newborn care as my responsibility, having absorbed messaging throughout my life that I was "made for it." Being the youngest in my family and only ever having experience with older kids as a teacher, I went into research mode. I asked friends and colleagues for tips. I read articles, bookmarked websites, and signed up for newsletters, and a few weeks before my due date, I signed myself up for a breastfeeding class at our local hospital. Though I figured the class was mostly for me as the one in my partnership with the necessary nursing anatomy, my husband opted to come, too.

The class was full of practical information and resources, but the most important lessons we walked away with were the many ways *my husband* could contribute to breastfeeding success. In the class, mixed in with lessons about nursing holds, clogged ducts, and latching, the instructor gave explicit instructions to nonnursing caregivers on how they played a part in the whole process. The instructors didn't treat my husband like a side character. They made it clear from the get-go that his role and participation in the process were essential. In my preparation, I'd been hyperfocused on ways I, as a new mother, could care for our new family member.

Fueled by antiquated ideas about gender and parenthood, I was compulsively creating inequity.

When the teacher told us about cluster feeding—when growing infants periodically spend multiple days nursing nonstop—they didn't just provide tips about treating chapped nipples. They were also direct with us about the need to take care of the person stuck under a baby. Feeding *me* was an important aspect of keeping a baby fed. They emphasized the importance of giving me time when my body was my own, when the baby's crying was out of my earshot, and when I wasn't being touched. They gave us tips for soothing a baby in the middle of the night, encouraged non-nursing caregivers to learn swaddling and shushing, and repeatedly underlined the importance of teamwork. They framed the discussion around how we, *as a family unit*, could work together to successfully move through the infant stage and meet our goals.

Prior to the class, I saw nursing the baby as something I was going to be responsible for and not something we were responsible for together. My husband and I knew we wanted to parent as equals, but I'd been imagining a complementary dynamic and not so much a collaborative one. Had we not had the concrete examples we were given in that class, I'm positive we would have relied on old patterns of imbalance. Armed with encouragement and examples, we were able to take a less black-and-white approach to that aspect of our lives. Rather than defaulting to our usual dynamic, we made an intentional shift and approached it as something to build together. Instead of my taking the lead and managing, we acted as coconspirators, strategizing and making joint decisions right out of the gate.

Until that point, we'd had very little experience having in-depth conversations about our priorities and goals. We fell in love and naively believed that everything would naturally work itself out. We'd absorbed the culture of competition that our society is built on. When we learn to see ourselves in constant comparison to neighbors or colleagues, always striving to be better or have more, that mindset often seeps into our closest relationships, too. A competitive culture frames everything from career decisions to who gets personal time within a partnership as a case of win or lose. Our culture discourages us from seeing the ways we could collaborate, so we all have our voices heard and our needs met.

The class prompted us to sit down and make explicit plans for how we could both contribute to feeding the baby. We had a discussion about what our short- and long-term goals were. I wanted to exclusively breastfeed for as long as I could, with a goal of introducing solids at six months. My husband agreed, and from there, we considered our work schedules and decided we'd prioritize my sleep. We agreed that at night, I'd nurse during wake-ups, and if the baby didn't go back down, he'd take her into another room and rock her so that I could get some sleep. We talked through scenarios and made plans as a team, establishing, even before the baby arrived, that we both wanted to be a part of the baby-feeding process. It wasn't me versus him; it was us versus keeping our baby fed.

We did a great job working together throughout our breastfeeding journey, but it wasn't a true light bulb moment for us. It was more of a one-off win. We'd been together for years at that point, with well-established imbalances in many areas of our lives. We stayed afloat and took some of what we learned from the teamwork approach we used with breastfeeding and applied it in other areas of our lives, but it took the compounding pressure of the toddler years, a second kid, and a new job for us to hit a point where we realized an overhaul of our entire relationship needed to happen.

We needed to shift, in every area of our lives, from a "me versus you" mindset. We had to reframe what it took to create a life together, moving away from a competitive understanding of our time and needs and embracing an approach that saw us as coconspirators.

ENTHUSIASTIC COLLABORATION

An alternative to the Nag Paradox that takes into account both logistical and emotional considerations is enthusiastic collaboration. By that, I don't mean we need to champ at the bit to clean the floors or put on fake smiles while we sign up for summer camp, but when partners are jointly invested, they work toward collective goals and ensure everyone's needs are met.

The Nag Paradox leans on outdated methods of list-making and complementary roles, while enthusiastic collaboration is rooted in recognizing the most essential work of our lives as a shared endeavor. When I thrive, you thrive. We thrive together. Or as Robin Wall Kimmerer puts it in *Braiding Sweetgrass,* "All flourishing is mutual." It's not about *equally* sharing the mental, emotional, or physical load; it's about approaching that load with the goal of consideration and care. It's about valuing each other equally, taking personal responsibility, and not letting expectations go unspoken. Enthusiasm is *eager interest.* Collaboration is *working together toward a shared goal.* That goal is everyone having what they need. That goal is a give and take. That goal is mutual flourishing.

Enthusiastic collaboration involves:

- accounting for the **mental and emotional loads** when considering responsibilities
- **consenting** to the division of labor in a relationship
- openness to have **ongoing** communication

- a commitment to personal **growth**
- noticing when **decision** fatigue is shaping decisions and addressing it before assumptions take over
- **trading mind-reading** for asking questions, asking for what you want, and noticing
- **curiosity**, approaching conflict and problems with creativity, self-reflection, and vulnerability
- **compromising** and problem-solving with a focus toward the best possible outcome for everyone, not a win or lose. Asking: How can we all have the most of what we need? Not solving for who is right or wrong, or who can have what they need or not.

We may start off with different skills, feel unique pressures, or come to the table with individualized expectations, but none of those things bar us from learning, growing, and taking personal responsibility. We can't let societal expectations or models of inequity trap us. How we talk about housework, how we divide tasks, and how we slip into roles of manager and managed keep us from connections we deserve. The damage that delegating does is insidious but avoidable.

The division of labor in our households and the ways we talk about daily tasks with partners are as much opportunities for connection or rejection as coming in for a kiss when you get home from work or giving words of affirmation. The Gottman Institute calls these verbal and nonverbal requests "bids for connection," and has found that the response to those bids has a major impact on the health of a relationship.

Asking to share in the chores, cook together, or navigate health insurance may not seem that romantic, but requests to work together to build a life is inviting someone to connect. If you've been groaning and fighting your way through conversations about housework, a reframe can make a difference. These are bids. They're opportunities for connection. Consistently *showing up* is a way of consistently *turning toward* each other. When you ask a partner to engage in conversations about the household and are repeatedly met with resistance, it can lead to emotional distance. When someone makes an attempt to show up through a care task and they're met with eye-rolling or negative feedback, it's a similar kind of rejection. Noticing and turning toward your partner's bids strengthens connections, and if that's what you want, keep your eyes open for them. When your partner comes to you about a concern or shares their feelings, if they want to work through a conflict so you can understand each other better, or even if they just want to review the weekly schedule, accept the invitation to connect. Date nights are important, but so are conversations about laundry detergent.

The prominent model for how we're supposed to divide our homes is imbalanced, and as a result, it's an unsustainable setup for resentment. One of the biggest lies our society has told us and has built into the framework of loving relationships is that one person can do enough of the work of loving to make up for someone else's lack of effort. Let's take ownership and agency of the ways we love, and see them as an active choice backed up by actions. Loving someone means wanting to grow and wanting *them* to grow, then doing what you can to support that. It means taking personal responsibility and allowing others to do the same. More important than who's actually checking off items on a to-do list is that we start from a place of wanting to meet each other in mutual love and understanding.

5 THINGS YOU CAN DO RIGHT NOW

1. Focus on a Goal

Where are you seeing the Nag Paradox cost you? Do you want to argue less? Do you want to feel less resentful or defensive around each other? Do you want to feel like you can discuss housework without arguing? Do you want to feel less stressed, alone, or overburdened? Do you want to feel less directed and more empowered? Figure out where the pain points are and use that as your motivation. "Working on improving this dynamic will benefit me/us by improving/giving me more _____." Set your sights on what the work will bring you!

2. Express Yourself

Don't expect other people to know what you want or need. Be clear, kind, and direct about how you feel. Practice taking ownership of your own emotions and let others do the same for themselves.

- *Take emotional responsibility.* Many therapists recommend using "I" statements to communicate feelings in a direct way while avoiding blame.
  - Example: Instead of "You didn't take out the trash again. You're always letting me down" try "I feel

overwhelmed and unimportant when you say you're going to do something and don't follow through."

- *Get comfortable being uncomfortable.* Disrupting patterns and establishing new communication styles may bring up tough feelings. You may feel guilty. The other party may feel upset. That's okay! Using care, empathy, and understanding is important, but we're each individually responsible for processing our hard feelings.

3. Abolish the Royal "We"

Don't just imply or assume when communicating about housework. In a household where one person is the manager and nothing gets done without them pulling the trigger, when someone mentions housework that needs to be done and says "we" need to do it, they usually mean one specific person.

If your partner notices the milk is running low and says, "We need to get more milk!" but has no plan to add it to a list or go get it themselves, what they really mean is *you* need to get more milk. If members of a household can just say things like, "Hey, I'm gonna be late on Thursday," and not make any plans for childcare or dinner in their absence, they're really saying, "I'm going to be late. I need you to handle things on your own. If you're busy, you have to figure that out." There's no asking, no agreeing, just implication and assumption.

Say what you mean:

- "We're low on milk. Do you want me to grab it, or can you get it when you go to the store tomorrow?"

■ "I've got a nonnegotiable meeting tomorrow. I can plan for a babysitter if you're not available. Let me know!"

Without clearly communicating about who will do something and what the expectations are, whoever *usually* does something is going to have to handle it or catch blame if it isn't done. Get in the habit of agreeing to a point person for tasks as they hit your mental plate. Just a quick, "You got the laundry this week or need me to handle it?" can help clarify expectations and chip away at any resentment around a history of one party taking on more than they signed up for.

4. Seek to Understand, Not to Win

One of the most common pitfalls in the Nag Paradox dynamic comes from directions and corrections being given without much explanation. Being told what to do without knowing *why* creates a sense of powerlessness. The imbalance of the dynamic creates misunderstanding, but our society has shown us very little representation of reacting with curiosity. When timelines or expectations are misaligned or priorities aren't the same, outcomes are bound to be different. If someone solicits help and the results don't meet expectations, conflict is going to arise. Instead, remember that there's a reason behind everything we do. "Why are you doing things that way?" can come off like an accusation when you've had tension around housework for a while. Make an explicit agreement that you're going to ask questions and give clarifications moving forward. Make it a habit to pay attention to what you're doing and why. Pay attention to how the other person does things. Ask questions about the details. Commit to the practice of seeking understanding and be open to making adjustments in how you do things once you have time to reflect or talk things through.

Be clear that you are not aiming to prove who is right or wrong or exactly how something should be done. You're working toward understanding. Our lives are busy, and it might feel hard to find the time, but a proactive minute is all it takes to get the ball rolling.

This sounds like:

■ "You usually do the bedtime routine, and I hesitate to jump in, because it seems like you have things handled. Can you give me some of the highlights of how you do it and why?"

■ "I'd like to understand more about how you manage the meal planning. Is there a reason you get certain things from different stores?"

■ "Hey! I'm about to do the dishes, and I realize I've never walked you through my process. You don't have to do it the same way, but I've learned I'm more likely to do a load of dishes in my free time if the rack is empty, so I try to put things away anytime I notice it's full."

■ "This morning, can we do the breakfast routine together and talk through the steps? I try to have the baby's lunch packed before bed, but whenever I forget, I make sure to feed him breakfast before I start making his lunch, so he's eating while I'm working. Since he's having blueberries this morning, I'll pack him a different fruit for lunch."

5. A Practice Project

Pick a project to do together and use it as practice in collaborating and compromising. Choose something with an outcome that packs a punch, like redecorating a space in your home, coming up with a weeknight dinner menu, or planning a vacation. Focus on coming up with an outcome that reflects everyone's interests and efforts. Make clear agreements about who will handle what, make an effort to gather everyone's input, and go through as much of the process together as possible. When planning, sit down together to sketch out ideas, add thoughts to a shared document, or create a shared Pinterest board. Don't do more than what you agree to! Practice asking clarifying questions and working through conflicts with openness.

As you do this, pay attention to what kind of communication works well throughout. Take note of moments when it felt like you were on the same team. What set you up for success? What kept you on track? Do you do well with prescheduled work time? Do you like learning together as you go, or planning and then going off in your own directions? Are you a planner or a doer? Do any of your strengths complement your partner's? Keep notes in a shared document or notebook and talk about them. Pay attention to how you felt throughout the process and what it felt like to have accomplished something together. Have an *actual conversation* about it and acknowledge the payoff. Carry those lessons forward into other areas of your life.

CHAPTER FIVE

Good Faith and Incompetence as a Weapon

The Power of Anti-Perfectionism

NOT FIFTY-FIFTY, BUT GOOD FAITH

Erin and Noah were in a long-term relationship; they were engaged, living together, planning a future, and expecting to be together for the long run. When they first connected, they had a ton of fun together—doing late-night karaoke and taking spontaneous weekend trips. Noah was passionate about helping people, and Erin admired the work they did volunteering with local organizations. Noah wrote Erin poems and made her playlists. Noah proudly showed Erin off to their friends—an experience that made Erin feel deeply loved, especially as a kid who grew up as a closeted queer in the Midwest. They fell in love hard. When things were good, they were good, and Erin saw any challenges they faced as minor hurdles and opportunities to grow together. A few years into their relationship, shortly after Noah started a rigorous training program to become a first responder, Erin found herself in a tough position.

Prior to the start of their program, Noah had been in charge of only a few chores around the household, mostly doing the dishes after Erin would cook for them and some weekly cleaning. But within the first few weeks of starting classes, Noah stopped doing their part with any consistency. First responder courses are notoriously stressful, and Erin understood there would be an adjustment period. Noah came home most nights on edge and irritated, and Erin wanted Noah to be able to unwind, so for the first few months, she avoided mentioning anything that could possibly put Noah on the defensive. Rather than potentially start an argument, she kicked the can down the road in hopes of things easing up at some point, and stepped in to fill the gaps.

As time went on, Erin got worried that the ongoing stress was turning into a mental health decline in her partner. Erin wanted to help, and as Noah's life partner, she saw it as her responsibility to support them in any way she could. Erin told Noah she'd handle their portion of the housework until further notice, hoping it would relieve some of the stress they were under. It wasn't ideal, but she'd already been doing it and officially agreeing at least felt like she'd had a choice in the matter.

She was careful to avoid giving any feedback that could be perceived as negative, and while she tried to make things as easy as possible for everyone at home, she encouraged Noah to get professional help for their mental health. Erin spent evenings researching types of therapy, made calls to their insurance, and presented Noah with options. She looked into support groups, packed them healthy lunches, and tried her best to get Noah what they needed.

It didn't matter which of the dozens of different angles she took, though. Noah said they didn't want outside help. If Erin brought up the impact of their stress on her, Noah told her they'd never made any demands. Noah had "never asked" for help. It was true that Noah had never asked for Erin to step in around the house or do the legwork to get outside help, but because Noah wasn't doing it, Erin was forced to either cope with the negative consequences or do it herself. Not only did Erin worry about Noah's wellness, but she was worried about herself. Her own mental and physical health had taken a toll trying to figure things out on her own.

Things weren't adding up for Erin. She trusted her own judgment in most areas of her life, but the inconsistencies and conflicts in her relationship often left her doubting herself. She wanted Noah to thrive. She cared deeply about them. The issue wasn't that she couldn't or didn't want to show up for them. What hurt so much was how dismissed and diminished she felt. Noah's not having the capacity to help out around the household was completely understandable, but they had just stopped doing their part.

Erin and Noah had been having the same conversations repeatedly long before the stress of first responder courses entered the picture. Erin had been more than just the lead at home; she'd often felt like she had to coach Noah through basic tasks like making sure they washed the top *and* bottom of plates or reminding them for the twentieth time where they could find the kitchen scissors. Anytime Erin hit her limit, Noah defended themselves by listing off times they'd tried to step up and Erin got mad at them for how they handled things. Conversations ended with Noah accusing Erin of attacking them and Erin feeling sorry she'd even brought the issue up.

Once, after one of their conversations on the topic, Noah offered to pick up ingredients for a chicken pot pie recipe Erin wanted to try. They came home with everything except for chicken, claiming they "couldn't find it," and after a brief argument, Noah sulked around the house, barely speaking to Erin for days. Erin felt guilty, wondering if she was expecting too much, and avoided sending Noah to the store in the future.

For most of their partnership, Erin had been picking up responsibilities that Noah had dropped—emotionally, mentally, and physically—and Noah had let her. Meanwhile, Noah claimed Erin was making her own choices. According to Noah, Erin wasn't doing anything she hadn't chosen to do.

But Noah was either unable or unwilling to do certain tasks, and the absence of effort or acknowledgment put Erin into a position she *hadn't* chosen willingly. She was boxed in, given no other option but to run herself ragged performing physical, mental, and emotional labor or face any number of negative consequences.

By the time first responder training entered the picture, Erin felt stuck. She didn't want to be cruel and ask Noah to push themselves beyond their limits to work on things at home. Besides, they'd been together for years and had talked about having kids. They'd tied their finances together. Erin had sunk time, effort, and money into the relationship and held on to the hope that she could fix things with more effort. The longer it went on, the more it felt like she would be losing if she left.

It didn't make sense that Noah was so capable in other areas of their life but wasn't applying the same skills at home. Erin wondered if something was wrong with her or what she could do differently to be worthy of attention and care.

WEAPONIZED INCOMPETENCE GETS much of its power from the reality that it would be cruel to expect someone to do something they're genuinely incapable of doing. Criticizing someone when they're trying their best wouldn't be kind. The question then becomes, *Where is the line? How do we know if it's been crossed and what can we do about it?*

Consent is an important element of all healthy relationships, and whether it's present or not can be a key indicator of whether a dynamic has left the realm of safe and secure and crossed into dangerous, depleting territory.

The issue with Erin and Noah's relationship wasn't that Noah needed support. Erin *wanted* to help Noah get their needs met. The issue was the way it was being handled. Erin was drained from the physical demands of running a two-person household, but also emotionally and mentally exhausted from managing her partner's moods and suppressing her own emotions while being told *none of it was a problem*. What made it all worse was she didn't feel like she could share any of her feelings with Noah. She felt isolated and unimportant. As she tried to sort out her feelings, she oscillated between feeling guilty and used.

In an ideal world, Noah would have put some effort into self-evaluation and self-advocacy. They would have noticed the impacts their stress was having on them, their partner, and their relationship and asked for or accepted help. It felt to Erin like Noah expected her to work around them and accommodate for what they needed without considering the needs of the household as a collective. To prevent that, Noah could have been more self-aware and considerate in their communication. They could have been realistic about their capabilities and taken personal responsibility to communicate their needs and seek sustainable support. Noah claimed they couldn't take care of things at home because they didn't have the skills, were too stressed from their courses, or were too tired, but they wouldn't take any steps to fix those issues—even with help. Erin was left to wonder if they weren't aware of or had simply accepted the destructive impact their behavior was having on her, and it felt *terrible*.

If Noah needed Erin to keep their lives running and help them meet their basic needs in order to get through their first responder training, they needed to have a conversation about that. Erin deserved a say in the matter. Her needs had to be part of the conversation. Even though the stress of training or the challenges of mental health struggles may have accentuated Noah's problems, they weren't what caused them. The trouble lay with the lack of transparency and communication, an imbalance of effort, and that Erin wasn't given the opportunity to give informed consent.

Each situation is unique, but beyond consent, an important piece of the relationship puzzle comes down to good faith. Good faith is an honest attempt rooted in good intentions. Forgetting to take the trash out despite saying you would, accidentally shrinking a dry-clean-only shirt, or forgetting to set up auto-billing are all behaviors that can happen to anyone, even when you're trying your best. Everyone's "best" is different. Everyone's *definition* of "best" is different. Everyone's "best" is also ever-changing and influenced by internal and external factors.

Some days my "best" is just waking up. Other days I can knock out a room remodel between sunup and sundown. Neither of those "bests" is better than the other. They just are. As someone who deals with depressive and hypomanic episodes, I have periods in my life when feeding myself and tending to basic hygiene are beyond my capacity. When I've felt well enough, I've come up with plans for how my loved ones can support me. I've taken preventative measures to make short lists of what I might need to keep me afloat, have had frank discussions with the people in my life so they know what to expect, and have taken responsibility for setting up supports, asking for help, and accepting it when it's given.

I've gotten better at noticing my patterns, but my needs aren't always predictable, and the manifestation of my mental illness isn't either. I try to take care of myself for my own sake, but I also consider the impact my mental, emotional, and physical health has on others. I rely on other people to show up for me, and they trust that I'll do the same in return. It's all very imperfect and human, and it's done in good faith.

WHEN WE TAKE seriously the task of communicating our needs and capacities with our loved ones, we can build relationships that are resilient against resentment. With open communication and an honest look at our resources and individual needs, we're able to adjust expectations and accommodate in a caring and considerate way. It's a delicate dance worth practicing.

Certain tasks are going to be a better fit for one person over the other. That's the beauty of being human. None of us should be expected to thrive in the same roles or fill the same shoes in the same ways. Our individual circumstances, our skills, resources, and schedules can impact how we do things. Adjustments, modifications, and negotiations might need to be made, and all of that is well and good. A big difference between weaponized incompetence and good faith effort is that with a good faith effort, when you try to pull something off and it doesn't work out, you don't just throw up your hands and expect everyone to deal. If a task needs to be completed or a need is left unmet, a good faith effort would include trying to find a solution or communicating about a need for support.

With weaponized incompetence, not knowing something acts like a shield against accountability and responsibility. With consent and a good faith effort, not being able to do something is an opportunity to learn, to adjust, or to problem-solve.

WEAPONIZED INCOMPETENCE

When Destiny and Eli were dating, she loved taking care of him. He lived in what she saw as a typical "guy apartment" with some friends: nothing on the walls, a sparse fridge, but nothing too alarming. She grew up believing the way to a man's heart was through his stomach and loved how appreciative he was when she cooked and cleaned for him. A year or so into dating, they moved into her place, since it was nicer, and she was more particular about how they kept it. Eli had agreed to be an equal partner when he moved in, but when it was his night to cook, he'd ask her what she wanted and order in. When Destiny asked him to handle the laundry, he tossed it in and left it in the washer for days until the entire apartment stunk of mildew. He was defensive when she brought it up and made a dramatic production of washing it all over again, folding it, and putting it away. For days afterward, he stayed on top of the dishes, picked up every sock off the floor, and did more around the house than he'd ever done, but he barely spoke a word to her. Even though the clothes he rewashed still stunk, she didn't mention it for fear of the fallout. Eventually, she apologized to him for bothering him about the laundry, and she never asked him to do the laundry again.

She filed that interaction away and approached him with caution moving forward. She noticed a pattern that anytime she asked him what the status of a task was, he lashed out, saying that her expectations were too high, or acted insulted that she'd doubt him. Sometimes after being prodded, he'd angrily rush through the task, do an inadequate job, and punish her by icing her out for days afterward. She felt like he was daring her to say something, setting a trap where her only options were to fix the issue without letting him know and never ask him to help again or bring it up and risk emotional damage.

She learned to pick her battles strategically and slowly took responsibility for his tasks in order to avoid arguments or major consequences. She feared her credit score would take a hit after he failed to pay the internet bill for months and ended up putting their joint bills in her name. She used her own money to pay for a monthly cleaning service, because she needed reliable help.

At one point, Destiny broke down and told him how unloved she felt, saying that at least if he took her out on a date occasionally, she'd know he loved her. A week later, he set up a surprise date at a five-star restaurant but failed to tell her about the dress code. When she arrived to meet him, she was in jeans and a T-shirt, and he was wearing his best blazer. She was so embarrassed she could hardly eat. The whole dinner, all she could think about was how she'd seen him meticulously plan for client meetings. His job in sales was to navigate these situations while making people feel comfortable, and she knew he was good at it. Why was this situation so different? Would he have put one of his clients in the same position? They had a huge fight later that night in which he told her she was ungrateful and that he wouldn't be planning dates in the future. She wished she'd never brought it up in the first place.

But Destiny hadn't brought it up to be hard on Eli. She'd raised the issue out of a sincere desire to communicate a core need of hers that wasn't being met. Eli's response to her voicing this need was to vilify that need instead of validating it. As a result, Destiny's desire to be loved was exploited. Her understanding of her role and responsibilities in her partnership were used against her. She believed she was doing her part by cooking, cleaning, and managing Eli's emotions. After all, he was charming, funny, and had a good job. He was upfront about not being well-versed in domestic skills and referred to himself as "not much of a feelings guy." Neither were most of the men she knew. She told herself he'd get there. Besides, Eli was well loved by Destiny's family and friends. She would sometimes test the waters with friends and vent about the mistakes he made, but they often countered with stories of their own issues at home. She felt unreasonable for even complaining. She wondered if she needed to be more patient or communicate better. She wondered if she was asking for too much. Was she really going to make a huge deal out of him not being good at housework?

The normalcy of it all concealed the destructive creep of Eli's behavior. As time went on, he continually refused to complete tasks in a way that met their household's needs and, even worse, made it impossible for Destiny to confront the issue. He was strategic in how he failed around the household, doing tasks poorly but also failing in his communication and emotional regulation. The hard truth was that Eli's inadequacies were purposeful. He failed at simple tasks that he was able to complete successfully in other contexts. Because he did such a bad job on the tasks that kept their household running and was hostile if Destiny talked about her needs, he left her with no other options but to do it herself or go without. He used a lack of effort and accountability not just to get out of things he didn't want to do but to control her behavior. He used his unreliability and emotional volatility as a way of dominating her. He manipulated social expectations and used them as a shield against accountability. Eli used his incompetence to dominate her time, energy, and actions. He used it as a weapon.

A FAILURE THAT SUCCEEDS

Incompetence is the inability to do something successfully. But weaponized incompetence is using willful ignorance or purposeful inadequacy to avoid effort or accountability. It's dropping the ball on purpose, through sabotage or a lack of care, to get out of something in a way that negatively impacts others. Weaponized incompetence might be walking past an overflowing garbage can day after day, claiming nobody mentioned it needed to be emptied, and then doing so without replacing the garbage bag. It could also look like ignoring sleep and feeding schedules or letting the toddler trash the house while Mom steps out to get her hair done. Not trusting her child in the hands of her partner may mean she stops going to the salon altogether, perpetuating the cycle of inequity and imbalance. Weaponized incompetence is breaking your partner's trust and making yourself unreliable, resulting in your partner sacrificing their time and energy to fill in the gaps.

Weaponized incompetence flies under the radar and often goes unchallenged because of how well it plays with existing social hierarchies and cultural norms. Even if two people enter a relationship seemingly as equals, power and privilege affect how each person is expected to behave and what consequences they'll face for transgressing.

Despite how Destiny rationalized Eli's behavior and contrary to what society tells us, weaponized incompetence is not a gender-specific behavior. It also isn't limited to a behavior that happens within romantic partnerships. Behaviors that could be described as weaponized incompetence include pretending not to know how to do a simple task, only doing part of the task, asking for step-by-step instructions repeatedly, or intentionally messing up the task to the point that you're not asked to do it again. By not putting in a sufficient amount of effort, you end up demanding the energy and effort of others. It happens in professional situations when employees act as if they don't know how to complete tasks or are purposefully inefficient, forcing other teammates to absorb their responsibilities or make up for their lack of effort. You see this with CEOs who refuse to learn how to use new software and force subordinates to do the work for them. Colleagues will drop the ball on small tasks so they're handed more important ones, climbing the ladder with incompetence. In a 2007 *Wall Street Journal* article, the journalist Jared Sandberg referred to the use of incompetence in businesses as a strategic power grab, claiming that, "Strategic incompetence isn't about having a strategy that fails, but a failure that succeeds."

Weaponized incompetence shows up in broader social systems when people whose identities are privileged and protected within the dominant culture—for example, able-bodied, white, straight, or cis-gendered individuals—avoid learning about and advocating for marginalized community members. When confronted with how their behavior causes harm, *not knowing better* is frequently used as an excuse to avoid accountability. The resources for educating oneself are out there, yet when members of the dominant, privileged groups choose not to engage in learning, their inaction perpetuates harm. Many willfully uninformed white people act shocked that racism "still exists," yet advocate for policies that benefit them while continuing to uphold systemic racism. This is weaponized, willful ignorance in action. It demands that the people being oppressed educate others and advocate for themselves in the midst of being harmed. We may not be individually responsible for the whitewashed history taught in schools or the creation of the systems themselves, but we are individually responsible for educating and advocating for better. To be ignorant of one's complicity in harm is one thing. Ignorance is not always a choice. To be made aware, to be given the opportunity to learn and do better, and to fail to take personal responsibility is using ignorance as a weapon.

We can disrupt the way weaponized incompetence protects power imbalances at home and in society by looking at what norms and behaviors are at play. On one section of her website, (divorcing) White Supremacy Culture, the author and academic Tema Okun lists several cultural characteristics that show up in our organizations and relationships that can uphold toxic and oppressive conditions. They're beliefs and behaviors that maintain the status quo, and we often support them unconsciously.

Some of the characteristics on the list are: perfectionism, defensiveness, only one right way, either/or thinking, fear of open conflict, individualism, objectivity, and the right to comfort. When it comes to weaponized incompetence, perfectionism can lead us to focus on there being one right way of doing things, placing very little value on learning from mistakes or taking new approaches. Defensiveness and the right to comfort lead us to protect the feelings of people in power and shield them from criticism or accountability. Either/or thinking and the fear of open conflict can discourage us from confronting issues and make us shy away from using conflict as a way of coming together and problem-solving. Individualism leads us to compete for time and to build self-reliance rather than connectedness. The belief in objectivity is the belief that it's possible for someone or something to be neutral, when in reality we each have unique perspectives, needs, circumstances, beliefs, and desires. The myth of objectivity often causes us to deny the existence of internalized biases and to view emotions or different opinions as unimportant or irrational if they stray from the dominant cultural narrative. For example, we're taught to believe that a job with a higher salary is "objectively" better than one that pays less, but that doesn't account for how the job makes us feel or if it actually improves our quality of life. The myth of objectivity erases individual circumstances and unique perspectives, and discourages us from flexible, empathetic thinking.

The myth of objectivity goes hand in hand with the lie that there could possibly be one right way of doing things. If it's "objectively" good to have a high-paying job, then we're encouraged to behave the "right" way to get it. *We should get to work early and stay late. We should take out loans to get college degrees.* We're held to social rules of respectability and professionalism that privilege those with access to things like generational wealth and legacy admissions to colleges, and who conform to standards of whiteness. These cultural characteristics help justify oppressive practices and normalize a society that treats some people as more valuable than others. Across the board, these cultural characteristics place blame on individuals for systemic oppression and fuel hateful, dehumanizing attitudes like sexism, racism, and ableism.

It's important to recognize and push back against this, because privilege and power remain protected when the people holding on to them remain ignorant. We need to be able to name what's going on in order to disrupt it. Systems of power keep us stuck and often discourage us from taking new, creative approaches to how we live our lives. They instill in us a rigid view of how things should be done and discourage us from questioning the status quo or rethinking how we do things.

We owe it to one another to take personal responsibility for reducing the harm we cause. When we discover that our behavior contributes to the harm done to others, we have an obligation to take the initiative to learn and do better. As participants in a society where our choices affect others, "I didn't know any better" does not excuse us from taking responsibility for our impact in any environment.

Not putting in the effort to seek understanding, whether it's about how we might be contributing to systemic oppression or how consistently failing to follow through on tasks causes anxiety, is as much a harmful behavior as knowingly sabotaging a task. Not knowing how to do something becomes an excuse not to take ownership of learning how or figuring out a different way to do things. Nothing changes if we don't take personal responsibility to learn and grow.

If nothing changes, the suffering will not go away or get any better. "Weaponized" is a strong word, for good reason. There's always some form of harm in weaponized incompetence. When someone chooses not to learn essential information or the skills necessary to provide proper care, there can be major mental and physical health repercussions. When dependents are in the picture, the damage can expand beyond the partnership and put children's emotional well-being and safety at risk.

THE RIPPLE EFFECT

Jamie and her husband, Paul, have a seven-year-old son who goes to an outdoor school. They tag-team bedtime—him on pajama duty and her handling brushing teeth—and as a part of her husband's nightly responsibilities, he agreed to check their child for ticks. One night about six weeks into the school year, Jamie discovered that Paul hadn't been following through. Instead, he'd been sitting in their son's room scrolling on his phone while their seven-year-old got into his pajamas on his own. When Jamie caught on to what was happening, she was livid, but she didn't bring it up right away. For a few days, she considered the best way she could approach the situation—planning for a good time to mention it, tinkering with her wording, and playing out Paul's possible reactions in her head.

She decided to confront the issue head-on at dinner one night. As calmly and directly as she could, she explained that she didn't think he forgot on purpose but would appreciate if he took the job seriously, then walked him through why it was a big deal. Jamie hoped the conversation would lead to changed behavior.

First, Paul denied that he'd agreed to do it in the first place, then went on to tell her he didn't appreciate being talked down to. When she responded defensively to him, he told her she was making a big deal out of nothing, *just like she always did*. The conversation ended with some bickering back and forth, and eventually Paul agreed that he'd check for ticks going forward.

She wanted to trust that he'd handle it, but the stakes felt high. To ease her anxiety, each night after their son got into his pajamas and came into the bathroom where Jamie was waiting for him, she asked him if his dad had checked for ticks. If he hadn't, which was two or three times a week, she sent him back to his dad and silently stewed. After a few weeks, their son started rolling his eyes and whining whenever Jamie asked, so she put her foot down and brought it up again. This time, she didn't hide her disappointment.

When she told her husband she needed him to take the task seriously, he got angry. He explained that he had been. He told her she was overreacting and attacking him. She, in turn, began listing off times he'd been unreliable in the past, and things escalated from there. For weeks after their argument, bedtimes were tense, but Paul did his checks more consistently. Jamie continued to check in with her son, who became the go-between. He made sure his dad looked each night and started confirming with his mom before she even asked. Eventually, she didn't have to send him back anymore.

Ticks are a big deal. They can carry parasites, viruses, and Lyme disease, which can all cause serious short-term and long-term health conditions. Everyone in Jamie's household knew the risks of missing a bite, including their seven-year-old. Without being explicitly asked to take on the responsibility of remembering and reminding his dad to check, he recognized it was something that needed to be done. If he didn't, he risked the stressful process of treating a days' old tick bite and doctor's appointments. Jamie stepping in as overseer solved the problem of making sure the check was done, but her husband's failure to follow through caused her to doubt that he could be trusted to keep his son safe in a reliable way. Over time, the issue came up in recurring fights. It remained unresolved and affected the mood around the household, where Jamie and their son filled in the gaps and moved carefully around him. Jamie wasn't the only one who noticed this. Their son did, too.

Jamie's story describes a situation that's more than just a minor mistake or "oopsy." Her husband's incompetence, inconsistency, and insufficient effort were far from harmless. He did not attempt to solve the problem or ask for help. His negligence had obvious risks for his son's health, but the absence of care reverberated through their household in other harmful ways. He did not take the issue seriously or accept responsibility for not meeting the family's needs.

Being forgetful or struggling to complete a task is one thing. Even with support in place, there will always be certain things we each excel at or struggle with. Jamie wasn't asking her husband for a flawless execution. She wanted him to try. She wanted him to take the responsibility seriously. He was aware of the risks of his inaction. He may not have acted outwardly violent, but his *inaction* was an act of harm. His neglect caused damage. Their son learned that his dad couldn't be trusted to prioritize his safety, a reality that shaped how he felt about his relationship with his dad and how secure he felt in general. He stopped asking his dad for help when he was sick or had a cut. He went to his mom with notes from his teachers, for help getting snacks, and even with life's big questions.

Jamie's experience is far from abnormal. In a man-on-the-street segment on *Jimmy Kimmel Live* called "Can Dads Answer Questions About Their Kids?" an interviewer asks fathers on the street to answer simple questions on camera in front of their children. Repeatedly, fathers fail to correctly respond to questions like "When is your child's birthday?" and "What is their teacher's name?" As children hear their caregivers answer incorrectly, the excitement of being interviewed on camera fades and you see smiles disappear. Some kids hide shock with surprised laughter, and some noticeably shut down.

When the clips are played for a studio audience, they're prompted to laugh. As a society, we've normalized absent and neglectful behavior from fathers so much that it's consistently presented as comedy (see sitcom syndrome). What's actually captured in those clips is cruelty. All the kids on-screen have to file away the knowledge that there are major aspects of their lives that one of their primary caregivers know nothing about. They all have to grapple with the reality that someone who's supposed to keep them safe and well cared for might not be equipped with the information necessary to handle that responsibility. These clips would never fly if mothers were being interviewed.

We're socially conditioned to roll our eyes at dads who fall asleep when it's their turn to watch the kids or don't book essential doctor or dental appointments. The same behavior exhibited by women, especially women of color, would be considered neglectful and might even run the risk of state intervention.

There are very real consequences to this kind of incompetence. Knowing what medicines your children take, how to put them in a car seat, what it looks like to dress them appropriately for the weather, what food is safe to feed them, and other basic care information is all essential to keeping a child safe. Some of the behavior presented as normal and funny in our culture is simply neglect. Behaving in a way that puts a child at serious risk of harm or death is abuse. It's less effort than you'd expect from a babysitter, *and yet* it exists within the realm of socially acceptable for some partners.

In addition to the harm this presents to children, there is also an effect on the consequently overburdened partner that goes beyond aggravation or resentment. Weaponized incompetence can cause people to quit jobs or pass up financial opportunities out of fear that leaving their homes and families in the care of someone else would result in unsafe or harmful situations. Not being able to work creates a barrier to financial freedom. Weaponized incompetence can be a tool to control and isolate, creating additional labor and stress on one person to the point where they lose connections with others. It can create an environment of physical and mental exhaustion and be used as a form of coercion.

When weaponized incompetence is present on an ongoing basis, *the harm it creates is ongoing, too.* All the domestic violence experts and psychologists I interviewed for this book agreed that when feigned incompetence or ignorance is intentional and part of an ongoing pattern, it's abuse.

We're responsible for caring for one another. We have an obligation to protect one another from harm. That includes considering the intentional *and* unintentional harm we cause. That includes listening when someone tells us we hurt them. Choosing not to work on certain skills or learn how to keep other people safe is *a choice.* Choosing not to put effort into something despite knowing it's going to cause harm is *a choice.* When you choose to behave in a way that will result in harm, even when it's because of a lack of action or effort, it's still *choosing harm*. When we're presented with opportunities to care for one another better, *it's our responsibility to try.*

BECAUSE OUR CIRCUMSTANCES are all so unique, and weaponized incompetence is a behavior that's so closely tied to social expectations, figuring out when it crosses certain lines can be hard. There are so many factors to consider—social conditioning, available resources, differing expectations or priorities, and so much more. Sometimes we don't realize the damage our behavior is doing. We may perceive a situation differently than someone else. We may have different standards or be expecting something we aren't verbalizing. We may be passing off a task in hopes someone else will pick up the slack without realizing the impact that has. We may be exhausted. We may think the other party's load is lighter—seeing no harm in shifting the scales. Because it's been sold as silly so often, we may just see things like using the last piece of toilet paper without replacing the roll as innocent avoidance even when we know how shitty it can be to reach for a square and find nothing. It *could* be that we don't see something as our responsibility, and it could also be that we really just don't see the issue. Inequity and skill deficits aren't always because of intent to harm. Even when a behavior is persistent or *seems* purposeful, it may not be.

Asking questions is essential. Not every partner who forgets that Fridays are "show-and-tell days" is trying to isolate, manipulate, or control. Knowing the full potential of the harm that's possible can keep us all safer in the long run. Asking ourselves questions about the nuances of impact and intent can help us set boundaries and draw lines for ourselves.

Consider: Do you notice inconsistencies in that person's behavior? Do they understand what it takes to maintain a client relationship but can't see why you're so upset about them forgetting your birthday? Do they research and plan detailed strategies for their fantasy football league but can't seem to figure out how to book a doctor's appointment? Can they tell you all the bands their favorite musicians have played in but can't remember you're allergic to shellfish? If you share your feelings or invite them to problem-solve, how are you met? If you point to a behavior and say, "When this happens, I feel hurt," do they respond with "Well, it doesn't hurt me, so what's the big deal?" Are there efforts being made to address concerns and reduce harm? Are all parties' needs being considered in seeking solutions?

Asking questions can help us recognize our internal alarm bells and make well-informed decisions. It can inspire reflection and help us stay more vigilant to nip things in the bud if we slip into harmful behaviors without realizing it.

In some situations, you may decide it's time to put together a safe exit plan. With a partner who's on board, it may come in the form of agreements to work on embracing creativity and accommodating for individual needs. In other situations, you might decide to make some personal changes—stepping back, communicating more directly, or no longer assuming unspoken responsibilities. Regardless of the answers, asking questions can be clarifying, and with clarity, we can better tailor our lives to meet our needs.

BUILD A FLEXIBLE FOUNDATION

Brittany and her husband, Harvey, were in their early thirties, married, with a three-year-old and six-year-old, when Harvey was diagnosed with Chiari malformation type 1, which required him to have emergency brain surgery. The brain malformation was corrected, but it has caused health complications, including a major spinal cord injury, the temporary inability to walk, ongoing migraines, loss of sensation in his extremities, a total lack of proprioception, and balance issues.

The two had been together since they were teenagers, had always wanted to have an egalitarian relationship, and did their best to stave off the preconditioned traps of inequity. It wasn't perfect, but they were both committed. However, leading up to Harvey's diagnosis and subsequent disability, while he was in crisis mode, Brittany took over full responsibility for keeping their household running. While Harvey focused on his health and they transitioned into a new postdiagnosis life, they learned to lean on support, adapt their expectations to fit their needs, and put a philosophy of "families help each other" into practice.

Their household dynamic has changed dramatically over the past few years. They attribute their ability to navigate the twists and turns with their commitment to communication and honesty. In their twenties, Brittany and Harvey fell into a frustrating dynamic where Harvey "didn't see" what needed to be done around the house. When she brought it up, he listened, and they worked together on a plan to address the issue. In an email, Brittany told me, "Mutual respect and willingness to assume goodwill on each other's part has been the foundation of our relationship." She was able to give him grace and support his growth, because he was open and honest about his skills and deficits.

Harvey isn't able to complete the same physical tasks he used to, but he does what he can. He can't haul in heavy groceries, but he's able to transport the kids the short distance to and from school. He also accepts more responsibility for mental tasks like planning meals, making grocery lists, and helping the kids with homework. He and Brittany communicate with each other about their capacities, adjust accordingly, and recruit help whenever they can. Brittany shared, "I think that spouses sometimes forget that they cannot be everything to their partner all of the time. Each person in a partnership needs other people, too. It took forced dependence for us to really come to terms with that." Getting clear on priorities and being realistic about what they need, want, and can handle has been key to their ability to make things work.

There's no perfect formula, and while the division of labor in their household may not be what they initially thought it would be, it's what fits their circumstances. It's a struggle they're in together. Brittany wrote to me, "Do I carry the majority of our family's mental and physical load when it comes to household tasks? Yes. But I also acknowledge that Harvey is devoting a huge amount of energy to keeping himself as healthy as possible so he can be a participant in our family. He is not a burden and I am not a superhero."

It's that balance that's so important. We can only give as much as we have available to us. We have an obligation and a responsibility to one another to care, but not beyond our capacity or capabilities. Brittany and Harvey redefined what "productivity" meant to them. They set their expectations realistically and structured their relationship around their needs rather than outside expectations. They looked at their unique situation, and the resources they had available, and figured out what would work for them.

It's important to acknowledge that not all mistakes or failures to follow through are weaponized incompetence. Sometimes life throws curveballs at us that force other duties to the side—unexpected illness, a promotion at work, or the death of a family member. Sometimes we just aren't skilled at something or don't have enough information or experience. Sometimes we have completely different ideas of what "done" looks like, who is responsible for what, and which tasks should take priority in our relationships. Sometimes we take on more than we can handle, make decisions that miss the mark, or just need more practice. But if you have a willingness to learn and get creative, then not knowing how to do something is an opportunity—an opportunity to learn, practice, and eventually master. When a need is unmet and certain approaches aren't working, it's an opportunity to look at things differently. We don't know what we don't know, but when we realize we have a gap in knowledge or a skill that needs some improvement or a different approach, it's up to each of us to figure out a way to do better or seek support until we have the capacity to do so.

The fact is, in long-term relationships of all kinds, including marriage, parenting, workplace, and friendships, our personal capacities will all be different and will also change over time. While one partner completes a PhD program, that might mean loosening up on the level of tidiness you expect around the house. You may decide to outsource laundry, pay for a cleaning service, or agree that takeout is going to be the meal standard until at least graduation. It's more important to acknowledge that adjustments may need to be made than it is to have all the minor details figured out. Life is full of surprises—fun and not so fun. Sometimes tasks need modifying, accommodations need to be made, or expectations need to be adjusted. And sometimes you're expecting yourself or others to do things that aren't realistic.

ANTI-PERFECTIONIST PROBLEM-SOLVING:
PROBLEM-SOLVE FOR THE *ACTUAL* PROBLEM

I have bipolar II, ADHD, and a reading disability. Some of the ways those disabilities show up for me are that I struggle to keep track of things, have a poor sense of time, forget important information, and deal with sometimes debilitating mood instability. I struggle with basic self-care tasks and can swing from hyperfocus to inattentiveness in ways that are costly to my work and personal life. Though I only got these diagnoses in my early thirties, I've dealt with the symptoms of these disabilities my entire life. I spent a lot of time feeling ashamed and inadequate, but I also found ways, some healthier than others, to accommodate myself.

Accommodation is a creative process—the opposite of the prescriptive blandness of perfectionism. One of the areas of my life where I've needed to accommodate myself is in keeping track of things. I pick things up and put them down in places they don't belong. My glasses end up in the freezer; my headphones end up in the wash; I forget to bring in the ice cream in the trunk and it melts into the carpet. This issue has made me late countless times and cost me thousands of dollars in lost items and replacement fees over the years. I'm constantly misplacing my keys, purse, and, to my family's frustration, the remotes.

I can't blame my family for not being able to hide their annoyed sighs when they reach for a remote on the coffee table and find nothing. Collapsing into the couch just to have to get back up and root around on the floor or dig between crumb-filled couch cushions is the last thing you want to be doing when you just want to turn on a comfort show.

That's a relatively low-stakes situation, sure, but we can still see it through the lens of weaponized incompetence, because the issue isn't about how seemingly big the issue is. If I had refused to acknowledge the ways in which my behavior affected my family or if I placed blame back on them, I would have forced them to stifle their frustration in order to keep me from getting upset. But as an equal participant in my household, it was my responsibility to look for a solution. I had to assess the situation, be realistic about my limits and what I was actually capable of, and take a stab at accommodating myself. If I couldn't figure it out, at the very least I needed to ask for help.

For years, my solution to the remote issue was that if I lost it, I'd be the one to get up and search for it. I'd feel guilty, promise to try harder to remember to put it back on the coffee table, and hope for the best. But the problem was never my lack of effort, so a commitment to trying harder wasn't going to fix it. After years of the same cycle, I just ended up feeling bad every time it happened, and my husband started to feel like maybe I just didn't care about how frustrating it was. Technically I was putting in a good-faith effort to remember, but I was focused on a solution that wasn't going to work for me. It didn't fit our family's needs and it didn't account for the resources we were working with.

After one particularly exhausting day, my husband and I put the kids to bed and settled into the living room to queue up some TV and again couldn't find the remotes. I tore things apart for ten minutes before finding them. At that point, I knew I had to do something different. I was incapable of being less forgetful. My brain is my brain. But my forgetfulness wasn't the actual problem that needed to be solved. We needed to be able to turn on the TV. We needed to be able to play movies and change the channels. Those were problems I could solve.

I started by racking my brain for what had worked in the past. I knew having a convenient and clear place for things had been helpful in other circumstances. I have baskets strategically placed throughout the house for miscellaneous items, hooks for keys at either door, and a rug in the place I have a habit of kicking my shoes off. After watching me break and lose a dozen pairs of glasses, my husband bought me felted cups and put them throughout the house in places where he's seen me take my glasses off my face.

I knew a basket on the coffee table would get in the way, so I thought of how I might make sure they stayed put without the bulk, dug up some Velcro stickers, and stuck one part to the table and the other to the bottom of the remotes. My issue with losing things is rooted in inattentiveness and distraction, and I tried to build support that leaned on my senses to help remind me of what I needed to do.

With the Velcro stickers in place, every time I picked up a remote I felt the scratchy bits on my fingers. This was a physical reminder to put it back. If that didn't get my attention, when I put the remote down on the couch next to me, the Velcro made a little scratchy sound. This was an auditory reminder to place it back on the table. If that didn't work, seeing the little white fuzzy Velcro stickers on the table acted as a visual reminder to pause what I was doing and look around for the out-of-place remotes before they got away from me. The Velcro was a solid attempt to solve the problem in a way that considered my support needs and didn't rely on my partner to figure things out.

But after a few months, I stopped noticing the Velcro as often, and the supports I'd put into place stopped being as effective. At that point, I asked for help. We brainstormed: we considered gluing them to a big board, painting them a bright color, or attaching them to the coffee table with a retractable cord. We eventually landed on buying a second set. I still have the Velcro on the main set, and it helps, but the second set lives next to my husband's spot and has saved us countless headaches.

TV remotes may seem trivial, but taking the time to analyze the problem and come up with a solution that accounted for our needs and priorities led to less frustration on my husband's part and less guilt on mine. Win-win. Do we handle everything so pragmatically? Absolutely not. But over the years, moments of curiosity and problem-solving like we had with the remotes have improved our lives and our relationships. Having clarity on what the actual problem was and being realistic and honest about the situation helped us come to the best possible solution.

OUR HOMES SHOULD take a unique, dynamic, individualized shape. They should function in a way that reflects our needs, our values, and our priorities. What that looks like is going to be different for each of us. Creating that means letting go of outside expectations, taking a critical look at *why* you do things the way you do them, and putting into practice a kind of homemaking that emphasizes your individual definition of home.

The home I live in is full of furniture we've pulled from the curb and put to good use for decades. Our dining room functions as a mudroom, library, artist studio, pinball arcade, and eating space. We leave things out—markers, sketchbooks, snacks, and chargers— while our walls are covered in pictures and prints and our shelves are stacked with games, books, and art projects. There are almost always a few dishes in the sink, at least one basket of laundry around, and a dozen half-drunk cups of water scattered about. We have postcards from loved ones stuck to our fridge with magnets we've found at secondhand stores, and our cupboard shelves are lined with kitschy mugs we've collected over the years. In the past, I've hesitated to invite people over without at least a day's notice, even my closest friends. I'd need at least a day to rush around and shove my mess behind closed doors and try to create the illusion that things always looked so put together. It's been a habit worth breaking. I get a lot more time doing the things I like to do with people I want to spend time with when I don't let my mess get in the way.

I love when friends have me over without going out of their way to do anything special beforehand. It's a gift to be trusted as an integrated part of their life. I'm happy to help with dishes or make myself a spot on their couch. I love being told to make myself at home. I love being invited into a space where someone lives, just the way they live in it, and I hope to open my own home to others the same way. To be witness to the shoes kicked off at the door, the toddler stool butting up against the bathroom sink, the candy wrappers left on the coffee tables, is to witness a life without unnecessary performance. Designing your life around your needs, then letting people in to share it with you can create a kind of authentic connection that comparison and competition could never create.

ACCIDENTAL EFFICIENCY

I'll say it until I'm blue in the face: *There is no one right way to do things.* There are ways things have been done and ways we think things should be done, but there's never just one right way. Being open to different ways of doing things and approaching tasks with creativity can lead to better systems overall. Taking an individualized approach to how we function in our households and within our relationships makes our day-to-day lives better and contributes to a wider cultural change in an essential way. Accommodation for our needs and desires is the opposite of so many of the cultural characteristics of white supremacy culture that Tema Okun writes about. The idea that there's one right way to do things is a myth; taking a more curious, needs-based approach can help move us beyond defaults and toward what truly works. When we accommodate our individual needs and center our humanity in how we live, we're actively disrupting oppressive culture. We're building a future where everyone has more of what they need to thrive.

An example of how this shift played out in our household revolved around the laundry. Typically, it's been a shared task. Anytime my husband or I noticed the laundry needed to be done, one of us would do it, simple as that. The unspoken expectation was that it was done at least once a week, folded and put away or at least in a basket in a bedroom, but we each did things our own way, and it was never much of an issue.

Then came the towels. When my husband did laundry, even after putting everything else in its place, he'd leave a stack of hand towels out next to the coffee table in the living room, where they'd sit until I put them away. It felt like he was leaving work out for me to do with no explanation. I couldn't wrap my head around why. The little pile felt like a middle finger in my direction, as if he couldn't be bothered to do that tiny part of the task. Each time he did it, I'd wait him out and see how long the pile would sit. After a few days of stewing, I'd take the stack, sort the bathroom hand towels from the kitchen rags, and put everything in its place with an unspoken irritation.

The hand towels in the living room were an opportunity to seek clarity. We needed to figure out what was going on and how we could bridge the gap between our different methods. I'd been working on my boundaries and communication, so in an effort to stop the resentment I was beginning to feel, I put the towels on the agenda for one of our weekly meetings. Because we were coming to the conversation as teammates, I was able to set my irritation aside and be genuinely curious about why he kept leaving the towels out, instead of approaching him in a moment of frustration.

In that conversation, I learned that he was leaving them out because, of the dozen or so towels that got washed every week, all of them had different patterns and textures. There were no clearly defined bathroom or kitchen towels. The times he'd try to put them away in the right place, I'd end up following behind him and moving them around, sometimes even rewashing them, adding to our workload. As I listened to my husband explain his thought process, I realized that what felt to me like him avoiding work and assuming I'd finish a task he'd started was actually his attempt at solving a problem. I didn't have to agree with his decision-making to see where he was coming from. Listening empathetically gave us both space to process what had happened and pull lessons from it.

He initially left the towels out to avoid a confrontation. To avoid the tension of me passive-aggressively correcting him, he neatly folded them and made it as easy as possible for me to scoop them up and sort them myself. He also noticed the silver lining of leaving them out almost immediately when, after one of our kids spilled a cup of water, he had a hand towel within reach to clean it up. Towels in the living room meant I wasn't following behind him correcting his mistakes, leaving them out meant we could avoid an argument about the issue, and nobody had to get up and run to the kitchen whenever there was a mess. Triple win in his mind. I was still annoyed that none of this was communicated to me, but I could see his points. Since my birthday-card moment a year or so prior, we'd been working on breaking our patterns of avoidance, blaming and shutting down, and the rewards of our work were obvious in how we moved through troubleshooting.

In that conversation, we each acknowledged the impact we'd had on each other. We listened to the other's perspective and allowed the other to share their feelings without judgment. He recognized how his lack of direct communication had impacted me and apologized for leaving the towels out without saying anything. He explained how he'd felt fearful and defensive based on our history of arguing over similar issues. I acknowledged how my past behavior had made him feel. We communicated without trying to prove each other wrong or place blame. We were on the same team, working toward the goal of improving our communication and simplifying how our household functioned. We wanted to feel less stressed and disconnected.

With an established sense that we had our eyes on the same prize, we could focus on the issue in front of us. We needed to do something about the towels. His complaint about the towels being hard to sort wasn't off base. The only reason I knew which ones went where was because I'd bought them.

As we talked, we were each mindful not to be dismissive of the other. We listened carefully for understanding and gathered information so we could brainstorm solutions. We decided to replace the bathroom towels with a full set we picked out together and got cute baskets to store extras in the living room. We created a simple sorting system: warm tones for the bathroom, cool tones for the kitchen. We got on the same page and ended up with a more efficient, functional home.

We also took the opportunity to talk through some of the other little hitches we'd gotten stuck on with the laundry. Instead of assuming the other person would handle it, we decided one of us should handle it and explicitly ask for help if needed. There were plenty of opportunities for the conversation to shut down, but we pushed forward knowing there wasn't one right way to do things. As a team, we came up with a plan to simplify things that ended up meeting everyone's needs more efficiently than how we'd initially been doing things.

CURIOUS, CLEAR, AND COMPETENT

The key to all of this is much more about attitude than it is about effectiveness or execution. When it comes to weaponized incompetence, you can ask someone to learn, set up meetings, and encourage them, but you can't convince someone to make a good faith effort if they're not willing to engage. *Willingness* is essential. *Curiosity* is essential. *Valuing the process of learning, growing, adapting, and connecting is essential.*

The more curious we are, the more we can learn. The more we learn, the clearer we can be. The clearer we are, the more competently we can carry out tasks.

Approaching our households with curiosity sounds like:

- "I'm struggling with this task. What's going on? Where is the issue?"
- "We have different expectations. What are we trying to accomplish? How do we want things done? Why?"
- "I don't have enough energy to dedicate to doing this well. What do we need to be successful? How can we do things more efficiently?"
- "We can't agree on what's most important. How could we gain a better understanding of each other's viewpoint?"
- "We're stretched thin. How can we adjust expectations to meet our needs? What accommodations can we make to be more successful?"

Approaching each other with curiosity and opening up a dialogue alleviates so much of the resentment, disconnection, and potential danger around weaponized incompetence. A willingness to consider the cause or explore different approaches shows an investment in making things better. Even if you come to the conclusion that there's nothing much you can do, an openness to discussion goes a long way. Shutting down a conversation can feel like a dismissal of the issue. When someone brings a concern to you, not engaging in a conversation about it can imply a lack of care or consideration. When you bring a concern to someone and they respond with "How can we try to solve this problem together?" it sends the message that they care about your comfort. If it matters to you, it matters to them. When they downplay the issue, claim there's nothing to be done, avoid engaging in a conversation, or otherwise reject the invitation to problem-solve, it can feel like what matters to you doesn't matter to them. It can feel like your feelings or the impacts a situation is having on you don't matter to them. It can feel like *you* don't matter to them. In contrast, meeting someone's expression of their needs or desires with curiosity, asking what could reasonably be done to accommodate those needs and wants, shows an investment in their well-being.

When something isn't working, asking what's going on is an acknowledgment that you think there could be a solution and you want to find it. Even more, it allows you and your partner to come up with your own "hacks," like the couch-spill towel basket that is now a permanent fixture in my home. Perhaps you get rid of the sippy cups that are clunky to wash. Maybe you buy all the same-color socks so you never have to match pairs again. Most important, you share these hacks, your mistakes, and the tiny wins so that the mastery and the mistakes are part of a two-way conversation. Working together on setting standards and finding ways that work around our homes and daily lives creates a unique opportunity to be seen by someone else. You get the chance to share the tiny things you struggle with every day, like losing your headphone case while the headphones are in your ears, and let other people consider what they know about you to propose solutions. Approaching each other with curiosity takes openness and vulnerability, and it creates a nurturing and supportive environment—at home, between friends, and at work.

When you have a clear understanding of what you or your partner care about, what matters the most to them, and what their short- and long-term goals are, you can make well-informed decisions that have a better chance of meeting their needs, ultimately caring for them in the best way possible. Clarifying expectations and finding the "right" way to do things in our homes is far less about setting rigid standards and far more about valuing the process of learning and gaining understanding. We aren't necessarily raising or lowering a bar when we define what works for us. We're taking the parts of us that make us unique and aligning them with our choices to create a life that reflects who we are.

We can all have more of what we need when we take an approach to the standards and inner workings of our households that center our humanity, not perfectionism rooted in patriarchy, capitalism, ableism, and racism. The solution to a society that has normalized and allowed for weaponized incompetence is to embrace a tailor-made kind of life that honors who we are as individuals.

5 THINGS YOU CAN DO RIGHT NOW

1. Play to Strengths

Everyone has skills they excel at and ones they don't, so be mindful of that when you set expectations and decide who should do what and how. None of us is working with the same resources, skills, or conditions. All of that must be considered when figuring out how you want things done.

A task like budgeting might feel easy to someone with an accounting background and impossible to someone who hates spreadsheets. Putting on an audiobook and folding piles of laundry might feel like heaven to one person and hell to another. If you hate making phone calls and your partner doesn't mind, let them show up for you in that way. If you deal with chronic illness and fluctuating capacity, get ahead of the issue and communicate about how you can account for that.

All we can do is work with what we've got, communicate often, and be proactive when possible. We can own our tasks, make considerate choices, leave room for different approaches, ask for help when we need it, and trust each other to try in good faith. When we hit snags, we can be open to new approaches, commit to troubleshooting together, approach each other with curiosity, and give each other grace.

2. Solve a Problem

Pick a recurring problem in your daily life and problem-solve with your humanity at the center. Let's imagine you keep forgetting to take the trash out. Focus in on the problem. When the trash doesn't go out, there's no space to toss things that need to get tossed. The house stinks. The bag overflows, drips, and leaves residue that requires scrubbing and scraping. It's gross, unsightly, inconvenient, and unsafe.

Next, observe. Mentally retrace your steps or spend a few days making a conscious effort to keep track of your movements. Keep a nonjudgmental eye out for what might be getting in your way. Where is the ball getting dropped? Is the kitchen trash in the back of the house, and you head out the front door in the mornings, so it's out of sight, out of mind? When you notice it's nearly full, do you tell yourself you'll get to it later and then get busy with something else and forget? What's your definition of a full trash bin that needs to go out? Is that different from your housemate's? What's getting in your way in following through?

Based on the barriers, identify support. Do you need to set yourself a daily morning alarm to check if the trash needs to go out? Do you need to make yourself an unmissable decorative sign to stick on the front door as a reminder to do your chore before you leave the house? Would it help to put a handful of empty replacement bags at the bottom of the bin so they're nearby next time the trash gets taken out?

Play to your strengths. Consider productivity support systems you put in place in work or school environments and put them to work at home. Be realistic about your capabilities and work with what you've got. Organize your home in a way that works for you. Spend some time labeling and sorting so that everything has its place; hang hooks and place baskets in areas of your home to help things run smoothly. Hone in on points in your process where things go awry and solve them. Try, fail, try again!

3. Priorities and Preferences

You can hone in on this practice and set flexible expectations by focusing on priorities and preferences. Pick a task and ask the following questions:

- What am I trying to accomplish with this task? What is the purpose?
- What needs am I trying to meet with this task?
- What are my top priorities?
- Do I have any preferences for how this is done or certain details?

Approach these conversations as if they're information-gathering sessions, not meant to come up with a rigid standard. Take notes in a shared document or add it into your "home manual."

The more you explicitly talk about your family's goals, your family's values, and the details of what makes you feel good, the more you can make choices that reflect those things. Try to understand the unique need or the personal story behind the details. If you had to choose, would you rather have dish soap that cuts through grime or is gentle on the ecosystem? Why? What do you want to save for in the long term and short term? If you were given $2,000 right now, what would you spend it on? Would your answer change if it were $100,000? Why? Talk about why you hang your clothes a certain way, why you stack the dishes a certain way, why you shop where you shop, where you store your important papers, and so on. The more questions you ask, the more answers you're open to hearing, the better. These explicit conversations help you as a family decide what "the right way" of doing things actually means to you and also give you the information you need to be adaptable and responsive to the ebbs and flows of life.

4. Emergency Plans

During major transitions in your life (birth of a child, career change), be proactive about what might impact your capacity and talk about how you'd like to handle things. If you have a personal capacity that fluctuates due to chronic illness, caretaking responsibilities, or any other circumstance, take opportunities when you do have the capacity to plan ahead.

Talking through the plan for when shit in your life hits the fan helps you be prepared and has the added bonus of opening up a conversation about how to show up for each other better in everyday moments.

Ask: When you're low on energy or time, where can you trim the fat? Can you outsource meals or hire housework or childcare help? Do you have friends or family who live nearby who can help with carpools or running errands? How can you make it easier to get the help you need? What are some bare-bones, easy go-to meals for you? Make a list of your top five delivery places, and write out your usual order so all you need to do is punch it in and press "Deliver."

Ask: How can you support each other through periods of low capacity? How can you consider the needs of the collective when planning ahead? Is there a support network you can tap into? How can you improve your communication to navigate low-capacity moments more smoothly?

Preventative care goes a long way, and after every tough season, taking time to reflect and update protocols can make a massive difference for future events.

5. Identify Your High-Impact Five

For each person in a household, make a list of five household tasks that could be completed in less than fifteen minutes that have an immediate payoff. Consider tasks that provide a sense of relief when they're done, that loom in the back of your mind, or that provide a positive sensory experience. Which tasks are quick but make a big difference in how you feel?

Do you feel a sense of relief when the floor has been swept or vacuumed? Do your shoulders drop when the grocery list has been updated? Do sparkly floors, sanitized doorknobs, or fresh sheets boost your mood?

Come up with your list of five, then give important details so anyone could pick up your list and pull off the task effectively. Be thorough and clear about the important parts!

For example, one of my high-impact five tasks is taking out the trash. I'm sensitive to smells, and I work from home, so having the remnants of the previous night's food taken out to the alley and the bag replaced has a significant positive impact on my mood and ability to focus. The details matter, though. If the trash is taken out and the bag isn't replaced, someone could toss something in without noticing and make a mess that will need to be cleaned. If the trash is put on the back porch, a squirrel might get it. Relief comes when the trash is taken out, the liner replaced, and the full bag goes all the way out to the alley. I've clarified those details on my list.

Other tasks on my list include clearing out clutter, doing dishes, picking up out-of-place items, and managing the recycling. On my list, I've explained the aspects of the tasks that matter the most. I explain what I mean by "clearing out clutter," define what I think the dishes should look like when they're "done," and give details. Managing the recycling means flattening the cardboard so that it fits in the bin, all bottles and cans crushed and put in the bin, and the back porch, where it's usually piled up, completely emptied. Without the details being addressed, the unfinished aspects of the tasks would still loom.

Having a high-impact five for yourself can act as a quick-start list to go to when the endless to-do list feels too overwhelming. It's also a great guide for when other people in the household want to pitch in but don't know where to begin. A detailed high-impact five list can be an incredible map of things you can do to make your partner feel cared for.

CHAPTER SIX

Happily Ever After

An Expansive Look at Love

GABRIELLA MARRIED HER high school sweetheart, Mark, when she was eighteen. They both started college together and moved into a little apartment off campus. In the summer after their first year, Gabriella got pregnant, and by the end of their sophomore year, she'd dropped her classes to handle the housework and childcare full-time. Mark finished his degree, found a job that paid enough to cover their bills, and they had three more kids. Gabriella had always been a skilled artist and kept her toe in the career pond by taking on freelance work, with the plan of going back to school or working full-time once the kids were in school full-time.

When their youngest was about three and it was time to consider enrollment in pre-K, Gabriella started looking into undergrad programs and updating her résumé. Over dinner one night, she mentioned her plan to Mark, and his shock and confusion took Gabriella aback. He threw questions her way: *Were the classes going to be during the day or was it going to eat into the evenings with the kids? How much was it going to cost? What if the kids were sick or needed to be picked up from school early? He thought she'd given up on "that." It had been six years since they had their first. Wasn't the periodic little design contract enough of a hobby for her?*

In the moment, she didn't even know what to say. She had been the primary caregiver for their family for nearly a decade, managing every aspect of the household, handling the childcare herself or acting as the primary point person for teachers and babysitters, even quarantining with sick kids anytime they caught a bug so that Mark wouldn't catch something and miss work. For nearly a decade, she'd put the family's needs first, and she was happy to do it, but she'd undoubtedly made sacrifices. She was ready to make a shift and she expected the kind of eager support she'd given Mark for all those years.

That one conversation over dinner changed how she saw her entire relationship. She and her husband had been living the same life, but their understanding of roles, responsibilities, and expectations were totally different. The future she imagined had similar elements but was ultimately drastically different than what he saw. She began to retrace her footsteps and apply her new understanding to their big milestones and quiet conversations. When had he stopped believing she wanted a career? How had that expectation impacted where he'd put his time and energy? What else were they misaligned on? She reflected on what motivated her and how it may be different from what motivated her husband. She asked herself what she felt she may have missed out on, what needs her decisions had helped her meet, and where she'd felt deficits. She and her husband had assumed they were on the same page, but they'd drifted miles apart without realizing it.

Gabriella spent months after that conversation trying to gain clarity on what she wanted to do moving forward. Initially, she felt so betrayed that she saw the only path forward as out. She looked up apartments, quietly opened her own bank account, and started putting away little bits of cash every week. She looked up jobs she could take, researched health insurance options, and seriously considered what it would be like to be a single parent. She ruminated, thought about all the things she'd missed out on over the years, and a few months after that dinner conversation she approached her husband again. She told him she was going back to school. If he wasn't willing to support her financially, she'd take out loans. She wanted to travel a few times a year. She hoped he'd make himself available for the kids, but if not, she'd drop them off with her parents. She told him what she wanted and that she wanted to do those things with his support. She loved him and loved their family and hoped that he was on board with walking the same path with her. A path that allowed for both of them to have what they wanted and needed. At that point, she could keep quiet and guarantee her needs wouldn't be met, or ask for what she wanted and gamble on him shutting her down or getting behind her. She had spent months grieving her past understanding of her relationship and the false sense of certainty she'd felt. But with the grief came the thrill of possibility.

When Gabriella confronted Mark, he was unsurprisingly defensive but told her he wanted to make things work, even if it meant major changes. Gabriella worried he was just trying to appease her but took him at his word. She started checking herself anytime she functioned on an assumption and spoke it out loud instead. When she caught herself putting herself on the back burner despite nobody explicitly asking her to, she started a conversation instead. It was uncomfortable, but communicating honestly allowed them to see, for the first time in years, where they stood and which direction they were going in.

In the years since their initial uncomfortable dinnertime conversation, their family roles and responsibilities have shifted. Gabriella has gone on to enroll in a local fine arts program, and on the nights she attends classes or needs to study, Mark handles things on his own at home. As a result, they've each gained new confidence—Gabriella in her sense of self, and Mark in his role as caregiver.

Gabriella's goal of opening up to Mark wasn't to save her marriage. She recognized that if she didn't let him in on what she was feeling and share her personal growth with him, whatever relationship they'd be saving wouldn't be an honest one. She was hopeful that he'd get on board with her as she grew and changed, but she accepted that she couldn't predict any particular outcome.

Overall, the shifting dynamics caused them each to ask themselves what they really wanted, and while the answers haven't been simple, their relationship has transformed from a stagnant partnership based on assumptions to an authentic connection where they each had more confidence to express themselves.

STORYBOOK ROMANCE

One of my favorite storybooks, *The Worst Princess* by Anna Kemp and Sara Ogilvie, starts with Princess Sue trapped in a tower, reading books about other princesses who have been freed, so she can find that freedom, too. She grows out her hair, sits by her window, and waits for a prince to rescue her from her tower. When a prince finally does arrive, he tosses her on the back of his horse just like she'd hoped for and takes her away from the tower where she'd been held captive. Quickly, though, Sue realizes her prince isn't rescuing her from captivity and giving her the life of adventure and freedom she'd been led to believe she'd have.

Instead, he takes her into his own castle and locks the gates. Inside the castle walls, he insists she follow the princess rules and do the things that *good* princesses do. She's been duped. She stares out the castle window, determined to find a way to give herself the happy ending that the prince did not deliver.

The idea of "happily ever after" became popular in the 1700s, and it's had a real chokehold on romance ever since. Through a romantic partnership, your life is supposed to get better. It's supposed to leave you feeling fulfilled, supported, and comforted. With marriage comes a committed partner who's looking out for your best interests, because you are family. Some people seek marriage in hopes that they'll find someone to witness life with, to share responsibilities with, or to make them feel desired and taken care of. Some seek marriage in hopes of finding safety and stability, purpose, or acceptance. Overall, most people seek long-term partnerships because they believe they will make their lives complete.

I knew that marriage was a thing I was supposed to want even before I could spell my name. Adults would accuse me of having crushes on the boys I was best friends with, saying one day we might walk down the aisle together. There was no consideration that I could simply want to spend time with a boy as a friend. Like breathing or eating, being lovesick was supposed to be a natural part of girlhood. Considering who I'd marry was a question that carried as much weight as what I'd do for a living.

I spent my entire life believing that I couldn't have it all if I didn't have a romantic life partner, and so the importance of that was always in the back of my mind as I made choices for myself throughout my life. By middle school, when I held hands or "went steady" with someone, I'd imagine I was at the beginning of a storybook romance in which I married my childhood sweetheart. With each breakup, I'd move on to searching for the "real" right one.

I don't remember ever being explicitly taught that it was my purpose to get married and have kids, but I still picked up on the importance of those things. As a member of the Spice Girls generation, all the "girl power" messaging convinced me I'd never *need* a man, but I still had a sense that no matter how good my life was, it would be even better if I had a partner. I pictured my life looking a certain way, and it included riding the roller coaster of life with someone. I believed it was something that would bring me a kind of happiness and fulfillment I wouldn't be able to find anywhere else.

With every crush, I imagined what our kids would look like. I tried on their last names, practiced the cursive version, and envisioned writing it on a check one day to pay the down payment on a home. I imagined the relief and sweetness that would come from being a part of a pair. Each other's entire world. I idolized the couples I saw on TV and dreamed about how magical it would feel to find the love of my life and settle down. I, like so many other people, thought that when you love someone enough, all the feelings of acceptance and belonging and trust and intimacy are automatically a part of the deal. I knew it would take "work," but I didn't know what that really meant. I didn't necessarily dream of an expensive wedding, a house on a cul-de-sac, or a marriage with traditional roles, but I still believed that the kind of life I wanted to live would include a long-term commitment and a little family unit where we were all we needed. My version of a fairy-tale life definitely included a true love's kiss.

When I asked my followers to share their motivations for partnership with me, a lot of their responses boiled down to believing it would make their lives better. They shared that loneliness and the desire to feel needed led them to couple up. Many shared the sentiment that they wanted someone to support and be supported by through the ups and downs of life. They believed they'd find understanding, intimacy, and companionship. Overwhelmingly, the responses I got expressed a clear desire to find a teammate. They were seeking someone to build lives with who shared their values and wanted just as much as they did to love and be loved by another. However, for people currently in long-term partnerships, there's often an uncomfortable truth to be faced when you go from asking, "What need did you want to be fulfilled by this?" to "Are those needs being fulfilled?"

NOT SO FANTASTICAL

Our society places a massive emphasis on the pursuit of romantic partnership, pedestaling the nuclear family unit and putting marriage and long-term commitment at the top of a love hierarchy. But we also get massively mixed signals around what we should want, why we should want it, and how to have or maintain it. Romantic love is supposed to feel like the stars are aligning. It's supposed to be great, to be easy, to be the most important and fulfilling thing at the center of our lives.

At the same time, the standards for what that actually looks like are a far cry from magical. After settling down, a lot of people find their realities falling short of the reasons they sought out a partnership in the first place. Initially, they have big dreams of sharing the ins and outs of their lives together, and for a while that's exactly what they do. They get to know each other, share their interests, and hang on to each other's every word. Intimacy comes easily as you connect over the songs you liked in high school and your shared distaste for something everyone else loves. This coming together is when the future is full of potential.

It's that potential that can be dangerous. Banking on what *could be* can have us overlooking what's right in front of us. We settle into the ease and comfort of initial chemistry and attraction. We write off misalignments as bridgeable gaps but slip into patterns that expand them beyond repair. Eventually, we feel like we're going through the motions, hitting the same snags, or treating each other like passing ships. What used to be dancing in the kitchen turns into exhaustedly collapsing onto couches to scroll.

Part of this is natural. After all, it would be silly to imagine that the butterflies you feel will flutter nonstop for fifty years. Different kinds of intimacy come from getting to know someone on a deeper level. Companionship and a sense of security may replace the exciting anxiety of learning the nuances of another person. Relationships all have their strengths and challenges. Our circumstances, understandings, and priorities change over time, and so do we. For our relationships to be resilient, they must evolve and adapt, but letting potential overshadow our reality can be a setup for never actually getting what we need. It can act as a barrier to being present and building the little bridges that ultimately maintain quality connections.

MARRIAGE IS WORK

Unlike in the movies, real loving commitments should include agreeing to do your part in building a life together, growing together, and doing what it takes to show up for each other through the ups and downs. It isn't just a commitment to "better or worse" that creates quality relationships. It's the loving acts within them that do.

It's unrealistic to think that happy relationships like the ones we all desire are built on commitment alone. Relationships that make us feel secure and stable, where care is reciprocated and teamwork is ever-present, come from ongoing communication, agreements, and shared values. But the message that I picked up as a teenager from movies like *She's All That* or *Clueless* is that you should be willing to transform yourself for love. An opposites-attract romance is about the most romantic dynamic you can have. Differences will work themselves out, even if they're clashes in core values. What I didn't realize at the time was that when two people are drastically different in real life, the work of building and maintaining a strong relationship is made much harder. The recipe for quality connection isn't a combination of attraction and a willingness to do anything. As humans, we seek to be understood, but those movies made it seem like if you loved someone enough, understanding would just happen.

This was a major issue for me when I entered relationships. In everything from communication to the division of housework, I just assumed that being on the same page was something that would come naturally. I was under the impression that all the things I'd wanted out of a partnership would happen if I did what I thought I was supposed to do and loved in the ways I was taught to love. I was willing and eager, and I thought that was enough. I'm sure you'll be shocked to discover that's not what happened. These beliefs led me to look past red flags in potential partners. Because I thought my nonexistent boundaries made me an ideal partner, I ignored or rationalized poor treatment and incompatibility and stayed when I shouldn't have. I was hurt because of this, and I hurt others.

Following the path that I thought I was supposed to follow and then playing the parts I thought I was supposed to play in trying to build the relationship I thought would bring me joy ended up leaving me resentful and burnt out. Trying to create my own fairy tale based on my understanding of what long-term partnership and marriage were supposed to be caused me to completely lose my identity.

Unlike what I had been led to believe about marriage, just loving the hell out of somebody wasn't enough. Enjoying spending time with them and *desiring* to be with them happily for the rest of my life wasn't enough to meet the needs I'd set out to meet by partnering in the first place. You can proclaim to have the same values, and still, the visions of what you want your lives to look like may not be the same. Even if you feel like you were made for each other, there are no guarantees things will ever just fall into place. There can be so many great things happening within a relationship and so many reasons to love and commit, but the idea that those things are *all it takes* to create a sustainable relationship is pure fantasy. As the old adage goes . . . marriage takes work.

BUT HOW MUCH IS TOO MUCH?

I've heard different versions of the phrase "marriage takes work" countless times in my life, as I'm sure so many of us have. It's a phrase and a concept that can take on different meanings depending on who's saying it and to whom, so I surveyed my friends and online community to get their take. Here are some of their reflections:

■ "Growing up going to church, when I heard 'marriage is work,' it mostly seemed to mean women should do the work of giving up everything and dampening their emotions for the sake of their husband's masculinity, career, etc. It was a sentiment that was taught from the pulpit, in women's groups, and in marriage and relationship books. It was usually the response given to women when they talked about how overwhelmed or isolated they felt at home."

■ "For people in healthy relationships, it can be a reminder to take caring for each other seriously. I think it's supposed to encourage equity in contributions and effort, like booking a date night or doing your own personal work to self-reflect and grow. It might encourage someone to take accountability or compromise to repair after a conflict. When it's in response to someone in an unhealthy relationship, it suggests, 'Even if the romance is gone, no matter what, you have to do what it takes to stay together.'"

■ "It's usually well intended, like a reminder to work through conflicts or invest in the person you chose to partner with. Mostly it sends the message that you should keep trying to stay together no matter how dissatisfied you are in your relationship."

■ "I told myself this for years and it took a toll on me! I had a partner who worked hard for our family at a good job, who never raised his voice at me, and was way more involved than my dad ever was. I was like every other woman I knew, and nothing was ever balanced, so it wasn't like I didn't know what I was signing up for. I thought 'marriage is work' meant doing it all and being grateful for what help I got. That phrase taught me not to have limits."

◼ "My first serious girlfriend and I stayed together for years past our relationship's expiration date because of the idea that 'relationships take work.' I dropped out of school and moved across the country to be with her even though I didn't really want to, then resented her for it. We fought constantly, but I thought the hard work of a relationship meant doing anything for each other. We split the bills and chores, so we were way better off than other couples, especially our straight friends, so I didn't really think twice about how much we were each enduring. I thought it was what love was about."

Standards and expectations shape how we view relationships. This idea—that anything that's wrong with our relationships is a result of not working hard enough—might, in some circumstances, encourage us to self-reflect and grow. Often, though, it takes the failures of the nuclear family unit and places them on individuals. It makes it seem like the best thing to do when a relationship is less than ideal is to make more sacrifices and suppress your feelings rather than pause and fully assess the situation.

Take this moment at a bar a few years back, for example. An acquaintance complained to a group of us that her new partner never included her in weekend plans with his friends, despite her telling him multiple times that it bothered her. On top of feeling like an afterthought, when he stayed out late and didn't answer his phone, she felt insecure and worried. Her friends consoled her but also reminded her that he'd been single a long time and probably wasn't used to considering other people. She was told to "just keep working at it. Maybe try approaching him differently. Eventually, he'll get it."

They were early in their relationship, and it was probably a good time for both of them to reflect on what their expectations were. If he didn't want to spend his weekends with his girlfriend, it was up to him to be honest about that; then it was up to her to believe him and accept it or move on. Her friends placed the emotional labor on her, and she was blamed for his lack of attention to her concerns. She was encouraged to put in more work rather than set healthy limits.

Erin, from the previous chapter, fell victim to this mentality. She loved Noah, and part of what she thought she needed to do to prove her love was be willing to give herself up. The belief that a successful relationship requires unconditional self-sacrifice stunted her ability to assess whether the relationship was a relationship she actually wanted to be a part of. Focusing so intently on proving her love caused her to miss out on red flags, and ultimately she ended up feeling abandoned.

Another example of the damaging messaging of "marriage is work" played out in a work lunchroom. A colleague confessed that his girlfriend had been begging him for a ring. He loved her and they'd been together for years, but he'd kicked the can down the road because she wanted kids and he wasn't sure. A married older coworker chimed in and said he used to feel the same way, but "a good partner is hard to find. If all it takes is giving her a few kids, it's worth it. Happy wife, happy life. Sometimes we have to compromise."

Multiple things could be true at once. He could love her, and also they may have been better off taking their lives in different directions. Appeasing his girlfriend and going through the motions of the wedding, the kids, and the house would have been dishonest and a self-denial of what he actually wanted. His partner deserved a partner who was all in, and he deserved to have *his* happiness factored into how he shaped his life.

Compromise is to be expected in loving relationships, but drawing the line between when it's healthy or harmful is important. There's a difference between compromising on the weeknight menu and compromising on your core values or giving up on having your basic needs met. Discernment around how much work is too much work is essential if we want quality relationships. How do we know when the turbulence of the day-in and day-out dynamics is just growing pains? How do we know if what we're dealing with is normal or if what's normal is okay with us? How do we cut through the mixed messaging around what love should or shouldn't be and decide for ourselves?

Taking a beat to ask those questions is a start. What do we want our relationships to look and feel like? Who do we want to have relationships with? Why do we get into relationships in the first place? What purpose do our relationships serve? What needs are we hoping they'll meet? What do we expect them to contribute to our lives? What kinds of connections would we like to have? What kind of work do we want to put into relationships? What do we want to get out of them?

The quality of our relationships matters. They may require compromise and effort, but tossing around "marriage is work" misses the opportunity to consider how effective we're being. Are we working together? Are we working in the same direction? Are we working toward a shared goal? Is the work we're putting in paying off the way we'd hoped? *How well is this actually working for us?*

Just because something isn't bad doesn't make it good. Just because your partner is physically present, contributes to rent, or pitches in when asked doesn't mean you are in a loving partnership. We should not be evaluating our partners using standards like "It could be worse" or "At least they don't . . ." We should not be measuring the success of a relationship by its existence or its longevity, but by how it makes us *feel*. There doesn't have to be violence or name-calling within a relationship for it to be worthy of critique. You're not ungrateful or incapable if you're honest about areas where your relationship doesn't feel like it's measuring up. Just because it isn't outright bad doesn't mean that it's good enough.

Working toward what I thought would keep my husband and me together and trying to perform my role better prolonged the mediocrity in my life. I took my relationship issues as personal failures and did what I could with the tools I had at the time, but I carried around the belief that something was wrong with me. Of course, we should all be taking accountability for our own behavior, but when following the social scripts leaves us wondering what's broken about us, we can't let the myths around love and marriage hold us back from taking a critical look beyond ourselves. I'd spent too long thinking it was me and my needs and demands that were a problem, not that the expectations of motherhood were bullshit or that the nuclear family structure was an unsustainable lie. I thought my boundaries were an issue, not that I'd been doing too much. I was so focused on making marriage work that I lost sight of what I was actually trying to achieve by being married. When I considered what needs my relationship was meeting, what needs I was trying to meet in that relationship, and which were being left unmet, a whole world opened up to me.

NO SUCH THING AS NORMAL

I want to be very clear that while subpar, mediocre cis-het relationships have plenty of representation in our society, they are *not* the only ones that can be mediocre. Mediocrity, or settling for less than what's desirable, is a cultural issue, not an issue of identity. Cis-het couples more easily slip into normalized mediocrity because of assumptions, models, and pressures, but nobody in a *normative* society is immune.

Normativity is something the author Angela Chen wrote about in her book, *Ace: What Asexuality Reveals About Desire, Society, and the Meaning of Sex*. I had the opportunity to talk with her about how it relates to mediocrity on a phone call. Normativity is basically the social definition of what's "good" or "normal." It's how we're taught things automatically are or "should be."

Our society is heteronormative, meaning, as Angela described it, "we're socialized to believe that, unbeknownst to us, being heterosexual is the default." As a result, many people spend their lives following the social rules, acting out gender in a prescribed way, and assuming they're straight out of fear or without much question in what feminist theorists like Adrienne Rich have sometimes described as compulsory heterosexuality. Essentially, doing what we're "supposed" to do without exploring if it's what we want.

Heteronormativity is just *one* of the ways our society is normative. *Ace* explores other kinds of normativity, like how we're taught to prioritize monogamous romantic love, and especially digs into *sexual* normativity, or the idea that all "healthy, normal" adults are sexual creatures that experience sexual attraction. The same way people grow older and begin to question their sexuality or gender, "some people have a realization sometime in their life, sometimes many times, that their experience of sex and sexuality is quite different than what they've been told is normal or from what they've been told it should be," Angela said.

There is nothing wrong with being cis-gendered or straight. There's *also* nothing wrong with identifying as something different from those things. Despite what *Cosmopolitan* may claim, there's no "right" amount of sex you should be having or "correct" way to be in relationships with other people. By exploring love and desire as it relates to asexuality, *Ace* challenges the idea that those things have to look a certain way. The problem of normativity is that it suggests there's one specific "normal" or ideal way to be. It discourages us from seeing the value in a variety of loving and fulfilling relationships or deepening the connections that really enrich our lives. Normativity and the harsh social enforcement of it convince us that an empty marriage is better than an intimate and loving platonic friendship. When we find ourselves following the path in a direction that leaves us with our needs unmet, it discourages us from even asking ourselves what *could* be.

Angela proposes that a less formulaic look at love would give us all more of what we need. The idea that the best way to be happy is to end up in a cis-het married nuclear family unit where you have sex a certain number of times a week leaves a lot to be desired for a lot of people. It ignores the importance of building relationships with people who are aligned with you, whom you can communicate with well, and who you can trust and build intimacy with. She pointed out, "We don't have a lot of nuanced, distinct words to talk about concepts like libido versus attraction, romantic attraction versus platonic attraction." We're misled to believe that *marriage* is a need instead of considering *what needs marriage is supposed to meet.* Sometimes doing what we "should" do can give us what we need, but when it doesn't, that doesn't mean we aren't doing it right. Just recognizing that there are a wide range of ways to love, to desire, to be attracted to, and to connect with people can be a step toward figuring out what you actually *want.*

I asked Angela what she thinks holds people back from self-investigating. "Maybe it's fear," she said. Fear of discovering something that will make you unlovable. Fear of finding out you want something and not being able to have it. Fear of being rejected or misunderstood, or of being seen as weird or unusual. Fear of not finding someone to compromise with and create something with.

Outside of fear, what holds many people back from asking themselves what they really want is the anxiety that can come with freedom. It's like going to a new restaurant and being handed a ten-page menu. Sometimes the endless options can be so overwhelming, you end up looking around and ordering what everyone else has, even if it's not that great. Stopping to self-investigate *every* step of the way in every decision we make isn't realistic. Knowing what you're supposed to do and having an idea of a certain outcome is stabilizing. There's power in being intentional about the commitments you make to people and clearly defining expectations, but there's also some comfort in not having to talk through every single decision and agreement.

The answer to the pitfalls of normativity isn't to blow up your life or, as Angela put it, "waking up every morning and redesigning our relationships." It's a willingness to take a more expansive look at how love and intimacy can show up in our lives. It's considering that our friendships and community connections can enrich our lives and meet our needs in ways our romantic partnerships may not.

Questioning the basics of what we've been socially conditioned to believe about love and sexuality is a powerful place to start. Caution is natural. There's always going to be a risk when it comes to choices we make. In *All About Love*, bell hooks wrote, "The practice of love offers no place of safety. We risk loss, hurt, pain. We risk being acted upon by forces outside our control." There's risk in questioning, but there's also risk in standing still. There's value in embracing a little bit of fear of missing out. If we ask ourselves what opportunities for love we could have, the risks of standing still can overpower the anxiety of the unexplored and propel us toward what we deserve.

Notice what areas of your life leave you feeling fulfilled and which areas could use some work. Without courageous self-investigation, we run the risk of languishing in mediocrity when we could be thriving.

FAR FROM BROKEN

Of course, if we see nuclear families as the solution to the struggle, we're going to fear an alternative. After all, nuclear families struggle, too. People with and without kids struggle. Caretakers of elderly and disabled folks struggle. Single, childfree people struggle.

Ashley Simpo is a writer, advocate, and mother whose work is rooted in a love for community and collective liberation. She lives in Brooklyn with her son, and though she's divorced from and no longer lives under the same roof as her son's dad, there is nothing "broken" about their home. She and her child's father live in the same neighborhood and are both supportive and engaged parents, but their child's support network doesn't begin and end with them. Their family, their friends, the people on their block, and familiar faces in their neighborhood are all a part of their lives. Their community is made up of intimate relationships and casual and consistent interactions at the bodega. Her village includes them all, and it's light-years away from anything you could describe as "broken."

The cringeworthy messaging that paints nontraditional family structures as lower quality is partially what inspired Ashley to write her book, *A Kids Book About Divorce.* She also wanted to push back on the culture of mommy martyrdom and especially the toxic stereotyping that single motherhood has to be a grueling and miserable existence worth avoiding at all costs.

In fact, creating a new family structure can be something beautiful. In 2018, after Ashley broke up with her child's father, she and her five-year-old son moved in with her friend Tia and her two kids, who were three and thirteen at the time. They eased the financial burden of the cost of living and leaned on each other during a season of their lives when that made sense for them. Their relationship and willingness to build such an intimate bond brought them relief through companionship, splitting bills, and logistical support.

Nothing about marriage, motherhood, or single parenthood has to be the exhausting experience it's made out to be. Single parenthood is not an inherently lower-quality version of life. Ashley's intimate friendships are essential aspects of her life that help her meet her needs. Her relationships—platonic, familial, or casual—are not stopgaps until she finds some singular romantic love. So much of the stigma and fear that surrounds divorce and single parenthood stems from what our lives might lack if we did things differently. But our culture of mediocrity leaves us lacking even when we're married. It leaves us lacking in rest, fulfillment, and connection.

What Ashley wishes we'd all collectively ask is *why* we think *the way things are* is *the way things have to be.* What has us so convinced that ending a miserable marriage would be more damaging than maintaining it? Why do we label nonnuclear families "broken" and push people to stay together "for the kids"? Where does fear and stigma come from?

The idea that divorce or single parenthood is something to avoid at all costs is a scare tactic that keeps us from disrupting the larger systems of oppression. The nuclear family structure, the pursuit of the American Dream, and the free and underpaid labor it extracts from us hold up capitalist structures. Being forced toward and then desperately clinging to white picket fences is keeping us from the community that can make us all safer when we fall.

Asking questions about our beliefs about parenthood and marriage can lead us to the even bigger questions of what is really to blame for the challenges we face in society as a whole. *It's not our families that are broken; it's our systems.* The reality is that for some, marriage really is a means for survival. It provides a safety net that may not be accessible in other ways. Fear isn't always unfounded. This is part of the problem. Collectively, we should be working toward creating a society that provides everyone with what they need regardless of marital status. The answer can't be for us to fix our individual marriages or just do less around the house. The answer is an *overhaul*: the intentional investment in creating a world that gives us the freedom to choose. The answer is a diversity of tactics: individual inner work to unlearn oppressive norms, interpersonal work to build and maintain sustainable relationships, a cultural shift with care and community at the center, and ongoing advocacy for systemic change that focuses on giving us all more of what we need.

The question is not if we can have a future full of loving connections, joy, and fulfillment, but *what that would look like* and *how we can make it happen.* This takes creativity, questioning, and experimentation. And courage.

UNTETHERED

During the two years following my birthday-card moment, I did a lot of work on myself and in my partnership. As a couple, we chipped away at old habits and made new ones. We communicated our expectations out loud to each other and took a collaborative approach to our household from every angle we could think of, and through trial and error of trading tasks and adjusting expectations, we ended up finding a comfortable balance of responsibilities and a new, more efficient flow. This freed up a lot of mental and emotional space and gave me back my time and autonomy. I felt like I had more choice over how I spent my time and where I put my energy.

I wanted to live my life in alignment with what I thought really mattered, and to do that, I had to figure out what that was. In all areas of my life, I learned to tolerate the discomfort of uncertainty and prioritized self-exploration. I learned to say yes to opportunities for work and play and embraced the process of dabbling. I read fantasy for the first time since I was a kid. I thrifted clothes with loud patterns that stood out against my closet full of black crewnecks. I brushed up on my boundary-setting skills and built up my tolerance for the discomfort of having to hold them. All the changes in my behavior and my priorities led me to start a seedling-growing operation with some great people, read books at a rate I'd never achieved in my life, and stop turning down invites to go on walks in the woods with friends. Following sparks of passion led me to reignite old interests and deepen friendships and gave me a better understanding of who I was.

As I found more freedom to experiment with who I was outside of just a wife and a mother, I felt empowered to release more and more of the demands I thought those roles were making of me. But for all that was different in my life, it took me until the fall of 2021 and the spiral that led me to quit my job to accept that a better division of labor and some individual self-exploration wasn't enough. I was under immense pressure at work, fighting with my district for basic resources and being guilted for needing to take time off to be with my own kids during ongoing childcare interruptions. My students were being denied what they needed. Their parents and their families were being denied what they needed. My then undiagnosed bipolar II had me cycling through highs and lows on a near daily basis, and I was barely sleeping or eating. While my division of labor was better than it had ever been, and I'd found space beyond my roles, the stress I was under at work and the lack of access to consistent childcare support beyond my husband and me meant I couldn't enjoy any of it. No matter how late I stayed after contract hours or how hard I tried to meet all of my students' needs, I was never going to make up for what our government and our society had failed to provide them.

I saw myself wasting away for a dehumanizing system. A system that didn't see the people who made it run or the people it claimed to serve as deserving of care. Accepting my disposability at my job was like cutting the rope to an anchor. None of what I'd been told to seek had turned out how I'd expected—partnership, parenthood, or my career. So many of the "truths" I thought I knew—about what I should want and where fulfillment would be found—had been falsehoods, and letting go of that last thread made me feel free to move forward.

Changes in my partnership and in my sense of self had improved my quality of life and made me feel more understood and connected, but the process I'd been going through was never really about making things work. It went beyond that. It was about letting go of socially imposed expectations. Not only in my role as a wife and mother, but in what I should want, what I should value, how I should structure my priorities, and how I should live. I didn't want to split chores more equitably just to turn around and overextend myself in other ways. I didn't simply want to fix my marriage or have more time for work or friends. I didn't want my husband to do things my way. I wanted to figure out what we needed and wanted and find ways to make those things a reality. I wanted to care and be cared for in a sustainable way. Figuring out how to improve our lives meant deconstructing what a "good life" meant—imagining better beyond our relationship, beyond our household, and toward a society where everyone has what they need. I wanted to do more than just keep afloat. I wanted that for others. I needed to be able to let go of what used to be before I could move forward in the new beginning I wanted. I had to realize I wasn't just making adjustments; all the learning and growing I'd been doing had been a part of a transition from one chapter of my life to another.

Transition is a natural process we all go through multiple times in our lives. Some transitions are big and noticeable, like moving to a new house or getting a new job. Some are invisible but profound, like learning something that changes your worldview or making a serious commitment. In his book *Transitions: Making Sense of Life's Changes*, the author William Bridges described it as "the difficult process of letting go of an old situation, of suffering the confusing nowhere of in-betweenness, and of launching forth again in a new situation." A transition is different than just changing how you do things; it's leaving something behind and fully embracing something new.

According to Bridges, every transition has three parts: an ending, a neutral zone, and a new beginning. The ending is a severing of ties with the way things were, like the closing of a door so that another can open. A neutral zone is a phase of exploration, expansion, and discovery. The neutral zone can feel chaotic and empty all at once, while old understandings are challenged but no clear path lies ahead. A new beginning can't be rushed or forced. It can happen only after the closure of an ending and the realignment of the neutral zone. Genuine new beginnings aren't just a change of location but an inner shift. Not just rearranged art on the wall but a whole new canvas.

After that spark of realization that I wanted something different for myself in 2019, I'd spent two years hanging out in the in-betweenness of the neutral zone, trying to force a new beginning. A lot of the changes we'd made were having a positive impact on us, but I was hanging on to the belief that we could fix what we had. In reality, I needed to let it end.

I LEFT MY job. I started the process of getting additional support to deal with ongoing mental health issues. I received bipolar II and ADHD diagnoses and found a medication that has been stabilizing and life-saving. I also started having the most honest conversations with my husband that I'd ever had. Until then, I'd been too afraid to admit to him that I'd been rethinking so many of my life choices. We'd been together for so long, and he'd been a part of so many of them. The process of questioning what I thought I knew had been painful, and I didn't want to hurt him. I didn't want to open up a Pandora's box of unprocessed feelings and cause harm.

I eventually realized that keeping my honest feelings to myself was holding us both back. I wanted out of our marriage the way it was. I wanted a fresh start. I hoped he'd be a part of it, but to say it out loud, I had to accept that he might not want to be. The risks were high, but so were the possible rewards. What mattered most was that whatever came next was a conscious choice. In the end, when I pulled off the Band-Aid, he chose to build something new with me.

In the fall of 2021, I started a new life. My marriage didn't end, but a version of it did. I opened up about regret and remorse and even after the most challenging conversations, we walked away with a sense of clarity.

In the years since that birthday card, I'd been reorienting myself and getting to know what I wanted. I'd been considering my needs and letting them guide my understanding of who I was and what I needed out of my partnership. So many of the imbalances and misunderstandings that had become a part of our relationship pattern had been the result of foundational beliefs I'd picked up passively throughout my life, and I had to spend those years figuring out which ones to keep or discard. I was ready for change in 2019, but it took me two years to accept that that meant letting go of something that no longer existed. To have what I wanted, I had to give myself room to create it.

Earlier in this book I told you about that cheesy TikTok video I made in which I referenced burning down my nest and hoping to build something new on fertile soil. That's exactly what I did. Some transitions are marked with rituals like weddings or funerals, but mine was captured in a TikTok. I know . . . how very millennial of me.

I made changes to my environment and within my relationships, but the biggest shift happened within me. I made a commitment to saying goodbye to mediocrity in myself, in my relationships, and in my life. I traded the anxiety of the unknown for the hopefulness of possibility. Saying goodbye to what *was* meant I could move forward untethered. It was like a veil had been pulled back, and because I had been honest with myself that the old version of my life hadn't given me the level of happiness I'd wanted, I could move forward unafraid of unraveling it. *It was freeing to realize it had already come undone.* Up until that point I had spent my entire life working toward the job and the house and the husband and the kids. I was living the American Dream, the modern version of the fairy tale, and I felt so much grief realizing it wasn't what I thought it would be. I couldn't begin to write my own story and build the kind of life or have the kind of love that I really wanted unless I was willing to say goodbye to what I had. The most loving thing I could do for myself, my husband, and my kids was to stop trying to jam my foot into a slipper that didn't fit.

MAKE IT (ACTUALLY) WORK

When I got honest about what needs were and were not being met in my relationship and looked at it like a problem to be solved, I was able to get creative.

I wanted to feel supported, understood, and comfortable. I wanted my life to feel rich and adventurous. I needed to feel safe, secure, and connected. Considering what I wanted and needed, I could dream up what steps I needed to take to have that. Focusing on the needs allowed me to see how important it was for me to create the relationship I actively wanted, not just maintain a marriage. There was still a lot of good in my relationship, but there were sacrifices I was making out of fear. Focusing on what I wanted gave me the courage I needed to seek the partnership I desired. In my relationship, that meant courageously advocating for what I wanted, not just what would "make things work."

I'd grown up believing that the most fulfilling kind of love would come from a partnership, and because I worried my honest expression of needs might jeopardize that, I recontextualized the risk by considering how I might find fulfillment in different ways. My local neighborhood groups and the community garden I'd started had brought me joy. My close friendships had brought me closeness and connection. I'd found companionship and fun with colleagues and casual friendships. I knew I could scratch my itch for belonging and contentment if the place where I'd been finding those things was affected by my self-advocacy.

I knew my relationship had the potential to be so much better because I showed up fully and honestly in it, but knowing that I could have fulfillment outside of it was what empowered me to be vulnerable and ask for what I really wanted. Just knowing I'd be okay gave me the sense of security I needed to move forward.

WHAT DO YOU NEED?

Relationships take work, sure, but what are you working for? Marriage isn't effort for effort's sake. It's meant to be fulfilling. It's important to consider if the investment we make in our relationships is bringing us closer to having our needs met or holding us back. If you're pouring yourself into your relationship and you still feel like you're drowning, that sensation is something to sit with.

A mediocre relationship is a bit like a sinking ship. If water is rising through cracks and holes, you can try to keep up by scooping it out one cup at a time. But that's an exhausting way to deal with a problem—especially if you're also coaching a reluctant shipmate through the process or watching them stay dry and unbothered. There are ways of dealing with a damaged boat that won't leave you collapsed with exhaustion.

The problem with endlessly bailing water is that you're treating the symptom, not the cause. When you're dealing with persistent issues, making small tweaks and adjustments like hiring help or implementing a date night might patch things up and make it easier to manage for a while. But if you step back and look at the big picture, you have to be honest about the vessel itself. Is it worth the effort to keep it afloat or is it time to rethink the whole thing?

What we don't want is to accept what one commenter on the BestOfRedditorUpdates described as "a tolerable level of permanent unhappiness." I first heard the phrase in a TikTok video by the writer Shar Henley, who had stumbled on the phrase during a casual scroll. In a comment, a Reddit user wrote that a friend of his had been complaining about being "blindsided" by a breakup. The commenter's friend admitted that he was aware that his girlfriend had been unhappy for a long time but figured her frustrations were a rough patch. The commenter wrote that the issue wasn't that his friend was "caught off guard. He just thought it was a tolerable level of permanent unhappiness." He, and by proxy his girlfriend, were victims of a culture that convinces us to focus on what we can tolerate versus what we could enjoy.

Thanks to Shar's video, which has racked up millions of views and tens of thousands of shares, the term has started working its way into the public lexicon. It's been featured in dozens of videos across Instagram and TikTok, the topic of conversation on podcasts, and written about in trending articles. It's resonated so much because it really hits the nail on the head in describing an experience a lot of people have been living with but unable to describe. Mediocrity is like a dull pain—the common cold of discontentment—and just as we brush off a minor cough or a runny nose, we brush aside dissatisfaction in what is often one of our most important relationships.

Social conditioning has a powerful way of distorting our expectations, but we can fight back when we focus. Every relationship has mediocre seasons when things feel a little ho-hum and disconnected. There are times when more demands are going to be made on one partner than the other. You might feel disconnected from each other for days or weeks at a time. Sometimes more. Life is messy, but true partnership means being on the same team, navigating the mess. True partnership means everybody's interests are considered in both the short term *and* the long term. Relationships require effort, but in partnerships, efforts are reciprocated. Efforts are made in good faith. Things may never be fifty-fifty in any area, but they shouldn't be sustained by one person always having less. Enduring hard times is inevitable in any relationship, but the relationship itself shouldn't be an endurance test.

Let's free ourselves from the lie of "happily ever after" and the oppression of "marriage is work," and just focus on what love *feels* like. If we expand how we see love, recognizing the many ways it shows up in our lives, we'll see that it already exists in many different forms. The friend who sends a meme they know you'd like, the neighbor who drops off food when they know your partner is on a work trip, and the nephew who can't wait to spend the afternoon with you are all different versions of love that can bring purpose to your life. Throughout our lives, we can connect intimately with various people and experience various kinds of love. Notice the relationships and the experiences that make you feel seen, heard, and loved. If we can recognize the ways closeness, reciprocity, and care already exist for us, we can acknowledge that not all relationships have those things. If we focus on the quality of our relationships and how they make us feel, we can build the kinds of relationships that actually make us feel good.

Feeling like you're dragging your partner to the table to participate in daily life can leave you feeling dismissed and lonely. Feeling forced into a role of consistently asking for help just to be met with resistance can make you feel reluctant and misunderstood. If you approach your partner about things that matter to you, and they downplay or dismiss them because the same things don't matter to them, it might leave you feeling like *you* don't matter to them.

You're not ungrateful or broken if you feel discouraged or frustrated. Your feelings are not wrong. It's not silly or high maintenance to have your needs considered. Your needs are your needs! They're not extra—*they're the bare minimum*. I can't define mediocrity or tell you what good enough is. What I can tell you is that you deserve to have standards. You deserve to have your needs met. You deserve to have relationships in your life that make you feel cared for, supported, and loved. You deserve to have your efforts reciprocated.

LIFE ON THE OTHER SIDE

Compromise is to be expected in loving relationships, but drawing the line between when it's healthy or harmful is important. There's a difference between compromising on the weeknight menu and compromising on your core values or giving up on having your basic needs met.

Even though self-abandonment in the name of love is often sold as romantic, when core values come into question, the integrity of a relationship's foundation comes into question. Our values are at the center of who we are. They're connected to what we find important, what motivates us, and all the choices we make. What we value impacts *everything we do* from how much time we spend making beds and wiping counters to whether we'll practice certain faith traditions. When you're with someone whose *core values* aren't aligned with yours, the compromises are less about whether to pack lunches for road trips or get fast food on the drive and more about whether to take a job that demands the other give up theirs. When your core values are misaligned, even if you make agreements or dream up futures together, the images you have in your heads may be drastically different. You may be saying the same words, but the definitions are light-years apart.

It doesn't matter how hard you love someone. If they're unwilling or unable to be the partner you need, loving them harder won't change that. You can advocate for yourself, and communicate about what you need, but if you and your partner are on different pages about how you want to spend your time, your energy, and ultimately your life, explaining yourself in more detail won't change things. You cannot convince someone that something matters if they don't want to be convinced. In a relationship, the loving thing to do is to be honest about what choices might make you both happier.

This is where an honest appraisal comes in. Do the benefits of being together outweigh the sacrifices? What needs are being met within the relationship and which ones aren't? Are there creative ways to hang on to those benefits and get certain needs met elsewhere? You might find that living in separate homes or spending more time with friends relieves pressure on the relationship. You might choose to live under the same roof but end the romantic portion of your partnership.

You might find that a partner making a career change or pursuing a passion changes the relationship dynamic in a way that makes it more sustainable. Sometimes tending to unmet needs in other areas of our lives can impact how we feel within our most intimate partnerships. If you can clarify what kind of love you want in your life and use some creativity to figure out what that might look like in action, you can find tweaks and shifts within the same relational framework that gets you what you need. Expand your outlook when problem-solving. We're complex, multidimensional beings, and it's not only unrealistic but also unfair to expect one person to fulfill your every need. We were meant to have varied relationships— platonic life partners who keep you grounded, groups of casual friends you have a raucous good time with once a year, neighborhood folks you adore despite different values. They all matter, and the more we embrace that, the richer our lives are all around. Allow for curiosity and creativity when considering changes. You may find that the way you feel about romantic partnership changes as you establish and strengthen relationships outside of one.

Ask yourself what you feel is missing in your life or what you feel held back from and consider how you might shift things around in your life to gain more access to what you want. You don't have to jump immediately to splitting assets as the first step toward a new kind of partnership, but sometimes the most loving thing to do is make room for each other by stepping away. *It is okay to want something different.*

Not to say that it's easy. The idea that it's better to be partnered than to be happy is deeply ingrained in our society. Overemphasizing staying in a partnership regardless of its quality makes us lose sight of the reasons we partner in the first place. We settle for "at least they . . ." instead of the true desires we started out with in our search for "the one." Unfortunately, because women are often tasked with the responsibility of home life and relationship tending, they're often judged harshly for holding boundaries around expectations. They're called high maintenance or blamed for "giving up." We heap marriage in with motherhood as something women are supposed to endure and not complain about. But I'm here to tell you that white-knuckling your way through a marriage is not protecting you from pain. Fear of losing something you worked so hard for can blind you to what's waiting for you if you dare to offer yourself more.

At least once a week I get a message from a follower who shares the joy they've found after making more conscious choices about what they wanted in life. In one email, someone told me that after years of being a stay-at-home parent, she went back to school. She'd been a domestic engineer for years and loved it, and she hadn't even considered college or a career because the housework never stopped and she wanted her kids to have someone available if they ever needed something. Eventually, she realized she didn't need to give up on her dream to make that happen. She worked it out with her husband that he'd shift his hours around to be available for school pickup. They clarified expectations around housework, and even though it sparked some tension, the change gave her access to more of what she needed. She'd also started connecting with more parents in the neighborhood. Building a network of trusted adults who could jump in as needed let off a lot of the pressure she'd been carrying.

Rachel and May, whose Nag Paradox partnership led to their divorce, found that separate homes and a custody agreement made their relationship better. When I asked her about it, Rachel told me the split has been painful, of course, but mostly it's felt like relief. She grieved what she thought things would be, but the end also felt like a weight being lifted. She got the sense that May felt the same. They were less on edge around each other, as if a pressure valve had been released.

They sold their family home when they divorced, and each rented their own apartment in the same school district. Rachel told me that even though it's less room than what they'd had before, she's found a lot of joy in creating a new home: decorating, putting together a patio garden, and meeting families in their new neighborhood. She explained that ending her marriage has given her space to breathe. Even with a tighter budget and less help with the physical task load at home, she still feels less stressed overall. It wasn't a decision she made lightly, but just by the measure of how much more present she is in her day-to-day postdivorce, she has no doubt it was the right choice for them.

Being a part of a fulfilling relationship isn't as simple as finding the right person, then settling in and holding on for dear life. And there's no single answer for what's right for everyone. We all have unique circumstances, different needs, and distinct ways of thriving.

The narrow narratives about what makes a "good" relationship fail to account for any of that.

We're all better off when we stop subscribing to rigid definitions of success and allow ourselves the freedom to shape love on our own terms. We thrive when we reject outdated ideals and embrace love as an active practice of care, consideration, and reciprocity.

When we do that, we can create relationships that honor who we are—whether that means adjusting them, ending them, or reimagining love altogether.

CELEBRATE NEW BEGINNINGS

The longevity of a relationship is a poor measure of its actual quality or value. On its own, it doesn't tell us much. It's not a reliable indicator of whether a relationship is healthy, fulfilling, or genuinely enriching for those involved. Letting the time you've invested hold you back from honestly assessing the situation can needlessly prolong a relationship dynamic that isn't working.

Sometimes relationships run their course, and that's okay.

Sometimes the terms of a relationship need to be renegotiated; sometimes they need to shift, change, or end. We can normalize changing our minds and encourage adjusting our circumstances to meet our needs by celebrating away the stigma.

When Olivia Dreizen Howell got divorced in 2019, she didn't want to have to eat off the same plates or sleep in the same bed she'd shared with her ex-husband throughout their marriage. When she went looking for a way to ask her support network for help, she came up empty-handed. Everyone's always so eager to give gifts for weddings and baby showers, but there are so many other moments of transition in our life when we would benefit from a hand up from our loved ones. Recognizing this, Olivia and her sister, Jenny, teamed up to found the Fresh Starts Registry, the first and only platform that helps people rebuild their lives after major transitions. The registry offers curated lists of home essentials—everything from kitchenware to bedding—along with a wide variety of on-demand resources and access to vetted experts like therapists, divorce coaches, career advisors, and financial consultants.

Beyond providing tangible support, they are also doing everything they can to push for a cultural shift that paints brave decisions in a positive light. We should be cheering one another on not just for partnering but for walking away from partnerships or dynamics that no longer serve us. We should be saying congratulations when someone makes a courageous choice to start over.

All new beginnings, whether it's a full restructuring of a relationship you've been in, a commitment to a dedicated period of self-discovery, or an ending of a partnership, deserve to be celebrated. In your personal life, next time you or someone you love draws a boundary or walks away, get some flowers and cupcakes. Say congrats! Send a card or throw a party. Whether it's quitting a job, getting sober, moving to a new place, or picking up a new hobby, make a big deal out of it!

REMEMBER PRINCESS SUE? As she sulks in her captive tower, she notices a dragon flying by and coaxes it over by offering it some tea. The two commiserate over their shared dislike for the prince, and while they chat, out of the blue, the dragon sneezes so aggressively that it blows them both out of the castle and into the garden below.

The prince, furious with the mess, tells Sue, "You really are the worst princess!" But Sue doesn't let his judgment bother her. To him, she might be bad. But to her, what was bad was giving up the freedom and adventure she'd spent her life dreaming of.

Pulling herself out of a garden bed and climbing onto the dragon's back, she laughs. "Perhaps I am the worst princess." Princess Sue leaves behind the life she thought would bring her what she wanted. She found the kind of authentic love and support she'd hoped for in an unlikely place. At the end of the story, Sue and the dragon fly off together to fight battles and live adventurously. Her messy hair and giant smile say it all. *Truly liberated, the two live happily ever after.*

The story of Princess Sue is more than just a twist on a classic. It's a beautiful example of the joys of living a life that aligns with what you actually want. Unlike Belle from *Beauty and the Beast*, Sue doesn't try to change the prince or adapt to his bad attitude. She's not like Ariel, who gives up her voice for the chance to be with someone whom she couldn't be her true self with. Sue doesn't put a certain kind of fairy-tale ending above what she wants.

The prince never would have been happy fighting knights alongside Sue. Sue never would have been happy brushing her hair and twirling around the castle all day. Neither of them was ever going to find what they needed by doing what they thought they were supposed to do. Princess Sue's fairy-tale ending looked different than she'd expected it to, but by closing the book on mediocre, she gave herself the happily ever after she deserved.

5 THINGS YOU CAN DO RIGHT NOW

1. Make It Work for You

In a normative society, taking the time to *wonder* gives you the opportunity to have what you want, not just what society tells you to want.

To go from "making it work" to "making it work for you," evaluate your relationships, think about what you really want, and ask yourself some questions:

What do I need? *A sense of belonging? Autonomy? Meaning? Am I looking for safety, companionship, or passion?*

What needs are being met right now? What needs aren't being met?

How do I want to feel? *Do I want to feel safe, content, or satisfied? Am I hoping to feel empowered, hopeful, or excited?*

How do I feel in my relationships now?

What do I want? *Do I want a singular partner in crime? Do I picture a life with various close relationships? Do I* *want to follow a passion, spend time tending to family connections, or get outside more?*

Now look at that list and play out two scenarios—one in which you get what you are seeking and one in which nothing changes. It can be daunting to initiate a major transition, but calculating what you lose by *not* making a change can be just as scary. If you're ready, map out your own ending, neutral zone, and new beginning. What do you need to let go of? What will your neutral phase look like, and how can you support yourself while you go through the necessary limbo stage? And finally, what lies waiting for you in your new beginning?

The first and second parts don't have to happen in order. You can try things out, take steps, and make changes. You can join a class, learn more about yourself, practice setting boundaries, or decide what feels good and what doesn't. You may feel like things aren't going well or improving, but rest assured that it's all part of the process. You can't rush it, and the parts that are going to hurt are going to hurt. This time is for growth and discovery. If it feels disorienting, that's because it is. You're in the process of finding new footing.

2. Renaissance

If you're single, have you ever opted out of an opportunity because it might limit your dating opportunities? Maybe you've thought, "If I weren't concerned with looking for a partner, I'd _____." If you're partnered, have you ever caught yourself thinking, "If I were single, I would _____."

The way we're taught to place romantic partnership at the center of the definition of a "good life" can have the consequence of holding us back.

If you put partnership completely out of your mind and make decisions without considering how it might impact other people, what would you fill your life with? Maybe you've had a fantasy of driving off into the sunset and hunkering down in a cabin in the woods where you read all day. Or you fantasize about a college degree, a new career, or simply experiencing the sweet relief of not having to do someone else's laundry.

If you were to take romance completely off the table, break up with a partner, or write off dating altogether, how would your life change? Would you train for a marathon, do weeknight dinners with friends, or take an evening class? Would you get more involved in your neighborhood or pursue a hobby? Are there any areas of your life where you feel restricted or repressed? What would it look like for you to be free of that?

You don't have to wait to decide if you're going to stay or go to start your renaissance. You don't have to have a clear plan for what's next to make more room for what you really want out of life.

3. Get Comfortable on Your Own

> *"Knowing how to be solitary is central to the art of loving. When we can be alone, we can be with others without using them as a means of escape."*
>
> —*bell hooks*, All About Love

The societal emphasis on fairy-tale romance can lead to projecting a kind of love or connection onto people or partnerships that isn't really there. Get comfortable with solitude as a way of grounding yourself in reality. Learning to be alone with ourselves should not be confused with slipping into self-reliance or hyperindependence. Learning to be alone means practicing self-reflection and familiarizing yourself with your needs, your feelings, your beliefs, and your behaviors. It means tolerating discomfort, learning to take accountability, and behaving in loving ways toward yourself. Learn to be alone by dedicating time, energy, and effort toward caring for and learning about yourself. Take yourself out to dinner and drinks. Visit a museum and linger in front of the art. Read books that inspire self-reflection. Journal.

4. Get More Baskets

The fear of being alone can scare us into tolerating discomfort. When all your eggs are in one basket, you might find yourself thinking, "I've put so much work into this. I have so much invested. I can't change things or walk away." Relieve the pressure by finding some more baskets to put eggs in. Invest in platonic, familial, and community relationships. Think about the friends you have who might like to see a movie, go on a weekly walk, come over and cook dinner or do laundry, or travel with you. Don't write off those relationships as nonessential or less important than someone you might marry.

None of us were ever meant to be everyone's everything, and the nuclear family was never meant to be sustainable on its own. The thick cloud of resentment that's caused by trying to make things work can place a black-and-white filter on how we try to solve our problems. My husband doesn't like seeing movies in theaters, but I do. Instead of skipping out on that activity, I call my friends to go with me. He likes big gaming events and conventions, and I don't. He goes with his friends while I cheer him on from home. Having a variety of connections that play different roles in our lives means we have more opportunities and support. We can be important to each other and meet many of each other's needs, but our connections with other people mean the demands and expectations we place on each other are more authentic and realistic.

Lean into the friendships you have; invest time and effort into them. Send a birthday card, invite them over for holiday dinners, or offer to do seemingly mundane things together. Our friendships, families, and community connections don't have to be placeholders for a future soulmate. They can be a part of a loving network.

By shifting our focus away from the narrow ideal of the nuclear family and romantic partnerships as the ultimate source of fulfillment, we open ourselves to the possibility of building something much richer—a network of friendships, chosen family, and community bonds that can sustain and support us. When we're intentional about where we put our energy and efforts, we can cultivate these connections and create the villages we need to thrive.

5. Expand and Reshape Your Map

In the sea of heteronormative nuclear family milestones, where so many other possibilities have been pushed to the margins, it can be hard to picture what we could have. But alternative models of care, commitment, and kinship have existed and thrived for generations.

If you're unsure how to reimagine your relationships or support system, look to the people already doing it. Multigenerational households, queer chosen families, community elders stepping in as caregivers, friend groups raising children together, single parents supported by a web of loved ones—these structures have always been here. Pay attention to the diversity of loving relationships around you. When we learn from people who've built expansive intentional networks of care, we can see how many of our limits are just inherited stories.

Start small. Ask: What roles do I expect certain people to play in my life? Where did those expectations come from? Could I open up more to a friend or release a partner from a role they were never meant to fill?

As Angela Chen writes in *Ace*, not having language for the wide range of connection styles can be limiting. But even with better words, we still need to get curious and clear about what they mean to us and to the people we care about.

Try having an explicit conversation with someone close to you about how you'd like to show up in each other's lives. Talk about how much time you want to spend together, what kinds of support you'd like to offer, and what you hope for. These conversations might feel awkward, but they're an act of care. They make space for relationships that reflect what you truly want, not just what you've been taught to expect.

Questioning everything at once might feel overwhelming. Move at your own pace. Taking it one little intentional step at a time will help you build tolerance for the discomfort of veering off the well-paved path. After reflecting, choose one or two people you trust or want to grow closer to, and start a conversation. It doesn't have to be a dramatic declaration. It can be an honest check-in, a shared intention, or a plan to show up more consciously. Let the awkwardness be part of it. That's how something deeper begins.

PART 3

Community:
A Future Rooted in
Collective Care

CHAPTER SEVEN

Becoming the Village

Cultivating Community as an Act of Resistance

THE THREE SISTERS

I grew up and still live in the Midwest, on the ancestral, traditional, and contemporary lands of the Anishinaabe—the Three Fires Confederacy of the Ojibwe, Ottawa, and Potawatomi peoples. One of the most well-known pieces of Anishinaabe agricultural wisdom comes from the story of the three sisters.

The three sisters are winter squash, maize, and beans, and when planted together, they act as companions, each one benefiting from the gifts of the others. Maize has a tall, woody stalk perfect for supporting beans as they climb. Beans have a unique way of processing nitrogen that keeps the other plants fed at the roots. Squash plants grow along the ground and have prickly vines and broad leaves that keep the soil moist and free from weeds.

Squash, maize, and beans are all nutrient-dense plants that mature at different rates and provide food for harvest continuously from early spring until late into fall. When they're planted together, they can keep communities well fed for a large portion of the year. Each plant is enriched by its proximity and connection to the others. The people who tend to the plants and harvest the food get what they need, the soil remains balanced and ready to support crops the next season, and the cycle continues year after year.

Interdependence is at the core of the wisdom of the three sisters. It illustrates an essential truth: Nothing in nature thrives alone—not plants, not animals, not people. The story of the three sisters is one of mutual flourishing and sustainability. It's a model for a future we can have—a future with care and community at the center. The story of the three sisters captures the importance of honoring our capacity and individualized needs, prioritizing connection, and living by principles of mutuality. It describes how ecosystems flourish when the individual parts have what they need and no one element takes priority over the others. It shows the harmony of homeostasis and how we can achieve it through an acknowledgment of our interdependence.

LIFE WIFE

"My neighbor Kate, we are each other's life wife," Sydney said. They met at their kids' school playground and formed a friendship that evolved from casual conversations at the park into watching each other's kids and sharing weekly family dinners. Because of the steady presence in each other's life, they're now at the point where their kids consider the other mom to be "mom-adjacent." They may not be related by blood or by law, but Sydney and Kate are family.

Sydney and Kate both have partners who are active and engaged in their family roles but are more focused on their professional lives and financial responsibilities. Sydney is divorced and recoupled, and she and her partner have three kids between them. Her partner works full-time away from the house, and she works part-time from home. Kate and her husband have three kids of similar ages to Sydney's. She works a few days a week outside of their home, and her husband works a full-time job that keeps him away from home for extra-long hours during busy seasons a few months out of the year.

Their partners appreciate what Sydney and Kate have on their plates, but they don't fully get it. As primary life builders, it's nice to have their efforts appreciated, but having someone who knows the spiral of anxiety that comes from discovering a class project is due the next day or the dread of having bought in bulk a kind of food the house has decided they're no longer interested in is next level. Beyond just sharing memes and chatting about TV shows, they've built a kind of platonic intimacy through truly doing life together. Sydney and Kate fill a role for each other that is enriching and essential. A shared understanding between the two moms has led to a beautifully symbiotic relationship, and their routine of weekly tag-team dinners has been a big part of it.

"It's always at her house since it's bigger and accommodates all of us being in a space somewhere," said Sydney. "We can sit and talk/vent/brainstorm things. Sometimes she comes up with the dinner plan, and sometimes I do. Sometimes she cooks, and sometimes I cook. If something needs to be addressed with the kids, we usually tend to our own child's massive blowup if there is one. But if we are at the end of our rope, we are okay with the other person stepping in. Example: Three years ago, even early on in our friendship, her oldest had a very explosive temper. He was seething one day and trying to physically go toward anyone who was close, but I stepped between him and helped. I didn't have to 'do' much except be there to co-regulate with him, while Kate was managing other things in the house nearby. To hold that kind of trust is remarkable. My kids love her like she's their mom. They hug her, speak to her with the same manners and vulnerability they speak with to me, and know she is the next safe space that's nearby they can go to outside our home. . . . She is a soul sister, kindred spirit to me through and through. I would not move from where we are *because* of her. Having each other is a vital lifeline."

Sydney and Kate's bond is logistical *and* emotional, forged through covering for each other during appointments as well as talking about healing from various traumatic things they've been through. It's a novel approach, not one that was modeled for Sydney as a child of divorced parents. Her mom worked long hours, leaving Sydney to be a latchkey kid by the time she was nine years old. "As a Chinese family, it doesn't mean community the way Kate and I lean on each other," Sydney said. "You listen to the grandparents ultimately, but they also stay back and let the parents each manage their own children. I hardly remember my cousins even having quarrels and having to work it out, outside their own sibling." They were physically present for one another, doing things together and helping each other out, but the family culture was to keep a certain distance. Sydney said, "You mind your own business. You don't express feelings of affection with much physical embracing. All this to say, my friendship with Kate is the most reciprocal relationship I have ever had in my life. Of *any* relationship. We share ups and downs very equally. When we know the other needs a win, we show up. When we know we need to survive, we try to do it together on those days."

DIVERSIFIED CARE

Sometimes what starts from a need to survive can grow into an opportunity to thrive. We could all use a life wife, but what would be even better is being a part of something bigger. So many beautiful possibilities open up when we broaden our definition of care and where it can come from.

Jessica Daylover is an educator, a performer, and a queer polyamorous mother of two young children. She lives with her polycule, which includes her two children (three and six), her husband (her children's father), her boyfriend, and her husband's other partner/ her co-mother (whom she lovingly calls Sis). Being mostly estranged from her family of origin and two thousand miles away, Jessica has surrounded herself with chosen family. Her best friend of eighteen years is the godfather to both her children and her eldest child's favorite person on earth. They call them "Titi." Then there's also Uncle Jetsy, another uncle by love. Outside of that inner orbit, Jessica's village spans far and wide and includes her highly engaged online community members. On social media, where she goes by @remodeledlove, Jessica has used content creation and storytelling as a tool for expanding the cultural narrative on healthy relationships and polyamory and has built a platform of more than 150,000 followers. Her personal and intimate social media presence has created a global following that functions as more than just outsiders looking in. They feel more like extended family. In times of need, for herself or her loved ones, Jessica has been able to post requests for help, and her international village has always gone above and beyond.

Jessica's youngest was born with complex medical needs. On top of other health issues with no discernible source, they were colicky and restless, struggled with reflux and chronic ear infections, and hardly ever slept. In the first few months, while they adjusted to life as parents of a toddler and a baby, Jessica and her husband, Joseph, looked for answers, scraped by on minimal sleep, and hoped they'd either find a solution or their youngest would grow out of it. As time went on with no solutions, their mental and physical health deteriorated. Not only were they both dealing with deep feelings of hopelessness, but after nearly two years of stress and sleep deprivation, Jessica developed an autoimmune condition from her thyroid shutting down. They were hanging on by a thread, trying to keep their bills paid, care for both of their children, and make it through each day.

Right around the time their youngest turned two, they made the decision to have Joseph's long-distance partner, Ash, move across the country to help. Shortly after that, Jessica met her now-boyfriend, who also jumped in to help. The relief from having two additional caring adults on deck was felt immediately. Though Jessica and Joseph maintained primary responsibility for the kids, especially during overnight wake-ups, Jessica's boyfriend and her metamour (partner's partner) physically and emotionally supported them in countless ways. They helped care for the kids, cared for the caregivers, and eased the demands of daily life by each taking on a share of emotional, physical, and mental labor.

When it came to their child's ongoing health issues, Jessica and Joseph put their heads together to design and execute a plan. They compiled research, collected documentation, and leveraged each individual's strengths to advocate for their child's care. Their global village pitched in, too. Jessica had been open on social media about the symptoms their toddler had been dealing with, periodically updating her followers on what had been going on, and she often received advice and feedback from folks with their own experiences and knowledge. At one point, after being told by a pediatrician that there were no ENTs available in their network, Jessica broke down crying in her Instagram stories. One of her out-of-state followers offered to do some searching and ended up finding them two doctors who would take their Medicaid.

The support Jessica has received from her village has made a significant impact on the health and wellness of her and her family. With her community's support, her child ended up accessing the medical interventions they needed. In turn, Jessica has been able to get more of what she needs.

Jessica is a passionate performer and artist who thrives on connection and creative energy. Festivals and events she attends, and where she often speaks, have been a huge source of fulfillment for her both before and since becoming a parent. In that first year, amid their baby's ongoing health issues, she accepted one of her favorite annual festival gigs that had her away from home for ten days. Her husband had always been more than happy to handle the household while she worked or played, but that year they overestimated how hard it would be and trying to do it solo nearly killed him. In theory, she could have continued to take gigs and travel, but they were left traumatized by the massive mental, emotional, and physical toll it took on everyone when she'd tried. After that trip, she knew she couldn't take similar opportunities without being racked with guilt, so she didn't. Losing touch with that part of herself only deepened her depletion, leaving her with even less to give.

Accepting Ash's help was a leap of faith for them. Their willingness to accept help was a vulnerable and brave move that went against our culture's obsession with conflating strength with struggle. Trying to manage on their own wasn't making them strong. They got stronger the more they opened themselves up for support.

Jessica has always been a passionate community builder, often orchestrating and facilitating connections. When she was struggling those first few years through her child's illness, she was running on fumes and unable to do those things. She was depleted in her personal life, in her close relationships, and in her community at large. The more help she accepted, the more she was able to show up as herself and as a member of a community. When she was supported, she was stronger, and when she was stronger, everyone around her was, too. When she accepted what others were willingly giving her, she could give in willing and sustainable ways, too.

The profound impact the care from her community has had on her through some of her hardest times has driven home the most essential elements of it. The people in her life didn't assume what she needed, sending her a bottle of wine or an Edible Arrangement. It took intention to build trust between her and the people in her life. She had to learn her limits and communicate them. She had to learn to notice what she needed, accept help, and give what she could, not what she thought she should. Being clear and direct about what you need and learning to tolerate an honest yes or no is not something dominant culture encourages us to practice. It is kind to be clear about what you want. It gives others an opportunity to show up for you. When someone tells you what they need, you don't have to do the work of guessing or projecting. Nothing is wasted when you're considerate and clear.

Part of what has kept Jessica's relationships healthy is that she's practiced saying no and has shown the people in her life that she values their ability to say no to *her*. Hearing no and being okay with it doesn't mean not being disappointed, but it means the no is not received as a personal attack or punishment. "No" is a loving word. She's had to unpack a lot of internalized social expectations and learn the kind of conflict resolution skills so few of us have had modeled to us. These aren't just skills and principles she puts to work in her closest partnerships. Knowing her limits and her needs has empowered her to build healthier friendships, set realistic boundaries around how she spends her time, and in general make choices that align with her priorities and values.

It isn't polyamory that allows Jessica to pursue hobbies and creative opportunities. It's intention and the ongoing practice of setting boundaries and maintenance. It's a worldview that values individuality *and* connection.

She may have a nontraditional family structure, but the principles she's built her village on are the ones that exist in any thriving connection or network. She and the people in her life have relationships that function in different ways and meet unique needs. None of them are sustained on a label alone, and no socially constructed definition necessarily reflects how they choose to exist within those relationships. She's something unique to each person in her life the same way they are to her, and her willingness to see the possibilities in that means her community can be rich and robust. The strength of her relationships is due to the ongoing work she does with herself and with the people in her life. Her story is just one example of the ways giving and receiving care, setting limits, and living our lives as whole, expansive people can give us and everyone in our lives more of what we need. This isn't a polyamorous thing. This is a community-centered thing. This is a care-minded thing. This is a balance and sustainability thing. This is a way of being.

PLANTING SEEDS

When my oldest was about nine months old, I was scrolling through the neighborhood Facebook group when I stumbled upon a post by a neighbor asking if anyone wanted to get together to swap seedlings. At the time, I was just an aspiring gardener with a small raised bed and big dreams and had gone a little overboard with seed starting. Gardening was something I'd always liked, and because I could do it from home, it became an accessible way for me to scratch a personal-interest itch as a new parent. I was thrilled to see the post, happy to hear I might be able to trade my twenty extra cucumber seedlings for something more exciting, and get to know my neighbors. Even better, I recognized the poster's profile picture as someone who lived a few blocks away. I eagerly RSVP'd yes.

On the day of the event, I packed up my seedlings in a crate, buckled my baby into a carrier on my chest, and walked a couple of blocks to the dive bar where the event was being hosted. When I arrived, my neighbor Christina reintroduced herself and ushered me over to her tomato starts, where she helped me pick some that would fit my needs, then introduced me to a handful of other neighbors.

Over the course of an hour, I got to know the ten or so neighbors who showed up to the swap and listened to them tell me all about their gardens and filled my crate with traded seedlings. I was a total novice, so I soaked up every word. It was incredible. Christina, who'd coordinated the whole thing, had been sharing seedlings and swapping her harvest with neighbors for a few seasons already. She told me she was hoping to host more events like the swap but needed to figure out how to get the word out. She had big dreams of hosting events, sharing resources, and making homegrown food more accessible. I loved it. I wanted to get involved.

I left that event with some heirloom tomatoes, a jade pumpkin plant, and Christina's contact info. We were both eager to get the group off the ground, and after a few days of back-and-forth, we met in person to start planning. We started with a Facebook group and grew its membership through word of mouth. We recruited new members by putting up flyers and mentioning the group to the neighbors we ran into on our respective walks, her with her dog and me with my baby.

As the Facebook group grew, so did the connections within it. In the group, people solicited advice, posted pics, and coordinated trades. Because of how hyperlocal the group was, it was the perfect place to ask if anyone had a push mower to borrow, offer up flats of unplanted flowers, or see if anyone had any extra okra seeds. We got to know one another and our little quirks through the posts and comment sections. It was a lovely place to linger, packed full of pictures of flowers, valuable information about things like companion planting and drainage problems, and reminders of when to start fall seedlings.

As the group grew, we started organizing in-person meetings where we'd get together in someone's yard and talk shop. As the same faces started to show up more regularly, we started to dream bigger. We committed to maintaining the connections we'd made, making more, and having fun. That first winter working together, we hosted multiple potluck-style events to which attendees brought, among other things, canned jam, local honey, fresh sourdough, rum cake, and home-brewed ginger beer.

Not only was the food amazing but so were the people. I met Angie, who was born and raised in the neighborhood, full to the brim with local knowledge. Betty, whose dry humor and outgoing nature are immediately disarming. I met Liz and Kavan, who live a few blocks away and told us about the incredible canning network they belonged to back in Boston. During that first year, these familiar faces—and so many others—continued to show up, post in the online forum, and bring the community to life.

The gardening group has continued to be such a rich and

valuable resource because of how important sustainability and connection have been in how it functions. The group's primary mission is to respond to the needs of the community, so as the capacity of group members shifts and changes, the group does, too. The group is made up of next-door neighbors, people whose kids share a classroom, and individuals who can text each other when they accidentally leave their garage door open. The people who participate in the gardening group aren't just passing through; they're a part of the community—and invested in the group's success, in the wellness of the neighborhood, and in their relationships with their neighbors.

Our gardening group played a hand in my neighborhood's resilience during the first few years of the pandemic. Neighbors checked in on one another, shared groceries, and helped get one another the resources they needed. Through long stretches of isolation, we dropped off produce on one another's porches. Where social and political policy failed so many, the power of connection held strong.

With every season, the garden group has adapted and expanded. As of today, the group handles the stewardship of a local community garden, tends to chickens at the local elementary schools, partners with summer bridge programs, organizes mutual aid efforts, contributes to food sovereignty organizations, hosts multiple well-established seasonal events, boasts a massive free seed library, and has over two thousand active group members. Its impacts have been profound and ongoing and expansive. The gardening group is an example of how communities can thrive when individual needs and capacities are honored, when resources are shared, and when connection, joy, and sustainability are prioritized.

COLLECTIVE CARE

The gardening group is a network that encourages everyone to show up with what they've got and take what they need. The culture promotes the redistribution of resources and encourages asking for support. The group is founded on a belief in abundance—that the world has enough for everyone. The expectation of receiving care isn't that the recipient should return the gift in kind. It's that they'll offer up what they have enough of to share in the future. And the group's resource sharing goes well beyond plants.

The group has functioned as a reciprocal care network in many ways. Here are just a few: When group members have lost employment, they've been able to crowdsource leads and even act as references for one another. We've helped each other find housing, helped each other access public resources, and formed childcare trades. We've coordinated to make sure we've had representatives at neighborhood meetings and organized political actions. Because of the connections made in our gardening group, our neighborhood now has a neighborhood-funded mental health facility where anyone, regardless of ability to pay or legal citizenship status, can come get the support they need. When a neighbor has needed something, the group has been there to pool resources and put effort into finding ways to provide it.

The gardening group functions on the principles of mutual aid and collective care. Mutual aid is an organizational model that trades the top-down approach for one that empowers community members to play an active role in how things function. It's a cooperative way of building communities that focuses on collective benefit. Mutual aid is a way of providing for people's needs through "solidarity, not charity." Unlike charities and nonprofits with governing boards and wealthy donors who have the final say over who gets what, mutual aid is organized by the people, for the people. The author and activist Dean Spade defines mutual aid as "the radical act of caring for each other while working to change the world." It's a way of showing up for one another that functions on the foundational belief that we are all worthy of care. Mutual aid can look like a response to an immediate need, like a group of friends pooling money to help a friend cover an emergency medical bill. It can also look like a more ongoing or involved project. For example, the Free Breakfast for Children program was organized by the Black Panthers in the 1960s and helped feed more than twenty thousand children. In Chicago, the Rogers Park Free Store was established by a group of neighbors to redistribute community resources so that neighbors can get what they need. Groups that fundraise to help members pay rent and community-organized holiday gift drives are all examples of mutual aid in action. So are neighborhood giveaway Facebook groups and meal trains for new parents. Mutual aid can involve redistribution of resources of all kinds—not just financial or resources in kind, but also information, time, energy, wisdom, emotional, or mental support.

There's no board president or red tape with mutual aid. There's no hierarchy. Living in solidarity with other people means that no person is morally superior to another; no person's experience and truth outweighs anyone else's. No one has to prove their inherent value or worth to be treated with dignity and support. We all have needs, and we all have something to give. Mutual aid is about giving what you can and taking what you need. You don't have to meet certain socially defined measurements of success or productivity to be deserving of care. *You just are.*

As the author and disability justice activist Leah Lakshmi Piepzna-Samarasinha points out in their book *The Future Is Dis-*

abled: Prophecies, Love Notes, and Mourning Songs, complex webs of care and networks of peer-to-peer support have always been around. Collective care, an approach to caregiving where each individual's well-being is seen as a community responsibility, has been an important way for marginalized folks, especially in Black, Indigenous, working-class, disabled, queer, and migrant communities, to survive and thrive in a society that does everything in its power to stop that from happening. When you can't trust the systems to keep you alive, you learn to rely on one another. You learn to navigate relationships and care for one another, even through conflict. When asking for help can lead to deportation, institutionalization, or death, mutual aid and collective care is a means of survival and beyond. "Mutual aid" and "collective care" aren't just buzzwords; they're ways of relating. They're ways of organizing and frameworks for living that envision a society in which we all flourish.

In a 2018 essay, the activists Rushdia Mehreen and David Gray-Donald explored the idea of collective care as originating from queer and Black feminist organizing like the Combahee River Collective. They describe it this way: "It means that a group commits to addressing interlocking oppressions and reasons for deteriorating well-being within the group while also combating oppression in society at large." Collective care emphasizes joint accountability, with the aim of collective empowerment. It's about contributing to the world in a way that helps meet everyone's needs. *Everyone is responsible for everyone.*

The future we build should be co-created, inclusive, and accessible for all. We deserve to have our needs met inside our homes, in our relationships, and in all other areas of our lives. *All of us.* Our current social and political systems certainly aren't doing that for us, so who better to learn from than the people whose needs have been most exploited and ignored? Collective care has been the answer for so many already. Surviving and thriving by giving and receiving care, through community building and resource sharing, is not a novel concept. Building our lives around care and community is the most natural thing we can do, even if society does its absolute best to convince us otherwise.

LITTLE DEVIL

One of my greatest ongoing battles in recent years has been learning not to listen to the little devil that society has placed on my shoulder. That whisper that tries to convince me I'm not valuable if I'm not giving and producing. The voice that tells me I should push past my limits, should try to do more or be more. The voice that urges me to withdraw, tells me to put up a wall and not ask for help, that tells me who I should be and how I should measure what matters.

Throughout my life, it's whispered messages in my ear about how important it is to be accommodating and low-maintenance while also being productive and helpful. As I found my footing in the world, I paid attention to what kind of behavior was rewarded or punished, what held value and what didn't. I shaped myself around what would make me good, worthy, and successful. That little devil told me that a good friend never needs anything and can always be there for other people, even when it hurts. That little devil explained that good girlfriends are cool with whatever. A good employee is the first one in and the last one out at night. Be professional, never challenge authority, and prioritize working your way to the top. A career and personal life are fine as long as everything else is taken care of first. And good mothers make their children their entire world.

We've all got our own version of that little devil, made up of the expectations that have been forced on us throughout our lives. Beyond oppressive circumstances, there are social pressures and cultural values we have to defend ourselves against. Stories about the best way to be seep into our subconscious. Messages we've learned along the way dull our ability to trust our intuition and aim for socially constructed measures of success. We're coached and coerced into denying ourselves the slowness, connection, and care we deserve.

The myth of meritocracy tells us that if we work hard enough, we can have anything we need and want. *You better get your grades up or you'll never get anywhere! Just put your head down! Be the peacekeeper! Your parents didn't work hard just for you to let them down! Climb! Win! Get ahead or you'll fall behind!*

Those little devils coax us into trading our time and labor for a chance at fulfillment, forcing our eyes away from what else could be possible.

It tells us to compare ourselves to others and give more and try to be better—but always by its definition of what that means. *Can't find childcare that doesn't cost more than your salary? Must be a you problem! Working full-time but can't afford rent? A personal failure. Isolated and depressed? Must be that you aren't trying hard enough. Get your priorities straight! Follow the rules! Don't be frivolous! Fall in line!*

The little devil we each carry around on our shoulder is a social construct, not truth. They're expectations and cultural norms rooted in capitalism, patriarchy, white supremacy, and ableism. They are meant to protect power, produce wealth, and keep us burnt out and busy enough that we don't have the energy to fight back. We are being exploited and pitted against each other by systems that thrive on our disconnection. We all deserve lives where we have what we need. We deserve to live in a society where that's the norm—the bare minimum. To create that, we have to recognize the influence the little devils have on us, how they direct our energy, and push back. Hyperindividualism, self-reliance, and hard work aren't what make a just society. The answer isn't to work beyond our limits, to abandon boundaries, to ignore our needs and give our labor to systems that don't see our humanity. It's the opposite: to fully embrace what makes us human. It's to put our efforts into care work. It's to invest in one another. It's to redefine success as sustainability. To value limits, connection, and the honoring of capacity. It's flipping mediocrity on its head and adopting our own definitions of "good enough."

One of the ways our social norms are so devilish and powerful is they exploit our very real needs. We need to be able to afford to live. We want to feel safe, secure, and comfortable. We want to belong. We want to feel challenged, productive, connected, and fulfilled. We want to nurture one another, to love, and to feel a sense of ease. We have needs, and we want them met.

When people don't have what they need, society blames them for not trying hard enough to get it. When someone does have enough, they're encouraged to keep pushing for more. No matter your output or effort, you're never enough. But it's a lie. We are not machines. We are not commodities. We are human. And we are not meant to do this alone. When we release ourselves from these impossible expectations, we make space for something better—a life where we belong to each other instead of the systems that drain us.

COMMUNITY

I started going to the garden group as an isolated new mom who wanted to invest in the community I lived in. I wanted to contribute to creating a future where my kids would feel like they belonged. I wanted to be a part of something, and the way I knew how to do that was to be of service. Volunteering, organizing, offering up what I could. My involvement with the group and all the opportunities, experiences, and connections it brought me taught me first-hand what it meant to really be a part of something. And in the last few years, post–identity crisis, I've come to understand that one of the reasons I've felt such a deep connection with the group is that I've gotten so much out of it. I had volunteered plenty, but the way I showed up in my neighborhood was different from how I'd shown up in other spaces. I wasn't just there to serve others; I was immersed in the community—a part of a flow of resources—tangible and intangible. From the connections facilitated by the group, I've received help with my kids, hand-me-downs, and rides. I've shared many meals in crowded living rooms and stood in front of many stoops chatting with people I've shown up for and who have shown up for me. My needs for security, connection, and care have been met in so many ways through the group. When I look around at the relationships and communities I'm a part of, it's the ones that are built on mutuality and reciprocity that are the most fulfilling and secure.

A liberated future isn't a pipe dream. A village isn't an inaccessible concept. My gardening group functions like a village. We all offer what we can, ask for what we need, and accept when it's offered. We don't expect each individual to contribute the same thing—in fact, we aim for the opposite. Biodiversity is essential to the success of a thriving ecosystem, and a community is exactly that—an ecosystem.

We can build the villages we want so badly through daily practices. We can create them through mindset shifts and the daily community actions of weaving our lives together. It happens through intentional acts of opening up, creating and maintaining connections. Community building is the work of noticing, nurturing, and continuing to show up. It's viewing the world with an eye for relationships, always looking for how we're connected and how we can continue to maintain those connections. It's asking questions, being curious and courageous. It's getting in one another's business and investing in people's well-being. In conflicts, it's asking how a situation can be improved rather than leaping to punishing or severing connections. In setting expectations, it's focusing on what needs need to be met. It's consideration of individual needs and circumstances in all our interactions.

Community is an action. It's maintained through noticing and nurturing one another. It's in knowing how much we can offer and giving within limits. It's in allowing ourselves to accept care. Community is a process. It's a flow. A web of care. It's being thoughtful about how we interact with one another, processing our own emotions, and working through conflicts. A future where we all have what we need is co-created and inclusive. **Nobody is left behind.**

It's achievable when we view the world through the lens of interconnectedness. It's achievable when we live by the principles of belonging to one another.

Just like our home systems, thriving communities function well when we think creatively about how to best meet everyone's needs. There's no one-size-fits-all answer. We don't all need to show up the same way. We can play to strengths and work with the resources we already have. For example, I work from home and can easily walk to my kids' school to pick them up. Meanwhile, they have friends whose parents commute from an hour away. It would be silly for me not to offer to bring their kids home with me on days when traffic is bad or they can't make it to pickup on time. Introducing myself to the parents of my kids' peers and establishing those relationships is a step toward becoming a part of their support network. It's a simple way to ease the burden on someone else while making use of the resources and capacity I already have.

My block functions this way during heavy snowfalls. If sidewalks aren't cleared of snow quickly, it can become heavy or melt and refreeze, and once it's compacted or icy, it can be treacherous for anyone trying to navigate the public way. In Chicago, each property owner is legally responsible for clearing their own walk, but on our block, anyone who can do more, does. Neighbors bundle up and head out when they have the time, not just stopping at the property lines but shoveling for their neighbors on either side. It's common to look out and see a neighbor carving a path down the whole block, even cutting a path in front of apartment buildings whose landlords rarely do their part, knowing someone else will inevitably return the favor a few hours later. This kind of teamwork means we don't each have to bundle up and head out every few hours when the snow falls. We take turns. Instead of everyone keeping up with just the snow in front of their home, the block is treated like a shared space. Keeping it clear benefits everyone.

Personally, I'm happy to bundle up, press play on an audiobook, and shovel the block whenever I can. Some days I don't have time to do more than clear what's in front of our home, but I give more effort when I've got it. Those of us on the block who can contribute with shovels or snowblowers do so. Not everyone has the same time, ability, or capacity to do that work, and there's no expectation for everyone to give the same effort. I don't shovel with the mindset that my neighbors all owe me something in return. The folks on my block show up when they can, whether to shovel, jump-start someone's car, catch a loose dog, or recommend a gutter guy. It's all part of the flow of community.

Maintaining that flow, whether it's in a gardening group or in a tight-knit family, requires vulnerability and a tolerance for discomfort. Our society discourages us from asking for what we need, and because of that, we end up out of practice and uncomfortable with communicating about our limits. Practicing the messy dance of saying yes and no when you really mean it can be challenging, but the outcome of that kind of honest boundary-keeping is trust and intimacy.

I feel more comfortable asking a friend for help with something if she's turned me down in the past. I feel the need to guess the other person's limits and predict their boundaries if they aren't communicated to me. If I ask a friend to go on a walk, but she's not feeling up to it, I want to know that. If I ask a friend to watch my cats while I go out of town, I want to be able to trust that they aren't saying yes then quietly stewing when they do it. Saying or being told no is not always comfortable, but honest, intimate relationships aren't made up of endless yeses. Saying yes all the time without discretion is a recipe for resentment. It's empowering to know that when someone says yes, they're giving freely. Honest answers give space for honest questions, opening the door for that flow of community to keep moving.

In our close relationships, in our communities, and on our blocks, showing up with what we've got and contributing to the common good is how we create the villages we're so desperate for. By embracing interdependence, we make space for everyone to thrive.

There's a common thread between what we undervalue in our

homes and in society at large. The cleaning, the maintenance, the organizing, the education, the learning, the connecting, the nurturing. We act like it's nothing in our homes and we underfund and undervalue it in our society. In the same way it's essential to give it the respect and attention it deserves for our wellness at home, it's essential to do the same for our community wellness.

VILLAGE LIVING

When I asked the author and activist Mikki Kendall how we might work toward a liberated future, she said, "We would have to create a society that didn't under-embrace the village concept, but not just 'it takes a village to raise a child.' It takes a village to *function*." When we raise kids in a village setting, they're seen as everyone's responsibility. She said, "You see the structure, sometimes in the islands, where the individual homes all surround the compound. The kids play inside that compound, any of the adults can correct the kids, and all of the adults feed the kids and tend to them, whatever. It's still a lot of work. But it's work that is shared."

A village is built like a circle. Houses on the outside and a space in the middle for the kids to play. Always looking toward one another. Whether or not a kid "belongs" to someone, they are our collective responsibility. A village is set up this way, with our eyes on one another, looking at how we're connected, not just looking out for ourselves. We ask for help, we take the risk to let other people care for us in ways we need to be cared for, and we contribute what we can. A village is a practice. It's an investment, a creation, something you maintain. It's infrastructure; it's mindset and worldview. It's relationships and connections.

A liberated future will be constructed from care work and

domestic, emotional, and mental labor. It will be built on a foundation of well-resourced communities. It will happen through investment in public education and affordable housing, childcare, and healthcare. We'll build safety by providing for one another. We'll connect and care rather than police and punish. It will require us to unlearn oppressive cultural norms and reject a transactional view of relationships. It will take a rejection of rigidity and an embrace of learning, changing, and growing. We won't build it on our own. We will build it together.

5 THINGS WE CAN DO RIGHT NOW

1. Lean in . . . to Your Connections

Start where you are. Look around and see where your connections already exist and what communities you're already a part of. Invest in your close relationships and your community. Next time you think of an old friend, instead of just letting the thought pass by, text them to let them know. Make a friend a playlist. Host a birthday party.

Lean into the ways you already support other people and let them be a support for you. Reach out to a friend to grab a coffee after being turned down for a promotion. Offer to drop off hot food when a friend is sick. Tend to the bonds that already enrich your life. Maintain and protect them. Work through conflicts, communicate boundaries, and treat your connections with the reverence and care they deserve.

Be especially mindful of boundaries. Giving more than you receive is one way of putting up a wall. Deep, authentic connection requires being on the receiving end of reciprocal care. The healthiest relationships aren't about going above and beyond. Boundaries and reciprocal care are what sustain and strengthen connections.

Show up. A party needs people. Every full room is full because of the bodies that fill it. Do not take for granted the power of your presence. Museums need visitors. Schools need children. Community meetings need community members to come and voice their opinions. Walk through the open doors. Accept the opportunities you're given. Your participation and presence matter even if you don't have a dish to pass. Attend community dinners, be a rational voice on your local community internet forum, take your kids to weekly park hangs. Be a host or a facilitator if that's what you want to be, but make sure you also show up and enjoy the experiences that are given to you.

Really *live* together—find the magic in the mundane and embrace mess. Don't wait to invite people over until the house is spotless or the laundry is folded. Leave the laundry to wrinkle or invite your friends over to do the "boring" stuff with you. Go grocery shopping with a friend. Get together to prep a few freezer meals on the weekend. Bonus: you can buy bulk and save by doing it together. Have a friend bring their laundry over and make a day of folding and sorting. Get help pulling weeds. You don't even need to talk, just be together. Don't do anything fancy, no big flashy meals, nothing beyond your limits—mac and cheese out of the pot, reruns on the TV, and doing chores. Find the magic in the mundane. *Live your everyday lives with the people who matter to you.*

2. Connect with Care

Care-centered connection starts with naming your needs and honoring others' in return. With friends, loved ones, and people you spend time with, open the door for conversations about what you really want and need. Have you ever bailed on a hangout because it was with a friend who likes to do expensive things that aren't in your budget? Have you ever winced your way through a group dinner at a restaurant that was too loud and didn't have something you could eat on the menu? Start having open conversations about what would make you feel comfortable.

Be open about your needs: Would dinner and a show stress your finances? Do crowded spaces make you uncomfortable? Are there certain topics you'd rather avoid? Explain your social battery beforehand and develop a code word so you can leave lovingly when you've hit your limit. Ask questions of others: What do you like to spend time doing together? Is there anything you want to avoid? What's your budget? How can we make our time together more enjoyable?

Make it a habit to communicate about needs—*yours and others'*—and make plans that consider them. Promote a culture that allows for individuals to have what they need with the least amount of barriers wherever and whenever you can. Having to ask for accommodations can feel daunting, and that fear of pushback can cause people to keep quiet about what they need. Be the first to start the conversation by bringing up individual needs early and checking in often.

Contribute to a societal culture of accessibility and inclusion by practicing open communication and consideration in your closest connections.

3. Take a Transformative Approach in *All* Your Relationships

The status quo needs to be challenged, and conflict is a part of the process. Conflict is an opportunity for connection and growth, and to grow means you're alive. We have to get comfortable with the messy, imperfect, challenging road of breaking apart and coming back together. We have to learn to get comfortable with conflict.

Approach conflict with *restoration* and *repair* in mind. A brilliant feature of being alive is that we get to change, grow, learn new things, connect, and gain understanding. Build relationships—intimate relationships and community relationships—on that foundation. Leave open the possibility that something new and better could come from conflict and harm rather than a repetition of it. Rather than looking for ways to punish or harm others as we've been harmed, we can look closer at problems and find solutions that prevent the same harm from happening in the future. Take lessons and turn them into forward motion, into healing, into a return to homeostasis. When harm is caused, ask how it could be repaired and prevented in the future. What was the cause? Where was a disconnect present? How could it be healed? What needs are unmet and how could we meet them? So often, the answer to those questions is care. When we have what we need, when we have the care and support we deserve, we're all safer and more secure.

A transformative approach in our relationship with the world asks us to consider the needs of individuals and communities when working through conflicts rather than meeting violence with more violence. It asks us to consider our impacts, self-reflect, and approach problems with creativity and care. It asks us to ask ourselves: How can we reduce harm? How can we use this as an opportunity to improve our circumstances? How can we make this better?

4. Borrow a Cup of Sugar, Lend Out Your Lawn Mower

Share with people—neighbors, friends, colleagues, and other people in your network. Establish a resource-sharing culture with the people in your life by asking for something small and returning the favor. If you like to cook but don't have enough garlic, text a neighbor instead of running to the store and see if they have some you can borrow. If they do and you make enough food to share, drop them off a plate to say thank you. When you get a chance to go to the store and replace the garlic you borrowed, make sure to tell them they can ask if they ever need anything. If you have a neighbor with a kid younger than yours, ask if they'd like to inherit your family's hand-me-downs. Before you drop clothes off at a thrift store, text a friend or neighbor who might have a use for them. Before renting an electric sander or buying your own leaf blower, ask a neighbor if they have one you could use. If they don't, buy one and tell them they can use yours if they need it.

Take inventory. Kick off the culture of sharing by taking stock of what you could freely offer to share and what you might benefit from receiving. If you have more than enough of something, offer it up. Check with others if you need something before you go out and buy it.

Ask yourself what resources you have to share. Skills? Knowledge? Time? Connections? Experience? Financial resources? Tools?

Over the years, we've inherited thousands of dollars' worth of toys, furniture, and clothing. We've furnished entire rooms for free. In turn, we've passed along bikes, cribs, diapers, clothes, food, and so much more. In a society that wants so badly to get us to work harder, buy more, and constantly compete, the willingness to share is a powerful act of resistance.

Divest from consumerism and keep money in communities. Our spending habits can have a major impact—globally and in our backyards.

If you can borrow, *borrow*. If you can shop locally, *shop locally*. Shopping locally and supporting small businesses is an investment in communities. Among other benefits, spending money locally helps keep resources local, reduces waste, and can strengthen a sense of connectedness. What minor shifts can you make that put money back into the pockets of neighbors?

Reduce the number of clicks it takes to shop small by starting a bookmark folder on your browser where you can collect small businesses with products you love. Frequent book buyer? Bookshop.org and Libro.fm are two online booksellers that directly support indie bookshops. Big fan of coffee or tea? Small roasteries and tea shops often offer subscription packages. Our brains are wired to be attracted to convenience. Make small adjustments in how you consume and try to automate or make a practice of intentional spending easy to maintain.

5. Be a Neighbor, Not Savior

Find your role as a changemaker. Future-building is ongoing, and we each have a role to play. Ask yourself where you excel and how you might lend your efforts to advocacy or action.

Start with your strengths and consider sustainability in your efforts. What do you excel at? What areas of your life are you already changemaking? How are you already investing in community and doing liberatory work? Are you community building? How? Are you an educator or facilitator? Are you a storyteller, a rebel, a chef, or a conversation starter? What passion, skills, and resources can you put to work for a better future?

For every social movement, there's been someone to watch the kids and pack lunches, someone to make the group laugh, someone with an inspirational voice, someone who can plan and coordinate, and someone with wheels. Not everyone has to be eager to field phone calls. Some people are going to have more money than time and vice versa. When we work together, we can pool our skills and resources.

Look into issue-specific advocacy groups like local mutual aid efforts, grassroots organizations, and nonprofits and ask what they need. Be realistic about your skills and capacity. What do you have an excess of that could benefit others? Do you have free time, expertise, or money? Could you set up a recurring donation? Do you have availability to help with Excel spreadsheets, compiling resources into a document, sorting through emails, language translation, or amplifying info on social media?

Work with what you've got and commit to forward momentum. Changemaking is a lifelong effort. There is space for you and your unique skills exactly as you are.

Get active on your block. We can effect a lot of change by getting involved in hyperlocal efforts. When we do that, though, we have to be careful not to speak over one another. On our blocks, in our neighborhoods, and in our cities, we can make a serious difference in the quality of life for us and our neighbors and do it effectively—solidarity has to be at the center of how we advocate.

Start a group text thread with the people on your block and keep in touch. Get into the habit of talking with your neighbors about what's going on. Learn about what affects them and what resources they need. Be mindful not to let your personal opinions or beliefs overpower those of your neighbors. Speak up for what you need and want, but do it with consideration of how it would impact others. Show up and advocate *as a neighbor*, not a savior.

Behave like you belong. See yourself as a part of an ecosystem and act accordingly. Behave as if you belong somewhere and are an essential part of the flow of energy through the world. *You are.* Self-reliance, or the idea that we could give ourselves everything we need, is a myth. We are meant to rely on one another. Our choices affect ourselves and the people, places, and things we interact with. We affect our families, friends, colleagues, and the people we pass on our morning strolls. We aren't just visitors in the world. We're essential elements of it. We are each an important part of the rich ecosystems of our environments. We aren't just residents of homes, on streets, in cities. We are what makes up the world.

Our society encourages us to compare ourselves, keeping us in constant pursuit of bigger and better. This framework for viewing the world focuses on how we're different and disconnected. We're all better for it when we reject that thinking and instead focus on our connections. Treat others as if they belong to you. Treat yourself as if you belong to them. Treat the world as if it belongs to all of us.

Keep learning. Our society does so much to try to keep us ignorant and complacent. Change happens when we educate ourselves. We owe it to one another to give a good faith effort. It happens when we make learning an integral part of our lives. We each come with our own embedded beliefs to evaluate and deconstruct. We've each got our own work to do to unpack the ways we may be contributing to harms in the world. New understandings don't just have to come from cracking open books or searching for answers. An important step in the learning process is loosening our grip on what we think we know. Asking "What else could be true?" and embracing curiosity and empathy creates space for understanding. If you don't know why someone is doing something, rather than judging, ask questions. If you notice patterns and trends, consider what might be influencing them. Many things can be true. There's no such thing as a singular truth or an unbiased perspective. It's an honor when others allow the world to learn from their experiences and stories. It's our responsibility to listen and learn from one another.

Holding space for learning and changing is essential for a better world. We don't have to fully understand something through our own limited viewpoints to trust other people's experiences. Defensiveness does nothing to change behavior or make us feel more connected. We can listen more than we speak and reflect often. We can diversify the stories we consume and witness. We can give ourselves grace and remember that growth makes us human. Read books, listen to other people's experiences, and make it a practice to gain new information and change your mind. Education is a great connector, and other people's stories are gifts.

Conclusion:
So, What's the Answer?

O NE MIDSUMMER FRIDAY, after a long week of edits on this book, I was walking to pick up my kids from day camp when my neighbor Liz stopped to talk. We've lived near each other for more than a decade and, in that time, have gotten to know each other well—as neighbors, co-organizers, and friends. Because our kids are about the same age and attend the same school, we pass each other almost daily, usually exchanging a wave or a quick hello before continuing on. But that afternoon, instead of walking past, she snapped me out of my end-of-day haze and flagged me down—one hand gesturing and the other gripping a backpack as she called to her kids to wait at the corner. She was on her way home after picking them up and asked if we were going to be at the block party that coming Sunday. Her kids were planning a bike race and were hoping mine would join in. I was so thankful she made the effort to get my attention. I'd seen flyers around, but I'd been so absorbed with work that I'd completely forgotten to do anything with the information. The block party was an event my family looked forward to every year, and we would have missed it if not for her reminder.

As we waved goodbye, I pulled out my phone, added the party to our family's shared calendar, texted my husband to put it on his radar, and set a 9 p.m. alarm to make sure we didn't end our night without checking in about weekend plans.

These small moments—showing up, making time for the things that matter, leaning into the connections we've built—are what we work toward. The systems we put in place at home, the patterns we break, and the ones we create are all part of learning how to live in alignment with what we value.

These days, this is our usual flow. We have a shared family calendar where we put events that impact each other or the family's schedule. We have a pretty good baseline idea of the things we all like to do and what we need to get done on any given day. Each of us takes responsibility for communicating with the other when we have things we want to do, and one person either handles the details on their own or asks for help. We try to maintain a balance of using the information we know about our family to make informed, considerate decisions, and not fall back on assumptions or old habits.

IT'S BEEN FIVE years since that birthday card, five years since I stood in my kitchen and felt the walls closing in around me, five years since that destabilizing, frantic moment.

On a Sunday afternoon a few weeks away from sending in final edits on this manuscript, I had another kitchen moment. I was standing in nearly the same spot, but this time, instead of holding a card, my hands were holding a coffee I'd wanted but hadn't asked for and a bag full of snacks I hadn't packed myself, ready to head to a block party I had the energy to show up to. I could hear my husband coaching the kids through putting sunscreen on their faces in the other room, when I suddenly became intensely aware of my surroundings. This time, the room didn't feel like it was getting smaller. I didn't feel panicked, lost, or invisible like I had years prior. I felt seen. I felt solid, rooted, and secure.

Those feelings weren't the result of having everything figured out. They were the result of ongoing effort. I still struggle with holding boundaries around my time. I'm still learning what my needs are, and finding creative ways to meet them. My personal identity is something I've become much more familiar with, but I continue to evolve. At home, my husband and I still fall into the nag paradox, and we have plenty of old dirt we still need to dig through, but we continue to grow in our communication. We go through periods when we find our division of labor is structured with clearly defined ownership over certain tasks, and periods when we each jump in when we see the other struggling. What keeps us on track is that we remain committed to being curious and flexible. Together, we've shifted our focus from what we think we're supposed to do toward what best meets our needs. We are building a life that prioritizes sustainability over obligation, and connection over convention. We are engineering our lives in a creative, organic, collaborative way.

My understanding of the world and my relationship to it are also constantly changing. I feel grounded, but not because I've reached a new milestone or gained a new achievement. I haven't unlocked a magic formula or a ten-step plan toward happiness. There's no easy fix. There's no finish line. There's also no such thing as having it all, because the world was never meant to be consumed.

I feel grounded because I'm hopeful. I do not want to settle for a life that could be better; I want to build it. I don't want to feel like I'm settling, and I don't want the people in my life to feel like they're settling either. I want to live my life in recognition that the issues we face each have a root cause and that change is possible. I want to live my life in the knowledge that we do not have to settle for mediocrity in any area of our lives.

Domestic inequity is a consequence of an uncaring world. The fight to find balance, to make invisible labor visible, and to feel more connected can start at home, but it cannot end there. The anthropologist David Graeber defines care as "action which is oriented to maintaining or increasing another person's freedom." Graeber's definition asks us to consider what freedom means and what work goes into creating and maintaining it. His definition asks us to draw connections between our actions and their impacts.

The process of looking for and asking questions about care has been an ongoing transformative experience for me. Searching for its presence has shown me how often it's withheld, exploited, and manipulated. Noticing where it is and where it isn't, then asking questions about why has been radicalizing.

In my home, I felt the weight of the work of the household and of childcare before I saw it, and when I began to notice, I saw it everywhere. The same culture that normalizes inequality in our homes normalizes inequality in society. It also normalizes:

- houselessness, food insecurity, and debilitating medical debt

- a lack of care infrastructure like accessible healthcare, childcare, elder care, and home care services, and protection for workers in those positions
- high rates of maternal death and the withholding of reproductive rights
- environmental destruction
- poverty, wealth inequity, and exploitative labor practices
- under-resourced education systems

No injustice stands on its own. Whether it's disproportionate demands within a household or disproportionate access to housing, the underlying problem is a society that doesn't value life. Our systems fail to prioritize the well-being of people, the planet, and all living things. If we want to truly transform our society so that the average household isn't screaming at each other about the laundry, we have to ask ourselves what else we've accepted as normal.

A disregard for care is at the root of our social problems, and a transformation of our understanding of it will be at the center of solving them.

When I look for care, I find humanity. When I look for care, I see what our world could look like if it took a new shape. I am radically hopeful. I am radically optimistic. Not in an unrealistic and delusional sense, but in a committed, creative way—with a deep understanding that there is enough in this world for everyone to have what they need. I know I won't solve the world's problems in my lifetime, but I will be a part of the transformation.

I find hope in imagining a world where we each feel responsible for one another. I find hope in imagining a world that functions on the principle that we are all—every last one of us—deserving of care. I can imagine a future with care at the root. This radical hope is what makes me feel grounded.

We transform the world when we reject the complacency of sitcom syndrome and use our emotions as motivation to do better. We transform the world when we set expectations that reflect our individual needs and capacities. By approaching our daily lives collaboratively and centering creativity and curiosity, we escape the toxic traps of domestic inequity and leave no room for weaponized incompetence. We transform the world by not being lulled by the many ways things could be worse but instead move in the knowledge that things can and will be better.

We do the transformational work of future-building when we learn new ways to manage conflicts. We do the transformational work of future-building when we set standards in our homes that honor our unique needs. We do the transformational work of future-building when we recognize the many shapes love can take in our lives and refuse to limit our imaginations.

SO, WHAT'S THE ANSWER?

The answer is to refuse to accept mediocrity as inevitable—to envision a future beyond it and take deliberate action to build something better.

Leaving behind mediocrity isn't just about picking better partners or convincing them to share chores fifty-fifty. We need to appreciate the work. We need to learn to notice the care and invest in it. Care is the work we do to get free. It's everything from clearing the dishes after dinner to protesting injustice in the streets. It's something we can all benefit from giving and receiving. Care is the work that builds and maintains strong communities, and when we have communities, we have freedom. Liberation comes from love and love is an action. It will come in the form of seemingly mundane tasks—like refilling the bathroom soap when you notice it's getting low or clearing the crumbs off the counter—the "rituals of care," as the poet David Gate calls them, that contribute to our well-being. It will come in the form of acts of village building—like accepting when a friend offers to swing by with dinner or showing up to help a friend move—that weave us into each other's lives.

We all deserve an overhaul. Beyond just "raising the bar" or shallow forms of individual self-care, we deserve the strength and security of community. A future that's free from mediocrity is one that's made by us for us. It's one where individuality, inclusivity, and accessibility are at the forefront, where we move through the world, never forgetting our interdependence.

We all have unique circumstances, different access to resources, and various opportunities to effect change. The nature of building a future for all of us is that there's no such thing as one size fits all for anything, including disrupting the status quo.

TO HELL WITH LOT LINES

We all have something to offer in the cultivation of community power, and there are so many approaches we can take. Learning how to live well with one another makes us all happier, healthier, and better equipped to thrive through hard times. Noticing the invisible care that nurtures you inside and outside your home and appreciating it *matters*.

The educator and organizer Mariame Kaba is widely recognized for her phrase "hope is a discipline." In *Let This Radicalize You*, she expands on this idea, writing, "For me, hope is not a metaphor; it's a lived practice. It isn't a thing I possess. Rather, I have to remake it daily. I don't have hope, I do hope. It's an active process that I have to regularly commit to—hope not as an emotion but as a discipline."

Care is hope in action. It's the work we do that ushers us into the future. It's the work that meets our needs and keeps us alive and thriving. Shoveling a neighbor's walk gives them a path outside. It communicates that you want them to move safely and freely through the world. Cleaning a sinkful of dishes ahead of a meal makes those cooking and serving tools available. It makes a future shared meal a possibility. When we cook, clean, change bedsheets, take out the trash, pay attention, plan, notice, and nurture, we do the work that makes our lives possible. The most hopeful thing we can do is to care.

This book was written in between meals and bedtimes and errands and endless loads of laundry and dishes. It has been fueled by meals sent by friends, processed out loud with friends on long walks and through voice notes, and has been edited and shaped with guidance and support from so many. This book was not put together in isolation. It's made its way into your life because of the care that has been poured into me—the Skittles lovingly left in my writing spot by my husband and the bags of muffins and surprise food deliveries dropped off on my doorstep by friends. This book happened alongside the rest of my daily tasks of living. I ate late-night meals off plates that were then washed and put away. I wrote while wearing fuzzy socks and oversize hoodies that were washed and folded and put back on the shelf to be worn again. This book is a part of my life. It exists because I lived while writing it. It exists because of my connections, because of care, and because of the flow of community.

I feel absolutely honored knowing that this book has become a part of your life, too.

We're all a part of the fabric. When we're intentional about weaving our lives together, showing up and doing the work to care for and nurture one another, we're all stronger for it. The future that we co-create together will be *more than mediocre*.

Acknowledgments

T0 THE DOMESTIC workers, unions, organizers, and activists—
especially the Black and Brown women, Indigenous people, immigrant women, disabled folks, and all those who
have been criminalized and marginalized—who have long been at
the forefront of this fight. To those who have struggled to survive
within unjust systems, who resist the harms of colonization, capitalism, white supremacy, and ableism; who fight back, disrupt, and
demand more. To those who practice care as resistance and take collective action for the rights and protections that are long overdue—
this work is, and always has been, built on your efforts. You have
shown us a vision of what is possible, and we will build it.

To my family—thank you for doing the daily work of building a
life with me. Jack, you've shown up for me in immeasurable ways
with time, attention, love, and snacks. Charlie and Frances, your
creativity, humor, and kindness remind me daily how lucky I am to
know you. Mom, I've learned so much from you, and I'm grateful
to be able to call you a friend. Gary, thank you for always keeping

us well fed. Steve and Jim—thanks for always doing more of the chores than me growing up. You continue to set the bar high as caregivers. Dad and Beth—thank you for teaching me to notice the little things.

To my dear friends—especially Crystal, Julie, and Nora—for the long walks, the shared meals, the verbal processing, and the camaraderie. To Lori, Rachel, Kara, Cait, and so many others whose friendships have shaped me through the years, I'm grateful for the ways you've shown up and helped me grow.

To my agent, Joanna MacKenzie—for seeing the vision and value of this project and encouraging me to keep going. I'm so grateful for your advocacy and for the way you championed both the work and me at every step.

To my editor, Maya Ziv—your insight and input gave this project the push it needed to really fly. To Ella and the entire team at Plume, thank you for guiding this book into the world with thoughtfulness and care. To my sounding board and support, Hilary Swanson—your insight, patience, and encouragement made this book stronger at every step. Thank you for pulling me back when I got lost in the weeds.

To Eve Rodsky—for being a fire-starter in the domestic equity movement, fanning the flames of change and bringing people together to push the conversation forward. Your passion is powerful and contagious, and it's been an honor to stoke the fire with you. To you and the whole team, especially Amanda, thank you for the many gifts you've given me—both personally and professionally.

To the authors, organizers, storytellers, experts, and individuals who shared their thoughts with me, expanded my understanding, and generously offered their perspectives—including Clare Brown, Angela Chen, Chelsea Conaboy, Jess Daylover, Tim and Jessica Durand, Pierre Fleury, David Gate, Rose Hackman, Olivia Dreizen

Howell, Markus Harwood-Jones, Mikki Kendall, Sophie Lucido Johnson, Nick North, Imani Payne, Ashley Simpo, and Dr. Han Ren.

To all the folks who shared their thoughts, answered surveys, emailed with me, and gifted me their time on Zoom calls—your perspectives and experiences have enriched this book beyond measure. While I can't list every single person by name, please know that your insights, generosity, and trust in me have made a lasting impact. Your contributions are an absolute gift, and I do not take them for granted.

To my friends and neighbors—on my block, in my neighborhood, and in my city—to my gardening group, mutual aid organizations, and all those who have embodied generosity and care through shoveled walks, shared food, and handed-down clothes, furniture, and bikes—I am grateful to be in community with you.

To the teachers, babysitters, friends, and loved ones who provide our family with essential childcare—thank you for being a part of our lives. I'm so grateful for you.

To my online community—none of this would have happened without you.

Finally, to my readers—this book is for you. Thank you for taking the time to engage with these ideas and for being part of a movement toward change. Thank you for being a part of my life and for allowing me to be a part of yours. I'm honored to be part of this movement with you.

With gratitude and care,
Laura

Resources

Relationships, Equity, and Communication

Books

Chen, Angela. *Ace: What Asexuality Reveals About Desire, Society, and the Meaning of Sex.* Beacon Press, 2020.

Franco, Marisa G. *Platonic: How the Science of Attachment Can Help You Make—and Keep—Friends.* Putnam, 2022.

Gottman, John, and Nan Silver. *The Seven Principles for Making Marriage Work.* Harmony Books, 1999.

hooks, bell. *All About Love: New Visions.* William Morrow, 2000.

———. *The Will to Change: Men, Masculinity, and Love.* Washington Square Press, 2004.

Rodsky, Eve. *Fair Play: A Game-Changing Solution for When You Have Too Much to Do (and More Life to Live).* Putnam, 2019.

Spade, Dean. *Love in a F*cked-Up World: How to Build Relationships, Hook Up, and Raise Hell Together.* Algonquin Books, 2025.

Tawwab, Nedra Glover. *Set Boundaries, Find Peace: A Guide to Reclaiming Yourself.* TarcherPerigee, 2021.

Wong, Alice, ed. *Disability Intimacy: Essays on Love, Care, and Desire.* Vintage Books, 2024.

Online Resources

Fresh Starts Registry: https://www.freshstartsregistry.com
The Gottman Institute: https://www.gottman.com
A Guide to Relationship Anarchy: https://www.therelationshipanarchist.com
/relationship-anarchy-guide
National Domestic Violence Hotline: https://www.thehotline.org

Domestic Labor, Care Work, and Capitalism

Books

Bhattacharya, Tithi, ed. *Social Reproduction Theory: Remapping Class,
Recentering Oppression.* Pluto Press, 2017.
Garbes, Angela. *Essential Labor: Mothering as Social Change.* Harper Wave,
2022.
Hackman, Rose. *Emotional Labor: The Invisible Work Shaping Our Lives and How
to Claim Our Power.* Flatiron Books, 2023.
hooks, bell. *Ain't I a Woman? Black Women and Feminism.* South End Press,
1981.
Jaffe, Sarah. *Work Won't Love You Back: How Devotion to Our Jobs Keeps Us
Exploited, Exhausted, and Alone.* Bold Type Books, 2021.
Nadasen, Premilla. *Care: The Highest Stage of Capitalism.* Haymarket Books,
2023.
Piepzna-Samarasinha, Leah Lakshmi. *Care Work: Dreaming Disability Justice.*
Arsenal Pulp Press, 2018.

Essays

Bhattacharya, Tithi. "How Not to Skip Class: Social Reproduction of Labor and
the Global Working Class." *Viewpoint Magazine,* October 31, 2015. https://
viewpointmag.com/2015/10/31/how-not-to-skip-class-social-reproduction-of
-labor-and-the-global-working-class/.
Nadasen, Premilla. "The Care Deficit." *Dissent,* Fall 2016. https://www
.dissentmagazine.org/article/care-deficit-hta-domestic-worker-organizing
-history/.

Organizations

CareForce: https://fairplaypolicy.org/careforce
Caring Across Generations: https://caringacross.org
More Perfect Union: https://perfectunion.us
National Domestic Workers Alliance: https://www.domesticworkers.org
Service Employees International Union: https://www.seiu.org

Raising the Next Generation

Books

Brown, Christia Spears. *Parenting Beyond Pink and Blue: How to Raise Your Kids Free of Gender Stereotypes.* Ten Speed Press, 2014.

Conaboy, Chelsea. *Mother Brain: How Neuroscience Is Rewriting the Story of Parenthood.* Henry Holt, 2022.

Madison, Megan, and Jessica Ralli. *We Care: A First Conversation About Justice.* Illustrated by Sharee Miller. Rise × Penguin Workshop, 2022.

Schenwar, Maya, and Kim Wilson, eds. *We Grow the World Together: Parenting Toward Abolition.* Haymarket Press, 2024.

Slice, Jessica. *Unfit Parent: A Disabled Mother Challenges an Inaccessible World.* Beacon Press, 2025.

Sugarman-Li, Lori. *Our Home: The Love, Work, and Heart of Family.* Illustrated by María Perera. Collective Book Studio, 2024.

Tamaki, Jillian. *Our Little Kitchen: A Board Book.* Groundwood Books, 2020.

Whippman, Ruth. *BoyMom: Reimagining Boyhood in the Age of Impossible Masculinity.* Harmony, 2024.

Feminism and Social Justice

Books

Beck, Koa. *White Feminism: From the Suffragettes to Influencers and Who They Leave Behind.* Atria Books, 2021.

hooks, bell. *Feminism Is for Everybody: Passionate Politics.* South End Press, 2000.

Kendall, Mikki. *Hood Feminism: Notes from the Women That a Movement Forgot.* Viking, 2020.

Lorde, Audre. *Sister Outsider: Essays and Speeches.* Crossing Press, 1984.

Piepzna-Samarasinha, Leah Lakshmi. *The Future Is Disabled: Prophecies, Love Notes, and Mourning Songs.* Arsenal Pulp Press, 2022.

Vergès, Françoise. *A Decolonial Feminism.* Pluto Press, 2021.

Ward, Jane. *The Tragedy of Heterosexuality.* New York University Press, 2020.

Online Resources

(divorcing) White Supremacy Culture: https://www.whitesupremacyculture.info

Organizations

Disability Visibility Project: https://disabilityvisibilityproject.com
Equimundo: https://www.equimundo.org

Community and Future Visioning

Books

Birdsong, Mia. *How We Show Up: Reclaiming Family, Friendship, and Community*. Balance, 2020.

Hayes, Kelly, and Mariame Kaba. *Let This Radicalize You: Organizing and the Revolution of Reciprocal Care*. Haymarket Books, 2023.

Kimmerer, Robin Wall. *Braiding Sweetgrass: Indigenous Wisdom, Scientific Knowledge, and the Teachings of Plants*. Milkweed Editions, 2013.

Klinenberg, Eric. *Palaces for the People: How Social Infrastructure Can Help Fight Inequality, Polarization, and the Decline of Civic Life*. Crown, 2019.

Krawec, Patty. *Becoming Kin: An Indigenous Call to Unforgetting the Past and Reimagining Our Future*. Broadleaf Books, 2022.

Solnit, Rebecca. *Hope in the Dark: Untold Histories, Wild Possibilities*. Nation Books, 2004.

Spade, Dean. *Mutual Aid: Building Solidarity During This Crisis (and the Next)*. Verso Books, 2020.

Organizations

Next River: https://www.nextriver.org

New Economy Coalition: https://neweconomy.net

Project NIA: https://project-nia.org

Notes

Chapter One: Domestic Engineer

37 **describes white feminism:** Marie Solis, "Koa Beck on Dismantling the
Persistence of White Feminism," *NBC News*, January 9, 2021, https://
www.nbcnews.com/news/nbcblk/koa-beck-dismantling-persistence
-white-feminism-n1253555.

38 **unions have fought:** Jennifer Guglielmo, Michelle Joffrey, and Diana
Sierra, "Strategies," A History of Domestic Work and Worker
Organizing, https://www.dwherstories.com/collections/strategies.

38 **live in poverty:** "Domestic Workers Face Poor Wages and Working
Conditions—Particularly in the South," Economic Policy Institute,
March 6, 2025, https://www.epi.org/press/domestic-workers-face-poor
-wages-and-working-conditions-particularly-in-the-south/.

39 **state's minimum wage law:** "Minimum Wage," Delaware Department of
Labor, October 10, 2024, https://labor.delaware.gov/divisions/industrial
-affairs/wage-hour/minimum-wage/.

39 **a few of the historical exclusions:** "Domestic Workers Bill of Rights
FAQs," National Domestic Workers Alliance, October 25, 2024, https://
www.domesticworkers.org/programs-and-campaigns/developing-policy
-solutions/domestic-workers-bill-of-rights/domestic-workers-bill-of-rights
-faqs/.

39 **disproportionately impact women:** "Domestic Workers Face Poor Wages
and Working Conditions."

39   **estimated $10.8 trillion:** Clare Coffey et al., "Time to Care: Unpaid and
      Underpaid Care Work and the Global Inequality Crisis," Oxfam, January
      20, 2020, https://policy-practice.oxfam.org/resources/time-to-care
      -unpaid-and-underpaid-care-work-and-the-global-inequality-crisis
      -620928/.

40   **median salary of $178,201 annually:** "How Much Is a Mother Really
      Worth?," Salary.com, May 2019, https://www.salary.com/articles
      /mother-salary/.

40   **97 hours per week:** "How Much Is a Mom Really Worth? The Amount
      May Surprise You," Salary.com, May 2021, https://www.salary.com
      /articles/how-much-is-a-mom-really-worth-the-amount-may-surprise-you.

40   **just under $185,000:** "How Much Is a Mom Really Worth?"

41   **full-time nanny in the United States:** Sheri Reed, "This Is How Much
      Child Care Costs in 2025," Care.com, January 29, 2025, https://www.
      care.com/c/how-much-does-child-care-cost/.

41   **between $300 and $800 a month:** Becca Lewis, "How Much Does
      Professional House Cleaning Cost?," Angi, September 26, 2024, https://
      www.angi.com/articles/how-much-does-it-cost-hire-house-cleaner.htm.

41   **weeknight dinners can cost:** David Watsky, "Wondering If a Meal
      Delivery Service Is Cheaper Than Takeout? I Did the Math," CNET, June
      14, 2024, https://www.cnet.com/health/nutrition/wondering-if-a-meal
      -delivery-service-is-cheaper-than-takeout-i-did-the-math/; Pocketbook
      Agency, "How Much Does a Private Chef Cost? And Is It Worth It?,"
      Pocketbook Agency, October 6, 2024, https://www.pocketbookagency
      .com/how-much-does-a-private-chef-cost/. Weeknight dinners costing
      an average of $20,000 per year is based on a conservative estimate of a
      $24,000 annual fee to hire a private chef for weeknight meals and data
      that estimates it costs between $14,000–$20,000 for takeout or delivery
      for a family of four for every weekday for a year.

42   **typical American family structure:** Paul F. Hemez, Chanell N.
      Washington, and Rose M. Kreider, "America's Families and Living
      Arrangements: 2022," United States Census Bureau, May 23, 2024,
      https://www.census.gov/library/publications/2024/demo/p20-587.html.

43   **American households are dual income:** "Employment Characteristics of
      Families—2023," Economic News Release, U.S. Bureau of Labor
      Statistics, April 24, 2024, https://www.bls.gov/news.release/famee.htm.

43   **more than their male spouses:** Richard Fry, Carolina Aragão, Kiley
      Hurst, and Kim Parker, "In a Growing Share of U.S. Marriages,
      Husbands and Wives Earn About the Same," Pew Research Center,
      April 13, 2023, https://www.pewresearch.org/social-trends/2023/04/13
      /in-a-growing-share-of-u-s-marriages-husbands-and-wives-earn-about
      -the-same/.

43   **increase in financial equity:** Sarah Jane Glynn, "Breadwinning Mothers
      Are Critical to Families' Economic Security," Center for American
      Progress, March 29, 2021, https://www.americanprogress.org/article
      /breadwinning-mothers-critical-familys-economic-security/.

43   **women averaged 4.6 hours more:** Fry et al., "In a Growing Share of U.S.
      Marriages."

44   **not the guaranteed result:** Glynn, "Breadwinning Mothers."

44   **the domestic care gap persists:** Melissa A. Milkie, Liana C. Sayer, Kei
      Nomaguchi, and Hope Xu Yan, "Who's Doing the Housework and
      Childcare in America Now? Differential Convergence in Twenty-First-
      Century Gender Gaps in Home Tasks," *Socius* 11 (2025), https://doi.org
      /10.1177/23780231251314667.

44   **doubled since 1965:** Kim Parker and Wendy Wang, "Chapter 5:
      Americans' Time at Paid Work, Housework, Child Care, 1965 to 2011,"
      in *Modern Parenthood: Roles of Moms and Dads Converge as They Balance
      Work and Family,* Pew Research Center, March 14, 2013, https://www
      .pewresearch.org/social-trends/2013/03/14/chapter-5-americans-time-at
      -paid-work-housework-child-care-1965-to-2011/; "Average Hours per Day
      Parents Spent Caring for and Helping Household Children as Their
      Main Activity," U.S. Bureau of Labor Statistics, June 27, 2024, https://
      www.bls.gov/charts/american-time-use/activity-by-parent.htm.

44   **more than five hours of leisure time:** "Table 11a. Time Spent in Leisure
      and Sports Activities for the Civilian Population by Selected
      Characteristics, Averages per Day, 2023 Annual Averages," U.S. Bureau
      of Labor Statistics, June 27, 2024, https://www.bls.gov/news.release
      /atus.t11A.htm.

44   **women generally do more housework:** Parker and Wang, "Chapter 5:
      Americans' Time at Paid Work, Housework, Child Care, 1965 to 2011";
      "American Time Use Survey News Release—2023 A01 Results," U.S.
      Bureau of Labor Statistics, June 27, 2024, https://www.bls.gov/news
      .release/atus.ht

44   **cognitive labor more evenly:** Caitlan McLean, Connie Musolino, Alice
      Rose, and Paul R. Ward, "The Management of Cognitive Labour in
      Same-Gender Couples," *PLoS ONE* 18, no. 7 (2023): e0287585, https://
      doi.org/10.1371/journal.pone.0287585.

45   **sleeplessness, mental health problems:** Amanda M. Pollitt, Brandon A.
      Robinson, and Debra Umberson, "Gender Conformity, Perceptions of
      Shared Power, and Marital Quality in Same- and Different-Sex
      Marriages," *Gender & Society* 32, no. 1 (2018): 109–31, https://doi.org
      /10.1177/0891243217742110.

45   **household's mental workload:** Elizabeth Aviv et al., "Cognitive
      Household Labor: Gender Disparities and Consequences for Maternal

Mental Health and Wellbeing," *Archives of Women's Mental Health* 28 (2025): 5–14, https://doi.org/10.1007/s00737-024-01490-w.

54   **Black men are more likely:** John Paul Wilson, Kurt Hugenberg, and Nicholas O. Rule, "Racial Bias in Judgments of Physical Size and Formidability: From Size to Threat," *Journal of Personality and Social Psychology* 113, no. 1 (2017): 59–80, https://doi.org/10.1037/pspi0000092.

60   **David Gate, whose writing:** David Gate, "Doing the Laundry," *A Rebellion of Care: Poems and Essays* (Penguin, 2025).

64   **creates relational satisfaction:** Jill Suttie, "How an Unfair Division of Labor Hurts Your Relationship," *Greater Good*, November 5, 2019, https://greatergood.berkeley.edu/article/item/how_an_unfair_division _of_labor_hurts_your_relationship.

64   **have open conversations:** Suttie, "How an Unfair Division of Labor Hurts Your Relationship"; Sinead Smyth, "Accepting Influence: Find Ways to Say 'Yes,'" Gottman Institute, March 11, 2021, https://www .gottman.com/blog/accepting-influence-find-ways-to-say-yes/.

Chapter Two: Sitcom Syndrome

79   **impacted their mental health:** "Workplace Stress," Occupational Safety and Health Administration, U.S. Department of Labor, accessed May 5, 2025, https://www.osha.gov/workplace-stress/understanding-the -problem.

79   **three hundred times that of the average worker:** Josh Bivens and Jori Kandra, "CEO Pay Slightly Declined in 2022," Economic Policy Institute, September 21, 2023, https://www.epi.org/publication/ceo-pay -in-2022/.

84   **one especially heartbreaking video:** Laura Danger (@thatdarnchat), "This dynamic is really common and it's ok to be frustrated by it. You both deserve rest and you should both be sharing in the grunt work. #domesticlabor," TikTok, June 13, 2022, https://www.tiktok.com /@thatdarnchat/video/7108746089641020718.

90   **Audre Lorde wrote:** Audre Lorde, "The Uses of Anger: Women Responding to Racism," in *Sister Outsider: Essays and Speeches* (Crossing Press, 1984), 124–33.

Chapter Three: Hey, Mama

101   **in a quick video:** Eilise Patton, "Mom IG bloggers Be like:," YouTube, August 3, 2023, 18 sec., https://www.youtube.com/watch?v =-tpYqMyDtFw.

108   **Dr. Raina Brands tweeted:** Raina Brands (@RainaBrands), "Our son has been in daycare since the beginning of the year. If he is sick and needs to come home early, they call me. If they want to give him paracetamol [acetaminophen], they call me. If he has injured himself they call me. So what? I have repeatedly asked them to call my partner first. I have asked them to put a note on my file about that. I have asked the manager. Today they called and I asked them to always call my partner first and 2 hours later THEY CALLED ME AGAIN. What makes this more absurd is the fact that my partner has always been the main point of contact! He filled out all of the forms, he did all of the settling-in sessions, and he drops our son off every morning. But they are incapable of viewing him as a primary caregiver. When I say gender inequality is a self-reinforcing system, this is what I'm talking about," Twitter (now X), March 2, 2022, https://x.com/RainaBrands/status/1499017089880834052.

110   **more likely to be contacted:** Kristy Buzard, Laura Gee, and Olga Stoddard, "Who You Gonna Call? Gender Inequality in External Demands for Parental Involvement," *SSRN*, October 1, 2024, https://ssrn.com/abstract=4456100.

112   **"myth of the maternal instinct":** Chelsea Conaboy, "Maternal Instinct Is a Myth That Men Created," *New York Times*, August 26, 2022, https://www.nytimes.com/2022/08/26/opinion/sunday/maternal-instinct-myth.html.

112   **"not uniquely maternal at all":** Chelsea Conaboy, *Mother Brain: How Neuroscience Is Rewriting the Story of Parenthood* (Holt Paperbacks, 2023), 17.

113   **girls already spend more time:** Gretchen Livingston, "The Way U.S. Teens Spend Their Time Is Changing, but Differences Between Boys and Girls Persist," Pew Research Center, February 20, 2019, https://www.pewresearch.org/fact-tank/2019/02/20/the-way-u-s-teens-spend-their-time-is-changing-but-differences-between-boys-and-girls-persist/.

115   **defined the Man Box:** Brian Heilman, Gary Barker, and Alexander Harrison, *The Man Box: A Study on Being a Young Man in the US, UK, and Mexico* (Promundo-US and Unilever, 2017).

118   **children's gender-role attitudes:** Tomás Cano and Heather Hofmeister, "The Intergenerational Transmission of Gender: Paternal Influences on Children's Gender Attitudes," *Journal of Marriage and Family* 85, no. 1 (2023): 193–214, https://doi.org/10.1111/jomf.12863.

121   **parental leave for fathers:** "Length of Paid Leave (Calendar Days)," World Bank Group Gender Data Portal, 2024, https://genderdata.worldbank.org/en/indicator/sh-leve?cid=gen_web_gdp_en_ext_homepage#idEconomyComparison.

122   **"sickeningly pathetic"**: Anders Anglesey, "Candace Owens Calls Pete Buttigieg Paternity Leave 'Sickeningly Pathetic,'" *Newsweek*, October 18, 2021, https://www.newsweek.com/candace-owens-pete-buttigieg-twitter-paternity-leave-supply-chain-crisis-1639801.

122   **"Paternity leave, they call it"**: Jake Lahut, "Tucker Carlson Mocks Pete Buttigieg's Paternity Leave as 'Learning How to Breastfeed,'" *Business Insider*, October 15, 2021, https://www.businessinsider.com/tucker-carlson-pete-buttigieg-segment-video-paternity-leave-adoption-chasten-2021-10.

126   **birthing parents often end up:** "How Parents Used Their Time in 2021," The Economics Daily, U.S. Bureau of Labor Statistics, July 22, 2022, https://www.bls.gov/opub/ted/2022/how-parents-used-their-time-in-2021.htm.

126   **in queer and same-sex partnerships:** Abbie E. Goldberg and Maureen Perry-Jenkins, "The Division of Labor and Perceptions of Parental Roles: Lesbian Couples Across the Transition to Parenthood," *Journal of Social and Personal Relationships* 24, no. 2 (2007): 297–318, https://doi.org/10.1177/0265407507075415.

126   **financial hit compared with non-birthing parents:** This report and the studies cited within it are referenced multiple times in this and the next paragraph on page 127. Eric Lindberg, Women's Salaries Plummet After Giving Birth. Here's One Way to Restore Their Earning Power," *USC Today*, June 24, 2020, https://today.usc.edu/women-giving-birth-child-penalty-salary-gap-usc-research/.

127   **costs more than the average rent:** "Child Care at a Standstill: Price and Landscape Analysis," Child Care Aware of America, 2023, https://www.childcareaware.org/thechildcarestandstill/#Landscape Analysis.

127   **uneven divide in childcare:** Goldberg and Perry-Jenkins, "Division of Labor and Perceptions of Parental Roles," 297–318.

127   **fathers spending less time on caregiving:** "How Parents Used Their Time in 2021."

137   **reduces prejudice and segregation:** May Ling Halim and Carol Lynn Martin, "Friendships with Different Genders Reduce Sexism," Society for Personality and Social Psychology, March 16, 2022, https://spsp.org/news-center/character-context-blog/friendships-different-genders-reduce-sexism/.

140   **raised by an LGBTQIA parent:** Wendy D. Manning, Marshall Neal Fettro, and Esther Lamidi, "Child Well-Being in Same-Sex Parent Families: Review of Research Prepared for American Sociological Association Amicus Brief," *Population Research and Policy Review* 33 (2014): 485–502, https://doi.org/10.1007/s11113-014-9329-6.

141   **traditional nuclear family:** Paul F. Hemez, Chanell N. Washington, and Rose M. Kreider, "America's Families and Living Arrangements: 2022," *Current Population Reports*, P20-587, U.S. Census Bureau, 2024, https://www2.census.gov/library/publications/2024/demo/p20-587.pdf.

141   **40 percent in 1970:** Hemez, Washington, and Kreider, "America's Families and Living Arrangements."

Chapter Four: The Nag Paradox

167   **"bids for connection":** Logan Ury, "Want to Improve Your Relationship? Start Paying More Attention to Bids," Gottman Institute, February 11, 2019, https://www.gottman.com/blog/want-to-improve-your-relationship-start-paying-more-attention-to-bids/.

Chapter Five: Good Faith and Incompetence as a Weapon

185   **"Strategic incompetence isn't about":** Jared Sandberg, "The Art of Showing Pure Incompetence at an Unwanted Task," *Wall Street Journal*, April 17, 2007, https://www.wsj.com/articles/SB117675628452071687.

186   **On one section of her website:** The complete list of fifteen characteristics: perfectionism, sense of urgency, defensiveness and/or denial, quantity over quality, worship of the written word, belief in one right way, paternalism, either/or thinking, power hoarding, fear of open conflict, individualism, progress defined as more, the right to profit, and the right to comfort. Tema Okun, "Characteristics," (divorcing) White Supremacy Culture, accessed March 4, 2025, https://www.whitesupremacyculture.info/characteristics.html.

191   **man-on-the-street segment:** "Can Dads Answer Questions About Their Kids?," *Jimmy Kimmel Live*, June 14, 2019, 3 min., 1 sec., https://www.youtube.com/watch?v=jHPbOGEUvZA.

Chapter Six: Happily Ever After

238   **William Bridges described:** William Bridges, Susan Bridges, and Michael Bungay Stanier, *Transitions: Making Sense of Life's Changes* (Hachette Go Books, 2021), 4.

258   **not having language:** Angela Chen, *Ace: What Asexuality Reveals about Desire, Society, and the Meaning of Sex* (Beacon Press, 2020), 113.

Chapter Seven: Becoming the Village

277 **idea of collective care:** Rushdia Mehreen and David Gray-Donald, "Be Careful with Each Other," *Briarpatch*, August 29, 2018, https://briarpatchmagazine.com/articles/view/be-careful-with-each-other.

Conclusion: So, What's the Answer?

300 **David Graeber defines care as:** Peterson Roberto da Silva, "Freedom and Anarchy: An Interview with David Graeber," AnarchistStudies.Blog, September 9, 2020, https://anarchiststudies.noblogs.org/article-freedom-and-anarchy-an-interview-with-david-graeber/.

303 **the "rituals of care":** David Gate, "Doing the Laundry," *A Rebellion of Care: Poems and Essays* (Penguin, 2025).

304 **"hope not as an emotion":** Kelly Hayes and Mariame Kaba, *Let This Radicalize You: Organizing and the Revolution of Reciprocal Care* (Haymarket Books, 2023).

About the Author

A licensed educator, facilitator, and domestic equity advocate, **Laura Danger** has worked closely with the Fair Play team and has been interviewed in *HuffPo, InStyle, Business Insider,* and others as an expert on weaponized incompetence and inequity within partnerships. You can find her online @ThatDarnChat.